STARETS PAISII VELICHKOVSKII
His Life, Teachings, and Influence
On Orthodox Monasticism

FR. SERGII CHETVERIKOV

STARETS
PAISII VELICHKOVSKII

*His Life, Teachings, and Influence
On Orthodox Monasticism*

Translated from the Russian

by

VASILY LICKWAR AND ALEXANDER I. LISENKO

NORDLAND PUBLISHING COMPANY
BELMONT, MASSACHUSETTS 02178
1980

By the Same Author

A Life of Amvrosii (1912; in Russian)

Optina Pustin (1926; in Russian)

Starets Paisii Velichkovskii (1933; 1938; 1976; in Russian)

The Significance of the Jesus Prayer in the Russian Orthodox Church
(in Russian)

Library of Congress Catalog Card Number LC 75-29632

ISBN 0-913124-22-2

© Copyright 1980

by

Nordland Publishing Co., Inc.

PRINTED IN THE UNITED STATES OF AMERICA
BY
ATHENS PRINTING COMPANY
NEW YORK, N.Y.

About the Author

Forced to flee Russia in 1919, Fr. Sergii Chetverikov was later invited to become the spiritual leader of the Russian Christian Student Movement in Paris. In 1939, he was researching the "Jesus Prayer" at the Varlaam Monastery in Finland when war broke out, forcing him to return to Bratislava where he died in 1947.

FR. SERGII CHETVERIKOV

Contents

PART IV

The Flowering of Starets Paisii's Brotherhood in
Moldavia: Dragomirna, Sekul, Niamets. Last Days
and Death of the Starets (1763-1794)

PART V

Starets Paisii's Pupils on Mount Athos, in Moldavia
and in Russia and the Growth of Orthodox
Starchestvo in the Eighteenth and Nineteenth

BIBLIOGRAPHY
ON STARETS PAISII VELICHKOVSKII

APPENDIX I

APPENDIX II

APPENDIX III

Preface

Hieromonk Paisii Velichkovskiĭ, the Moldavian starets and archimandrite of the Niamets Monastery in Moldavia, occupies a special place in the history of Orthodox monasticism and of the Orthodox Church.

His personality astonishingly combines the holiness of his own personal life, his love for learning, his remarkable ability for organizing a monastic commune, his skill in attracting and spiritually educating his numerous disciples who later constituted a great school of Orthodox spirituality, and finally his great literary talent which helped him to accomplish an important and necessary task: the correction of old translations of patristic and ascetic literature and the production of a new spiritual literature.

Because of his divergent genealogy and activities Paisii Velichkovskii belongs simultaneously to the Orthodox Churches of Russia and Moldavia. As a native of Little Russia, he spent his early childhood, his school years and his youth in Russia studying in the Theological Academy of Kiev and wandering about monasteries of the Ukraine in a fruitless search for spiritual guidance. At the age of twenty he moved to Wallachia and four years later to Mount Athos where he lived for seven years, at first in absolute solitude and later as the leader of a gradually growing monastic commune with which he moved to Moldavia. There he remained until the end of his life, deepening and expanding his activity, his spiritual influence and his fame in both the Orthodox and non-Orthodox worlds. Truly Paisii Velichkovskii can be called a reformer of spiritual life in the monasticism of Moldavia, Wallachia and Russia. He defined clearly the fundamental goals of monastic life, indicated how those goals could be attained, and thereby prepared people to be capable of realizing those goals. By the influence of his good example, his labors and his translations, Starets Paisii activated a tremen-

9

dous spiritual movement in Orthodox monasticism, which was especially noticeable in Russia where it affected not only monastics but people in all classes of society. The condition of spirituality in the monasticism of the Russian Church and among the Russian people in the eighteenth and nineteenth centuries cannot be conceived of correctly without taking into account the spiritual influence of Starets Paisii and his disciples. Their influence spread throughout more than one hundred monasteries and thirty-five dioceses of the Russian Orthodox Church through the efforts of more than two hundred of the starets' followers and their successors. Under their influence the cast of monasticism in Russia changed: the significance of internal spiritual accomplishments was exalted. The *starchestvo* of Optina Pustyn and its portrayal in Russian literature (*The Brothers Karamazov*) verifies this. The most remarkable Russian writers, Nikolai V. Gogol', Ivan V. Kireevskii, Fedor M. Dostoevskii, Lev N. Tolstoi, Vladimir S. Solov'ev, Konstantin N. Leont'ev and others, followed this spiritual movement in Russian monasticism, studied it and felt its influence upon themselves.

The first biography about the starets to be published in Russian, a translation of a biography written by the starets' disciple, Hieroskimnik Platon, was done by Optina Pustyn in 1847. Starets Paisii's first biography, which was written in Slavonic by his cell-servant Mitrofan, who lived close to him for thirty years, was composed some twenty years after his death. The next and quite extensive biography, which was published in Moldavian, was composed by Isaac. Gregory, the future metropolitan of Moldavia, abbreviated this Moldavian version. Finally, in 1836 Platon, using the versions by Mitrofan and Isaac, wrote a new biography in Slavonic. It was printed in several editions, and it served as a source for a series of other biographies about the starets, which were released in Russia at various times.

In 1913 Sil'vestr, the Bishop of Prilutsk and the auxiliary of the Poltava Diocese, conceived of the publication of the *Poltava-Pereiaslav Fathers*, a work composed of biographies of many ascetics who were born or lived within the boundaries of Poltava. The compilation of the biography of Starets

Paisii Velichkovskii was commissioned to the compiler of this present book. Thanks to the co-operation of Bishop Sil'vestr, Archbishop Feofan of Poltava and the Poltava Diocesan Brotherhood of St. Macarius, we had the privilege to use the rich manuscripts preserved in the libraries at the St. Petersburg Theological Academy, the Petersburg Academy of Sciences, the Moscow Synod, Optina Pustyn, the Novyi-Niamets Monastery in Bessarabia and the Archives of the Orlov Diocese.

The war and the revolution that followed discontinued our work until 1921, when our notes which were salvaged from Russia were brought into order in the quiet and solitude of a Serbian Orthodox parish in Yugoslavia. We had high hopes of visiting Rumania and the dwelling place of Starets Paisii, the Niamets Monastery, and to collect additional accounts about the starets there. We were not privileged to have our desire fulfilled until ten years later, in 1931. Due to unexpectedly fortunate circumstances, we were able to visit the ancient habitations connnected with the starets' name; i.e., Niamets and Sekul, to spend time in their libraries, to visit the Novyi-Niamets Monastery on the Dniester River, to work in Bucharest and to collect in all these locales additional information about Starets Paisii.

We express our deepest gratitude to all those institutions and persons who everywhere, sympathetically, attentively and obligingly rendered us their assistance in our work.

We acknowledge the shortcomings of our book written in the unfavorable conditions of émigré life, and we ask pardon for them.

Protopresbyter SERGII CHETVERIKOV

Part One

Life at Home and in School
(1722-1739)

"For thou, O Lord, art my hope,
my trust, O Lord, from my youth
... from my mother's womb thou
art my protector."

PSALM 70:5-6

CHAPTER I

The Homeland of Starets
Paisii Velichkovskii

The homeland of Starets Paisii Velichkovskii was the blessed Ukraine. In the beginning of the eighteenth century the entire left bank of the Ukraine was a prosperous and flourishing land. Neither the cossack wars of the seventeenth century, the Tatar plunderers nor the Swedish invaders were able to undermine such prosperity. The yet virgin country was known for its invigorating air, its exceptional fertility and its abundant variety of God's natural gifts. The population was great and it increased especially in the second half of the seventeenth century when the inhabitants of the right bank of the Ukraine, ravaged by endless wars and the oppression of the Turks and the Poles, left their old habitations for the left bank of the Dnieper River, the free untrammeled steppes of Poltava and Kharkov, where they formulated the settled Ukraine. In this vast, free expanse of land belonging to no one, the ploughmen had little time to cultivate the fields. Many fished, moved hay and tended fruit orchards. They made their living by manufacturing hemp, flax, tobacco, honey, beeswax, wool and salt. Many domestic animals, poultry and swine could almost always be found on the farmsteads and in the villages. But more so than their prosperity, the spiritual peculiarities of these Little Russians at the time attracts our attention. They were devoted to Orthodoxy, they loved learning and they cared for the poor. These were times of great spiritual ascent. The Little Russians had just lived through the heavy ordeal of a two-hundred year war for their faith and their country, along with dangerous incursions of the

15

Poles, Jesuits and Uniates. These struggles aroused a tremendous enthusiasm among the Little Russians, producing among
them a line of great figures famous for personal holiness, great
learning and love for their homeland. The Little Russians
lived their faith consciously, possessing a way of life that was
simple, humble and winnowed by the spirit of a natural
Orthodox churchliness. Groves of churches towered everywhere over the land, distinct for their individual beauty,
architecture and iconography. To this day the refined com-
plexity and subtlety in design of seventeenth and eighteenth
century iconostases, and the beauty, richness and durability of
embroidery of church vestments remaining from that time are
astonishing. The excellently harmonized and touching liturgical singing was a distinct local characteristic of church services
of the time.

The piety of the Little Russians was not limited though to
their love for churchly beauty. Their endurance of great misfortunes and sufferings for their faith and homeland cultivated in them a strong sense of charity. In every village one
could find hospitals and shelters, adorned with icons within
and without, for the aged and the orphaned. Widows and
orphans, almost always the results of ceaseless wars, were
extended charity by every household.

The love of the Little Russians for learning was remarkable. Almost all of them, including the majority of women,
were able to read and knew the order and rubrics of church
services and the liturgical chants. The priests educated the
orphans and would not allow them to become idle know-
nothings. After the Ukraine's liberation from the Poles every-
body began to learn liturgical reading and singing ambitiously
in special parish schools. Each parish community had a parish
school that was maintained by parish brotherhoods, which
were organized everywhere for the defense of Orthodoxy
and the Orthodox way of life from the onslaughts of Roman
Catholicism and Uniatism. Such brotherhoods existed not only
in cities and boroughs but in villages as well, unifying Orthodox Christians in a close, friendly bond. The brotherhoods
had their own meeting houses, where they assembled for discussing parish activity, stored brotherhood funds and conducted

a brotherhood court. Here, on the eves of great feasts, people gathered to prepare a cooked honey beverage that was sold for the benefit of the parish school and hospitals. The schools were not only used for educational purposes but also as shelters for the orphaned and impoverished and as hostels for itinerant teachers, wandering monks and chanters. They also housed young people who earned their food and shelter there by teaching in the parish school, frequently wandering from one school to another. Such young people had not yet decided upon professions for themselves and they moved from place to place seeing more of the world and ways of different people, as was the practice then. With time some of them became scribes, and even priests, while others became clerks engaged in commerce or joined the Zaporozhian Cossacks. Parishioners freely furnished shelter to the wandering church singers and pedagogues on the condition that they assisted at church services by singing with the choir or taught the children in the parish school. The parish warden paid them accordingly with funds collected from benefactors and parishioners. Due to the existence of such parochial schools and the concern of clergy and parishioners sometimes even the poorest and most neglected children received enough training to be capable of making their own living. Amid such conditions of life the Little Russians developed a spirit of self-sufficiency and independence and an obstinate character.

The public actively participated in all social events and was concerned about all issues. Until 1722, even the bishops and the metropolitans of Kiev were chosen by the unrestricted voice of the clergy, the cossacks and the middle class. For governing purposes the left bank of the Ukraine was divided into regions, each with a major city as its center. Besides the ten major centers of the Ukraine there were almost one hundred and twenty-six boroughs and many large and small villages and farmsteads. The official literate and even colloquial language of the upper educated classes of Little Russian society then is significantly distinguishable from the Russian language of today. It included many Polish and Latin words and clichés. Poltava, the birthplace of Starets Paisii Velichkovskii and a major city in the Ukraine was at that time a small fortress in the southern outlying districts of Little Russia, on the border of the vast steppes beyond which were the lands of the Tatars and the Turks. Two hundred years ago no one would have recognized Poltava as it is today. On the summit of a high steep hill from which one beholds a magnificent vision of the Vorskla River and the distant regions beyond it, Poltava reveals all those advantages that made her the foremost stronghold in defense of southern Russia from the assaults of wild plunderers coming out of the steppes. The strategic watchtower position of Poltava had been valued since the times of the ancient Russian princes. Even twelfth century chronicles refer to Poltava as a protective bulwark on the frontier. At the beginning of the eighteenth century Poltava occupied a small area surrounded by a moat, a soil rampart, and a timber palisade with five bastions and five fortress gates. After the Battle of Poltava in 1709, the fortress was restored and it remained standing until the nineteenth century. The buildings in the town were not particularly noted for any special dimensions or unique beauty. Even after the passing of many years Poltava was described as a small city of a thousand or so white-washed wooden houses, two or three of which were stone, and not having the usual streets or any formal mapping-out of urban plans. The public gardens that enveloped Poltava in a certain splendor were the best decorations the city had. Many churches stood out against the scenery of the city. The then wooden Dormition Cathedral stood almost on the same place where a later stone structure was erected in 1748. The Church of the Savior which stood next to the now non-existent Church of the Transfiguration was preserved in its original appearance but was later faced with stone to preserve it from the destructive effects of time. Peter the Great ordered a *Te Deum* to be served in this church following his victory over the Swedes. Many defenders of the homeland and of the city were buried in the cemetery next to the Church of the Savior.

In the country district of Mazurovka, the Holy Virgin Protection Convent was founded at the beginning of the eighteenth century by nuns from Podolia, and in 1721 it was moved to the village of Pushkarevka, four versts from Poltava. About a verst from the city the Monastery of the Elevation of the Cross was situated on the summit of forest-covered mountains. This monastery was founded in 1650 through the efforts of a certain Colonel Martin Pushkar in commemoration of his victory over the Poles. The main church of the monastery, built soon after the Battle of Poltava, was erected according to some accounts by Kochubei, the general of the Poltava forces and the son of the executed Vasilii Leont'evich Kochubei. According to other accounts Vasilii Leont'evich founded it himself at the end of the seventeenth century.

The population of Poltava, insignificant in number, did not exceed four thousand people. The city was surrounded by many villages, towns and farmsteads. Because it occupied a strategic locale at the crossroads of many cities and the powers of Turkey, the Crimea, Poland, Moscow and Persia, Poltava carried on extremely busy trade and commercial activities. Merchants and traders from Great Russia, Latvia, Poland, the Crimea and the Orient came together at Poltava's two great markets. Book dealers came from Kiev and Nezhin, indicating that there was a demand for books there. Many Jews (who lived in Poltava) were involved in commerce and handicrafts and wandered about the market places. Paisii Velichkovskii writes in his notes about Jews who were among his own maternal kin. The military officers, the cathedral protopresbyters, the district courtiers and the cossack hetmen were considered the notables of the city.

Such were the time and place of birth of the future Starets Paisii. He left these places while he was still a young boy but he never forgot them to the end of his life. He remembered his homeland, his beloved Poltava and the Ukraine, and he retained his knowledge of the Ukrainian language. At the end of his letters and other writings he added after his name, "a native of Poltava."

CHAPTER II

Early Life

Starets Paisii was born in Poltava into a very old, pious and respected Little Russian family. His father, grandfather and great-grandfather were protopresbyters in Poltava. His maternal great-grandfather, a certain Mandia, was a famous and wealthy Jewish merchant who, along with his entire household, accepted baptism. His maternal grandmother, the daughter of a Jew who also received baptism, entered a convent and consequently became the abbess of the Holy Virgin Protection Convent. Agafia, the sister of Paisii's mother, was also a nun in that convent. Consequently, the starets' mother, after being widowed and losing all her children, was tonsured with the name Iuliana, in the same convent. In such a way an entire generation of Velichkovskiis was distinguished by its peculiar religiosity. In addition they were gifted with talents. The chronicler Samuil Velichko describes the grandfather of the starets as a man who was "filled with the grace of God and wisdom," and writes that when, in 1687, the Hetman Ioann Samoilovich was leaving for the Crimean Campaign and riding through Poltava, the starets' father greeted him with syllabic verses of his own composition. It is also known that Paisii's father was a graduate of the Kievan Brotherhood College.

Starets Paisii was born on December 21, 1722, the feast day of St. Petr, metropolitan of Kiev, and he was therefore named Petr. He was the eleventh child in his family. The only younger child was Feodor, who died at age seven. Petr's godparents were Vasilii Vasil'evich Kochubei, whom the Velichkovskii family referred to with great favor. Petr was four when his father died. Then his brother Ioann was made protopresbyter of the Cathedral. Soon after Petr started to be trained in grammar. Sent to school by his mother, most likely to the parochial school of the Cathedral, Petr studied the primer, the *Horologion* and the *Psalter* for a little more than two years, and his elder brother, the priest, taught him how to write. As soon as Petr had learned how to read, reading became his favorite activity. He read and re-read all the spiritual books, the only books, he could find in his home and in the Cathedral library: the Old and New Testaments, the Lives of the Saints, the homilies of St. John Chrysostom and St. Ephrem the Syrian and others. Petr was a very peaceful, meek, serious, silent and profoundly religious child. Under the influence of his continual reading of spiritual literature and especially the lives of the holy ascetics, he was inspired with love for the monastic life. The exemplary pious life of his own family, stories about pilgrims who wandered about holy places, and attendance at church services strengthened Petr's devotion. He began to seclude himself in his room, giving himself to avid reading and prayer. His silence was amazing. For whole days at a time his family would not hear a word from him. Petr was neither morose nor despondent, but on the contrary a joyful friendliness shone on his face. He was fully immersed in his inner life, in his treasured prayerful abiding within God. In the presence of people Petr was, in the words of his biographer, so shy and meek that even his own mother rarely heard his voice. On great feasts when the relatives gathered at the Velichkovskiis', the children could not compel Petr to play in their games nor could even adults tempt him with gifts to join in their conversations. Perplexed at receiving no answer from the boy, they asked his mother if he was dumb. She answered that she herself frequently hears no more than a few words from him because of his usual silence.

Petr lived at home, continuing to behave in the same way, until he was twelve, when his elder brother, the Cathedral protopresbyter, died. His mother wanted to keep the priest's position at the Cathedral, as was the custom then, for her youngest son Petr. The people of Poltava sympathized with her wish. Supported by letters from Petr's godfather, Kochubei, and other respected citizens, the mother and her son, along with his uncle, set out for Kiev to visit the Archbishop Rafail Zaborovskii, in whose jurisdiction Poltava was then included. As was the custom then, Petr memorized some verses that he would recite upon meeting the archbishop. His mother and uncle prevailed upon him to recite them for them beforehand, but because of his usual shyness their insistence was in vain. When they had arrived and appeared before the archbishop the boy, much to the astonishment of his uncle and mother, recited the verses loudly, distinctly and without the slightest bit of timidity. The archbishop was so pleased with Petr that he readily granted the mother's wish that her son become the successor.

The appropriate credentials were prepared immediately and the Kievan Brotherhood School was directed to accept Petr as a student. The gladdened mother returned to Poltava with her son to prepare him for the path he was to follow, and when the time had come in 1735, she sent him off to Kiev again. The Kiev of that time was very different from the Kiev of today. The houses were low, the streets unpaved and there was a dense forest between the lavra and the Podol', the southern lower section of Kiev. The renowned bell tower of the lavra had just been built then. The famous Church of St. Andrew the First-called had not yet been built. Not long before this Kiev had been devastated by a terrible fire. A large part of the lavra's buildings were destroyed, and along with them an ancient and very valuable library containing manuscripts of Iaroslav the Wise. The Theophany Monastery and Academy also suffered from the fire.

Those places destroyed by the fire were rebuilt slowly. In 1733 Archbishop Rafail adorned the monastery with a new building, a dormitory for the needy students of the academy, and he added a second story with a huge colonnade in Tuscan style over the stone Mazepa wing. The academy Church of the Annunciation was set up on this floor. Starets Paisii's contemporaries, partially due to the teaching of the academy and to living in Kiev, subsequently became famous: Georgii Konisskii, the archbishop of Mogilev, G. S. Skovoroda, a wandering Ukrainian philosopher, Simon Todorskii, the archbishop of Pskov, a linguist and catechist of Empress Catherine II, Arsenii Matseevich, the metropolitan of Rostov, and others. In Kiev Paisii discovered the future bishop of Belgorod, Iosif Gorlenko, then a hieromonk in the residence of the metropolitan of the Sophia Cathedral, and Pavel Konuskevich, then the protodeacon of the Kievan Lavra of the Crypts who later became the metropolitan of Tobolsk. The names of these remarkable churchmen and holy ascetics demonstrate to what extent family, school and everyday life conditions favored the spiritual upbringing of young Orthodox at that time.

Of course the concentration of spiritual life in Kiev and the chief source of piety and Christian asceticism was the Kievan Lavra of the Crypts. St. Michael's Monastery, where the relics of the Great-Martyr Barbara were kept, and other monasteries radiated with the exalted life of many ascetics. The Kievan Brotherhood School, where Petr was a student, maintained a complex educational institution. It was a combination of lower, middle and higher schools housed in one section of the Theophany Monastery under the name of Kiev Mogilianskii Theophany Brotherhood Academy. This educational institution, founded as a small school at the close of the sixteenth century for the purpose of educating Russian Orthodox boys, was gradually transformed into an institution of higher learning due to the efforts of generous benefactors and protectors. In 1633, Metropolitan Petr Mogila made it a college and in 1701, by a charter of Peter the Great it became an academy. By the beginning of the eighteenth century the academy operated according to the plan of higher European schools and it became the center of higher learning and the nursery of educators of glorious Russia. The academy produced churchmen who were renowned not only for their learning and talents but also for their holiness of life, such as Feodosii of Chernigov, Metropolitan Dimitrii of Rostov, Bishop Innokentii of Irkutsk, Metropolitan Ioann of Tobolsk, and others. Created through the labors, cares and efforts of the metropolitans of Kiev, generous benefactors and all the Little Russian people, who saw in it a stronghold against the onslaughts of the Jesuits and the Uniates, the Kievan Academy was not a narrow-minded institution, but opened itself to children from all classes of society, spiritual and secular, rich and poor, notable and simple. It received foreigners too, but only if they were Orthodox Christians. Anna Gulevich, bequeathing her estate to the Kiev Brotherhood Monastery in 1615, wrote in her will that she was transferring her property to the childrens' school for the nobles and middle class of the Orthodox confession, and from that time on the all-inclusive character of the school was strictly maintained and confirmed by repeated resolutions of the brotherhood members and the bishops of the Kiev Episcopal See. The following figures show what great numbers of people were educated in the Academy: in 1715, 1,100; in 1742, 1,234; in 1744, 1,160, 388 of whom were from the clerical class and 771 from the aristocracy and gentry. The educational program at the academy was formulated in a special instruction composed by Archbishop Rafail in 1736 for professors and students. In the four primary classes major attention was devoted to the study of languages, i.e., Latin, Greek, Slavonic and Polish. The first class was called the *anlogiia* or *fara*, the second *infima*. These first two classes provided training in reading, writing and basic grammatical analysis of the above-mentioned languages. The next two classes were called the *grammatiki* and the *sintaksimi*. As the names indicate these pupils were trained meticulously in the grammar and syntax of these same languages. In addition some classes were trained in catechism, arithmetic, music and sight reading. From here the pupils were matriculated to the middle school in which there were two classes: the *piitiki* and the *ritoriki*. Both classes were completed together after one year and the pupils were then passed into the upper division of the academy which was composed of two courses of study: philosophy, which lasted for two years, and theology, which lasted for four. Upon their transfer from the middle to the upper division the pupils were designated as students. The rector of the academy, always the abbot of the Theophany Monastery, taught the courses in theology. The prefect, the rector's closest assistant, taught the courses in philosophy. Each of the other classes had its own instructor who taught all subjects. In the transfer process from one class to the next higher one, each pupil was examined by the instructor into whose class he was a candidate for transfer. The superintendent of schools cared for the discipline of the pupils. The monitors who visited the quarters of those students living in the monastery, the seniors, elder students living in the dormitory, and the censors who cared for the behavior of the pupils while they were in church, were assistants of the superintendent. The students were seated in classrooms according to their performance, the more successful ones toward the front and the less successful ones toward the back. Wealth and reputation had no meaning here: all the pupils were equal and they were distinguished only by capabilities and self-application. To help the instructors, because the classes were so large, the better senior pupils were chosen to observe and direct the success of their fellow pupils and were obliged to quiz their knowledge daily before the usual lessons were begun. Such assistants were called auditors. They were held personally responsible for recording the quiz results and submitting them to the instructors. Any carelessness on the auditors' part was severely punished by expulsion from his auditorship, or sometimes by subjection to physical punishment. Four censors were assigned each week, of which two were to list those who were improper in church, improperly behaved in public or incorrigible in something or other. The other two were responsible for coming to school earlier to sweep the floor, to heat up the furnace, and to check for tardiness by sitting at the door. Special attention was given to Latin. All pupils of the lower classes were obliged to speak to each other in Latin. Anyone who broke the rule was penalized. Various kinds of competition were practiced to encourage a greater interest for studies. The younger classes had contests in writing letters. The pupil submitted the name of the classmate with whom he wanted to compete or of the pupil whom he thought was unfairly considered to be better than him. If the claimant turned out to be correct in his claim and won, he received his due recognition, but if he lost he was subjected to a penalty according to the discretion of his opponent. In the upper classes, the divisions of philosophy and theology, there were no examinations, but debates instead. Debates were scheduled weekly for the students. Sometimes the professor himself assumed the position of the defendant, allowing every student to raise any objections to his lectures, which had been read during the previous week. Sometimes, when the professors were present or participating, the students entered into debates with each other over issues touched upon by some professor.

The annual debates were especially festive events. The metropolitan himself functioned as the chairman of the debate and the most notable personalities of Kiev participated. The following is an account of one such debate in the 1740's, around the time when Petr Velichkovskii was studying in the academy:

On the day scheduled for the debate the most notable and influential dignitaries of Kiev and all the
landowners of the outlying districts, having gathered
for the festivities, departed early in the morning for
the lavra, where the metropolitan had been since the
night before. About nine o'clock a festive procession
moved from the lavra to the Podol'. The metropolitan
rode in a carriage that was drawn by eight horses. The
procession was so long that while its beginning mount-
ed the top of Aleksandrovskii Hill its end was still at
the lavra. At that moment, all the belfries in the Podol'
resounded with their peals as the metropolitan's carriage
slowly approached the Brotherhood Monastery, which
was surrounded by flags, each with the insignia of some
department of the academy, and by crowds of people
filling the entire square and monastery courtyard.
A huge and artfully decorated placard which announced the subject and times of the scholarly debate
hung above the monastery gates. As soon as the metropolitan's carriage came to a halt at the entrance to the
monastery the monastery bells were silenced and the
bells that were pealing throughout stopped immediately. In the same moment two academy choirs standing at the sides of the monastery gates thundered
out the traditional 'Many Years,' while one student came forth to extend a welcome to the metropolitan on behalf of the student body. The metropolitan made his way into the hall preceded by the

choirs, while the academy orchestra seated in a wide
gallery welcomed him by playing a march. When the
metropolitan reached the center of the hall, the music
stopped and the choirs sang 'O Heavenly King.' Then
various greetings were extended in various languages
both in verse and in prose, while the rest of the participants gradually filed into the hall. Once the metropolitan and the other notables were seated in their
places, the prefect presented them with a thesis draft
of the forthcoming debate. The following are some
examples of the theses: in philosophy—'The goals of
philosophy are man's acquisition of happiness on earth,
the knowledge of truth and man's perfection through
good works'; 'The subject of logic is essentially to
harmonize the activity of reasoning and to apply that
harmony to known forms'; in ethics — 'Ethics is a
science whose subject is the activity of the will which
is directed toward ethical goodness'; 'Wild animals do
not act according to a definite purpose'; 'A person
entering a duel does not thereby prove his prowess';
'There is no known reason for which man can deprive
himself of his own life'; in physics—'A reasonable
soul is created and it enters into a man from God Himself and in its own essence is immortal'; in metaphysics—'Metaphysics is a science the subject of which is
being that is alien to materiality'; 'God is an entity
existing in Himself; but His being is made known by
revelations.'

The thesis draft was announced under the direction
of Professor Kazachinskii of the Mogilo-Zaborovskii
Academy of Kiev. The thesis was defended by A.A.Z.Z.,
and one of the most meritorious students of philosophy in the Academy, Vasilii Dumnitskii, was the
opponent. The program could not be completed entirely
because of the vastness of the subject matter; therefore
the metropolitan designated what thesis be selected.
During the time intervals between the debates the choir
and orchestra performed and pupils from the primary
classes recited dialogues and verses. After the debates

the metropolitan and the dignitaries were invited to the rector's quarters for refreshments.

All the academy students and pupils were divided into two groups. The smaller group was housed in the dormitory of the academy and the larger group, to which Velichkovskii belonged, was housed in quarters off the academy grounds. The pupils of this latter category usually spent their time around the church and the school. Under the supervision of the parish priest they were held responsible for learning liturgical reading and chanting besides performing their regular studies. The senior who was assigned to every such dormitory detailed two pupils per day, and three or four when more pupils were available, to read the psalms and the canons at the church services. On feast days all the pupils who lived at the school were obligated to attend church services at their own parishes, and those who were capable had to sing from the choir stall. In return for their help the parish paid for the heating of the students' quarters, which by the way, was quite a meager sum of money. The following record was found to be kept in one such parish: "Two kopeks paid to pupils on the Feast of the Protection; two kopeks paid to one school for work by students on the feast day of Pascha."

Because of their extreme poverty, many students went from house to house collecting donations on the great feast days. The school boys lived in very tight quarters. Sometimes they had to squeeze into one room along with the parish reader's family and some homeless children off the streets who were his pupils, and one table served as the only inviolable property of the school boys. Unsurprisingly, many unpleasant and often humorous incidents occurred between the boys and the housemaster in these cramped and uncomfortable conditions. The schoolboys however, endured everything, even if only for the sake of not losing the name or social status that they acquired by merely belonging to the school. At vacation time and even throughout the academic year, the students went on leave to all parts of Little Russia, but they continued to consider themselves a part of the student body of the academy. Other students succeeded in earning their daily bread by singing re-

ligious verses. They went about the streets of Kiev at dinner
time daily, singing at the windows or the gates of homes and
asking for alms.

In the evenings the school boys would often gather together in the square before an assembly of merchants who
were spending the night near their shops, and there they
sang polyphonic odes in honor of the saints, miraculous icons
and especially of the Theotokos. The music and words of such
songs were always the compositions of the students themselves.
With the arrival of the summer vacation, when some students
went to the homes of parents and relatives, and the homeless
and shelterless gathered together in wandering troupes in
order to somehow earn their food until the beginning of the
next academic year, these hymns and verses were spread into
the villages, cities and countryside throughout the Ukraine.

At the time of Metropolitan Petr Mogila, in the first half
of the seventeenth century, the students of the colleges wrote
and performed dramatic presentations of biblical events. The
future St. Dimitrii of Rostov contributed greatly to the production of such religious drama. The academy hall often served
as the theater for these plays, if they were not performed in
an open field or grove where people came two or three times
a year to enjoy such recreation.

Certain feasts and special days were observed with unique
festivity in the academy. On Palm Saturday all the students
and administration of the academy gathered together in the
yard of St. Sophia's Cathedral before Vespers. After they received the blessing of the metropolitan they sang the festal
troparion. "Today the grace of the Holy Spirit has gathered
us together. . . ," holding willows in their hands and making
their way in procession to the Podol' where Vespers was celebrated and they were preached to in the great monastery
church. On the major feasts, the students at the academy stood
holding candles through the church services and participated
in the Entrance at the Cherubic Hymn. In funeral processions
the students walked together in groups according to their
classes, and on the flank of each class a standard-bearer carried
icons of the Savior and the Theotokos on a star shaped placard.

The following is a description of the apparel and external appearances of academy students in those days.

A student's outer garb consisted of a kind of hoodless overcoat, a *kireia* with turned up sleeves that reached down to the heels. The summer uniform was made of silk or taffeta depending upon whether one was rich or poor. The winter uniform was made of broadcloth and trimmed with red or yellow cord. In the winter sheepskin was worn under the *kireia* and girded about the waist by a silken or woolen sash. In the summer the students wore a short kaftan that was fastened from the top with metal buttons. Those who were extra conscious of appearance wore wide and billowing pants, usually blue or red in color. They wore astrakhan hats, the tops of which could be any color. Their boots were of various colors: red or yellow with turned down tops, thick heels and ringing stirrups.

Such was life in the Brotherhood Schools of Kiev when Petr Velichkovskii was brought there by his mother in 1735. It was the only school, not only in the Ukraine, but in all of Russia, that was comparable to better European schools because of its level of education. In addition however, it was a strictly Orthodox school for the people, the cause of consolation and pride among the Ukrainians. It is understandable that to enrol in such a school was the cherished dream and happiness of every talented and inquisitive Little Russian youth at that time.

CHAPTER III

Attraction to Monasticism

Neither the intellectual and festal activities of the academy nor its comradely life had any attraction for the young Velichkovskii. His heart was instead captivated by beautiful churches, sacred places, silent caves and the solitude of conversations with friends about the ascetic life. In his early school days, Velichkovskii studied conscientiously and was passed to successively higher classes each year but, in the depths of his heart, special things were happening and certain decisions maturing. His prayerful contacts with God were strengthening him and his thoughts about his complete self-dedication to God and his absolute turning away from the world grew firmer. By this time he had already established three rules for himself. The first was not to judge those who were near to him, even though he saw with his own eyes that they were sinning. The second was not to have hatred toward anyone. The third was to forgive any insults or abuses with his whole heart. After becoming accustomed to those near him, Petr found friends among them who shared his same thoughts. They often gathered together in some unnoticeable corner, planning in quiet conversations for whole nights until the matins bell to leave the world and to become ascetics. They even made oaths to each other never to cut their hair, or to live in wealthy monasteries where to imitate the poverty of Christ and to live in intimacy and suffering were impossible. They agreed together that to remain in the world is better than to deny themselves worldly pleasures in order to live affectedly without cares in a monastery, thus misleading the laity, making a mockery of monastic life, and thereby securing eternal condemnation for their own souls on the Day of Judgment. In the monastery here Petr found his first spiritual counselor, the pious hieromonk Pakhomii who had spent many years of ascetic labors there. Petr loved to listen to his stories about the efforts of searching in monastic life and about the advantages of being there for a silent and prayerful life with God. Pakhomii supplied Petr with books on spirituality which strengthened Petr's inclinations to monasticism all the more.

During the summer from July to September Petr journeyed to his native Poltava where he continued to live his own peculiar spiritual life. By this time he had formed the habit of recording in a notebook the more remarkable passages that he found in his readings.

By the time of his third year at the academy Velichkovskii's academic efforts were beginning to weaken more and more and his desire for monasticism was overcoming him more strongly. One day some of his friends disappeared from school. Pondering their possible whereabouts, he was sure that they fled to a monastery and, most likely, to the Kitaevskii Skete of the Kievan Lavra of the Crypts. He decided to search for them and, when he found the chance, he quietly stole away from his superiors and set out for the Kitaevskii Skete. It turned out that his friends were there and they were overjoyed to see him. They fed him and, after the evening service, they joined the other novices in reading the writings of St. Ephrem the Syrian. When the long readings were finished they bid goodnight to each other and left Petr to sleep in the refectory. Following the Liturgy on the next day, Velichkovskii was invited to a common meal for all the monks by the superior of the skete. A reverent silence reigned throughout the refectory and the attention given to the readings there left a deep impression upon Petr. It seemed to him as though he were sitting not on earth but among God's angels in heaven. After the meal Petr's friends talked with him again but this time at some length in an attempt to persuade him to stay at the monastery. Petr was ready and willing, but he feared his mother who, as he knew well, would not agree to his entering a monastery but would remove him immediately. On the third day Petr took leave of his friends and returned to the city. His three day visit to the skete served only to strengthen his intention to turn away from the world. When the summer of 1738 had come, Petr did not return to his home but remained in Kiev, intending to visit all the sacred places there and to find the opportunity to realize his wish. At the time he was living in the Podol' near the Church of St. Nicholas the Good, at the place of an old widow who loved him and cared for him as though he were her own son. Taking advantage of his free time during the school vacation, Velichkovskii steadily and enthusiastically attended church services. He loved to go to the St. Sophia Cathedral to pray at the reliquary of St. Makarii and to visit the Monastery of St. Michael to pray at the relics of St. Barbara, the Great Martyr. Petr's favorite place was the Kievan Lavra of the Crypts. He went there mostly on Sundays and feast days for the early and late liturgies. Sometimes he went there in the evening to spend whole nights in the catacombs with other pilgrims or to spend a night in the lavra near the great bell tower. While standing in the church and seeing many ascetics all around him Paisii was moved immensely and so filled with gladness that he would praise God for finding him worthy to be in such a holy place. After the service in the great church he went through the catacombs with the other pilgrims and he delighted in the silence and peacefulness there, which was impossible even to imagine out in the world. His heart burned with desire to remain in that holy place forever, but remembering his mother, he felt that Kiev would not be the place where his desire could be fulfilled. The summer had passed by almost unnoticeably and Petr wanted to visit the Kitaevskii Skete once more. He remembered the pale, emaciated faces of the monks there and the exceptional beauty of their singing. There at the Kitaevskii Skete not only the special festal hymns but even the simple refrains, "Lord have mercy," "Grant it O Lord," and "Amen" were sung with sweet and gentle feeling. It seemed to Petr that even the cruelest and most obstinate heart would become softened and pour forth tears when hearing such singing. The very location of the skete, its modest wooden cross-shaped church dedicated to the memory of St. Sergii of Radonezh and adorned with icons of the great saints of Russia, its profound serenity and quietude created a prayerful and soul-pacifying atmosphere. Petr had great hopes that he perhaps would succeed in entering the monastery at this time and that his mother might yield to his wish. For the second time Petr crossed the threshold of the monastery. With joy and trembling upon entering, Petr first of all saw the superior of the skete standing near the church. Petr approached him, bowed to the ground and asked for his blessing to remain in the monastery for good. The superior led Peter to his cell where he bowed to him again and stood humbly at the door. The superior invited Petr to sit near him but Petr was frightened so he bowed still another time and remained standing in his place. This time the superior ordered Petr to sit with him but Petr only bowed and persistently remained in his place.

> You ask to be received into our monastery, [the superior said], but I see that you have not the slightest bit of ascetic humility, obedience and self-detachment. I ordered you three times to sit near me and you did not obey. At the very first word of my order you should have obeyed. How can you dare to request entrance into our monastery? Whoever is disobedient is not worthy of the monastic way of life.

Seeing that his words embarrassed Velichkovskii severely, the superior changed to a more gentle tone:

> My dear child, I just subjected you to an experience so that you will never forget, as long as you live, that the beginning, the root and the foundation of true monasticism lies in obedience and self-detachment. Whoever decides to leave the world and everything within it must leave behind his self-attachment and reasoning and take on obedience unto God in all things and unto his superior. Do not be embarrassed by the experience to which I have subjected you. Do not lose spirit and do not be disobedient to me out of stubbornness. God will forgive you child and I a sinner forgive you.

The superior proceeded to question Petr about his hometown, his family and whether or not they approved his entrance into the monastery. After Petr had told him everything the superior said,

> My child! Although you seek to be received into our monastery, I cannot permit it because of what you tell me. The outcome could be very unpleasant for you and for us. When your mother learns of your whereabouts, she can easily remove you from here with the help of the authorities. Do not be sad, but put all your hope in God. Believe me that He will not leave you but will help your wish to be fulfilled.

With these words the superior blessed Petr and dismissed him from the monastery.

September came and, with it, the new academic year. Petr was in the class of *ritoriki* but he barely occupied himself with his studies. At this time, following a truce with the Turks, Metropolitan Anthony of Moldavia had arrived in Kiev and was welcomed by Archbishop Rafail to visit the lavra. During his visit, Metropolitan Anthony noticed an acquaintance, Hieromonk Pakhomii, and with Archbishop Rafail's permission took him to his room. Because Petr was visiting his instructor, as he often did, he had the chance to receive the Moldavian metropolitan's blessing. Petr liked how Metropolitan Anthony served the Liturgy in Moldavian and this led him to develop a love for the Moldavian language and the Moldavian people. At the end of January, a fellow student and townsman of Petr noticed that he was not studying too diligently. He went to the prefect, Sil'vestr Kuliabka and told him that Velichkovskii was not studying and that his mother was spending money for nothing. The prefect immediately sent two students to fetch Velichkovskii. When Petr came to the prefect, he inquired very sternly as to why he was not studying. Contrary to his own timidity and bashfulness, Petr answered with a certain boldness that he himself could not understand.

> The first reason is that, because I have a firm in-

tention of becoming a monk and being conscious of
the unexpectedness of death, I want to be tonsured as
soon as possible. The second reason is that I see nothing
useful for the soul in external learning. I hear only the
names of pagan gods and wise men—Cicero, Aristotle
and Plato. By learning their wisdom people of today
have become blinded to the end and have digressed
from the true way. Intellectuals utter words but, internally, they are filled with darkness and gloom, for their
wisdom is of the world only. Not seeing any purpose to
such learning and fearing how I myself cannot but be
corrupted by it, I left it. The third and final reason is
that, in evaluating the fruits of such learning among
those who belong to the monastic ranks, I notice how
they are similar to worldly officials who live in great
honor and glory, decorating themselves with expensive
clothes, riding around on splendid horses and in exquisite carriages. I do not say these things in judgment.
After being trained in such external wisdom, I fear and
tremble that I, being a monk, will fall into worse infirmity and feebleness. For these reasons I left external
learning.

After hearing the young *ritor* attentively, Sil'vestr answered
him with a verbose speech in which he explained Velichkovskii's ignorance. He explained to him the great benefit of external learning and that if he did not recognize it, then it is
hardly surprising, since he did not apply himself to it in the
first place. He told him how the Three Great Fathers of the
Church, Basil the Great, Gregory the Theologian, and John
Chrysostom studied those pagan poets and wise men and that
external learning will not hinder him becoming a true monk
since it was no hindance to these Great Fathers who were lights
of Orthodoxy and true servants of Christ. Noticing that his
words did not produce the intended effect upon Velichkovskii,
Sil'vestr became angry and threatened him with severe physical punishment for disobedience.

Vacation time had come so Petr left for his mother's home
in Poltava where he had not been for almost two years. That

was the last summer which he spent in his homeland. He
finally decided not to return to the academy but instead to
begin the wanderings of a pilgrim. It was sad for Petr to
part with his homeland and its familiar places. What was
even more difficult for him was his imminent parting with
his mother. He knew her thoughts and plans for him and
what a great shock his leave taking would be for her. He wanted
to prepare her for it somehow so he began talking to her about
the matter by gradually making known his intention. Nevertheless she was overcome by great sadness. With bitter tears
she tried to convince him that he should not leave her. Petr
tried to calm and console her, begging her not to be sad but
to rejoice because the Lord had instilled such a desire within
him. Then Petr began speaking to her from a different per-
spective. He told her first of all that it was an absolute necessity
for him to finish school before he could choose his ultimate
path. Such ideas made her feel a bit happier and she began to
hope that he would change his mind. Petr had a friend, Dimitrii, who also lived in Poltava and who shared the same ideas
and intentions. So together the boys left their homeland.

As vacation time drew to an end Petr and Dimitrii arranged
to go to Kiev together to study but their real motivation behind
the move was to leave the Ukraine. Petr became ill though, so
his friend Dimitrii set off for Kiev alone to make the necessary
arrangements for their journey. Once Petr regained his health,
his mother sent him on his way seeing him off as far as Reshetilovka, about thirty-six versts from Poltava. There Petr
and his mother stayed through the night and when they finally
parted she cried bitterly, feeling that they were parting forever
in this life. Again she begged him not to leave her, to study
hard and to return to Poltava every summer so that she could
see him. Petr knew that he would never see her again. He
broke into tears and then fell to his feet asking for her maternal blessings. He kissed her hand and they parted at last. Petr
went on to Kiev and his mother returned to Poltava. Petr felt
a certain dualism within himself then. On the one hand he
felt a deep grief but at the same time he felt a joyful consciousness of liberation from the bonds of the world. While
en route to Kiev he suddenly and with great amazement saw

his friend Dimitrii standing before him. Dimitrii was returning from Kiev. He told Petr that he saw no purpose for remaining there since he was finished with all the necessary preparations. Therefore he decided to return to Petr in Poltava.

"You should have awaited my arrival in Kiev," said Petr, "but, since you did not the Lord helped us to meet. Take up your belongings and hurry with me to Kiev so that we can attend to our affairs."

"Since we are not far from our hometown," answered Dimitrii, "let me drop by there to bid farewell to my mother and to receive her last blessing, then I shall come to you in Kiev immediately. I shall even catch up to you along the road."

Petr shuddered. How strong are the ties of people with their parents and the world. He asked his friend not to leave him and not to go to Poltava but seeing how Dimitrii was insistent he said bitterly,

> I see my friend that the fervor for God in your heart has died out and that your love for your mother and the world is greater than your love for Christ. The world has bound you so that, even though you will repent and will want to leave it, you will not be able to. You will take a wife for yourself, be burdened by worries about her and your children and then you will finish your life in this world.

"Who will keep me back in the world if I want to be a monk?" answered Dimitrii. "I would sooner die than surrender to anyone who prevents me from fulfilling my desire. As you know my people are not like that. Believe me I shall return only to receive my mother's blessing and then I shall return to you."

"Let no one compel you to remain in the world but nevertheless I still say without any inhibition that your love for the world which is hidden within you and which you do not recognize will keep you in the world forever. Believe me, we shall never see each other in this life again, and therefore I shall not expect you but I shall follow the path alone, to wherever the Lord, Christ my Savior will lead me."

The friends kissed each other and parted. Petr continued on his way to Kiev, grieving that the envious world had snatched his best friend away from him.

Upon his arrival in Kiev, Petr dismissed his coachman and immediately wrote to his mother that by the help of God and her prayers he had made his way successfully. Then he began to think about where his next steps would take him. The first decisive turning point had occurred in Petr's life. His carefree childhood, that peaceful security beneath his mother's wings and in the school, had come to an end. From now on he would have to sustain himself. Having surrendered himself to the impulse of his heart, Petr divested himself of his strongest attachments to the world and stood singly in its vast abyss, alone before the face of God, putting all hope in Him only and adhering to Him with his whole heart. At that time Petr Velichkovskii was one month short of age seventeen.

Part Two

Years of Wandering in Search of Spiritual Guidance
(1739-1746)

"We went through fire and through water; yet thou hast brought us forth to a spacious place."

PSALM 66:12

CHAPTER I

Wanderings

After leaving his home, the academy, his country and its peaceful security, and taking upon himself poverty and wandering, the youth, Petr, clearly knew what he had to do. He saw the frightening strength of the world and feared that such a world might bind him and confuse his soul with its habits and needs and extinguish the holy fire of the love for God that was in him. Once and for all, decisively breaking asunder his bonds to the world and renouncing everything that would hinder his internal freedom, Petr followed the example of St. Aleksei the Man of God, confident that the Lord would not abandon him, as He did not abandon St. Aleksei. That divine fire of love for God, which he made the main purpose of his life, was kindled a hundredfold. Let us now follow our young pilgrim and see what he met in his wanderings and in what measure he fulfilled his cherished thoughts and wishes.

While Petr pondered where his steps would direct him, he was struck by the idea of visiting Chernigov, where a spiritual guide, the Hieroschema-monk Pakhomii lived. He hoped to find advice and receive a blessing for his forthcoming journey. Petr found a fellow traveler, one of the academy students who was passing through Chernigov to visit his father. They found an old boatman who agreed to take them to Chernigov for a certain price, bought all the necessities for their journey, and departed. After moving down the Dnieper for awhile they came into the Desna and went upstream with some effort until they reached the big city, Ostra, where they stayed for ten days. Great hardships accompanied them along the way. It was October and the weather was becoming quite

inclement and at times severe. Not having warm nor sufficient
clothing, Petr shook from the cold and he suffered especially
from the snow and the cold rain carried along by the strong
cutting winds. When night fell, the travelers hoisted their
boat onto the bank, kindled a camp fire and warmed themselves
as long as they could. Petr suffered more than the other two
because he did not have enough clothes. While he warmed
himself on one side, he froze on the other, so that turning
about from side to side the whole night, it was impossible for
him to get any sleep. The greatest difficulty was that the travelers always had to sail against the current and therefore continually work the oars. Petr's fellow travelers were stronger
than he and he was naturally weak from the time of his
childhood, having never known hard physical work. But Petr
worked beyond his strength and his body ached all over, especially in his arms and legs. Their boat was so small that it
was scarcely able to hold together during the journey and was
continually filling with water about four inches deep. The
travelers had to bail the water out even as the high waves
brought more in. At one point the boat almost completely
capsized near a sandbank in the middle of the river. They
jumped out, and standing in water up to their knees scooped
water out of the boat while struggling to keep it from sinking.
A rapid undercurrent caught them unawares, flushed out the
sand from under their feet and pulled them down river. Petr
nearly fainted from fear, but somehow they succeeded in
grasping onto the boat while they were being swept away.
After being washed up onto the bank and bailing out all the
water they continued on their way. As they rowed into Ostra,
they saw a man standing on the bank who watched while
the boat pulled in half submerged in the water. While the
travelers climbed out from the boat onto the shore the stranger
immediately began to scold the boatman: "Have you no fear
of God that you dared to take these youngsters out onto this
dangerous river in such a little boat? You are already old and
have no fear of death, but had these young fellows perished
you would have had a heavy sin on your soul. You not only
deserve no pay but you should be punished."

After scolding the boatman, the good stranger took the

boys into his home and took care of them for several days. The boys took the stranger's advice and parted with the boatman. He told them to pay him only half the fare but Petr, not wishing to anger the old man, gave him the full fare to Chernigov. Their host then found another boatman and paid him to take the youths to Chernigov. Having thanked their good protector, the young travelers went on their way.

They resumed their journey with enough food and really not needing anything more. Within a few days they came to Boldinskii Mountain, covered with dense forests, where the venerable Antonii of the Caves once lived and where the crosses of the Chernigov churches and monasteries glistened on the horizon. They joyfully thanked God for their safe arrival in Chernigov. After Petr bade farewell to his fellow travelers he made his way to the residence of the bishop where, upon finding his spiritual father, Hieroschema-monk Pakhomii, he was overcome with great joy. Petr stayed with Pakhomii for several days, telling him about his plans and asking advice about the best way to cross the border and to finally begin his pilgrimage.

"It would be best for you," Pakhomii advised, "to go to a certain monastery near Liubech, the homeland of the venerable Antonii of the Caves. There you will find a certain Hieroschema-monk Ioakim, who will tell you what to do. The Liubechskii Monastery stands over the Dnieper River along the Polish border so it will be easy for you to leave the country there. Stay on with me until market day, when you will easily find someone to take you to Liubech."

Petr stayed but he found no one to take him, so he hired a peasant who lived halfway from Liubech and who agreed to take him there. After spending the night in the peasant's village, Petr asked if he would drive him further. The peasant refused and Petr continued on his way and prayed to God. He was filled with fear because the road went through a dark and dense forest. This was the first time in his life that he traveled alone, and he was very afraid of meeting wild animals. Nevertheless, he went along calmly and before long his fear turned into joy as he saw the Liubechskii Monastery through the trees. He was not more than three versts from the

city. As he approached, he noticed a company of guards
standing at turnpikes, which marked the way from the Dnieper
River to the city limits. In order to reach the monastery Petr
had to pass them, and they were sure to stop him. He had
no official identification and feared being turned back by the
guard. Petr prayed intensely in his heart as he approached
them. Suddenly a monk who was going to the monastery appeared near the toll gate. He turned and gazed at the approaching boy. The guard then shouted at the boy asking who
he was. Not giving Petr a chance to answer, the monk re-
buked the guard.

"Why do you ask who he is? Can't you see that he's a
novice returning to the monastery?" The guard immediately
allowed Petr to pass and seeing that the monk was a hieromonk approached him then for his blessing.

The hieromonk, called Arkadii, brought Petr to the
monastery and accommodated him in the cell of the hegumen,
who was away. Petr, having noticed that Father Arkadii was
a spiritual man, was happy that they had met and he even
wanted to remain with him. As the hegumen was returning
to the monastery, Father Arkadii pointed him out to Petr
through the cell window.

"Look brother! There is our hegumen standing in the
middle of the monastery. Do your hegumens in Kiev walk
around like that?" Petr looked out through the window and
he saw the respected grey-haired starets in a wide black coat.
He was very impressed by his simplicity and humility. It was
the first time that Petr had ever seen such a poorly dressed
hegumen. Petr approached him for a blessing and the hegumen
asked:

"Where do you come from, brother? What is your name
and why have you come to our monastery?"

"I come from Kiev to be a novice and my name is Petr."
Hearing his answer the hegumen rejoiced and said:

"Glory to God for sending you to us. We used to have a
steward and cell servant here whose name was Petr. He left
the monastery two days ago. You bear his name and therefore I assign you to his duties. Be our cell servant." Father
Arkadii was astonished by what the starets had just said.

"Holy Father, this brother is only a new arrival at our monastery. He does not even know our duties. Allow him to live with me for awhile until he learns our ways. Then you will be able to determine which duty is necessary for him."

"I would be glad," said the hegumen, "to take your advice, but there is no one in our monastery who is suitable to be my cell servant. You know that yourself. Even against my will, I must not delay to assign him to this duty." The hegumen led Petr into the cell (dormitory) to show him what he had to do and to explain to him all his responsibilities, and he handed the keys over to him. Petr's duties were to ration to the cooks the amount of food, poppyseed, groats, fish, etc., that they would need to prepare meals. Petr prostrated himself at the feet of the hegumen and received his blessing.

Thus began the monastic life of Petr. He was led to a cell near the place of the hegumen. It consisted of two rooms. The same Hieromonk Ioakim, to whom Petr had been sent by Father Pakhomii, lived in the smaller one, and Petr lived in the bigger one, along with an old monk and another novice. Petr began attending to his chores energetically, but they were not very easy for him. He had to gather and store heavy stones which were used for covering storage vats. This tired him quickly but he dared not tell anyone. Instead he patiently fulfilled his responsibilities, asking God to give him strength. In the beginning Petr remained in his secular clothes, but later he was given an old cossack made from coarse black fabric. Upon receiving it he was beside himself with joy. Some time after the old monk who lived in the cell with Petr had died, the hegumen passed on his coarse grey cassock to Petr. "If you like these clothes, you may take them to wear." Petr accepted the gift gratefully, and after he returned to his cell, he kissed the old tattered cassock like a sacred object. He wore it until it was nothing but rags and threads.

Petr's duties began during Matins and ended late in the evening. When he finished he had to read the cell-servant's rules to Hieromonk Ioakim. By living so close to the starets, Petr always had the best opportunity to turn to him about those questions which occupied him most, but his natural shyness and timidity inhibited him and restrained his free

and open self-expression. Meanwhile the hegumen transferred Father Ioakim's residence to the monastery skete, about
five versts from the monastery. Consequently, Petr lost his
opportunity to seek his counsel. Father Ioakim's cell was given
over to Petr. The hegumen cared very much about Petr's
external and internal life, and did not leave him without direction. He gave him the book of St. John Climacus saying:

"Take this book, brother, read it with attention and acquire
holy steadfastness and every virtue. This book is of great use
for the soul." Petr took the book gladly and began to read it
immediately. He liked the book so much that he decided to
copy it for himself in his free time during the night. Petr had
no candles so he made wood slivers, about a *sazhen* or more
in length. He lodged them into the cracks in the walls and lit
them. By their light he sat down and copied the book. The
smoke from the splinters filled his room, and made his eyes
smart and his breathing difficult. Occasionally he would open
the windows for awhile to let out the smoke and then resume
his work.

Petr was fortunate enough to get a lamp after awhile, and
then his copying proceeded much more rapidly so that, by
the time he left the monastery, he succeeded in copying more
than half the book. Petr liked the monastery very much but,
unfortunately, his emotional tranquility did not last too long.
Before long greater temptations befell him, and added great
disorder to his life. The other monks in the monastery, watch-
ing after Petr, noticed his soft character and his consequent
inability to refuse favors to people. Almost all the monks,
from the lowest to the highest in rank, went to him to get
what they needed: poppyseed, millet, groats, etc. The hegumen
said nothing about this in his previous instructions to Petr,
so he did not know how to approach him. He was afraid that
the hegumen would forbid it and Petr, because of his weakness in not knowing how to refuse people, would appear to
be even more at fault. At that moment, his conscience would
no longer permit him to issue food rations without the knowledge and blessing of the hegumen. But seeing how the most
respected senior monks were coming to him, who was the
least among them, to ask for whatever they needed, he had

not the courage to look them in the face and, consequently, deafening his conscience, he could not dare to refuse their requests. The cooks took advantage of Petr, persuading him to give them a double ration and assuring him that their meals would therefore be much tastier. The food actually did turn out better and all the monks were so satisfied that they praised and thanked Petr for caring about them. They were even saying that the Lord would bless the monastery with an abundance of goodness because of Petr. Petr rejoiced with them affectedly but deep within his heart he was disquieted and his conscience continually tormented him.

The hegumen continued, however, to refer to Petr with invariable favor. It was his habit to invite a novice to his cell for supper and Petr was invited often. Petr entered the hegumen's cell and found him sitting at a meal with another older monk. Petr modestly remained at the door, not daring even to come near them. At the hegumen's call Petr timidly sat down at the table and partook of the meal. The food that was on the hegumen's table was the simplest: a certain kind of sour soup and buckwheat porridge. They drank the same pear juice or sour kvass that was given to the rest of the monks. The hegumen often charged Petr to read during meals in the refectory. Whenever there was an especially touching life to be read from the *Lives of the Saints*, Petr read it, as he learned to do in school, in such a way that many monks stopped eating and were moved to tender emotion. Some even left their places at their tables and sat around Petr, listening to him with tears. What moved Petr more was how the hegumen managed the lives of the monks in love, peace, meekness and patience, like a true father. Whenever a monk fell into transgression the hegumen forgave him immediately if he saw only the slightest indication of repentance. The hegumen instructed the penitent with helpful words, giving him a rule adequate to his strength and maturity. With such a wise and gentle teacher, the monks lived in peace and deep gratitude toward God.

This peaceful and happy life came to an end. Three months following Petr's arrival in Liubech, Bishop Antonii, metropolitan of Moldavia, who was then governing the Diocese

of Chernigov, assigned another hegumen to the monastery.
This was German Zagorovskii, a certain scholar. After his
arrival in Liubech, he soon began to manage the monastery
not according to the example of the gentle Nikifor, but quite
imperiously, as Paisii Velichkovskii's biographer writes. After
discerning the disposition of their new hegumen, the monks
grew fearful and some even fled away to unknown places.
Petr went about fulfilling his duties, but ever fearful that
he might do something to anger the new superior. Before
long those fears were quite justified. Once, during the Great
Fast, the new hegumen ordered Petr to give the cook a special
kind of cabbage for his table. Petr did not hear too clearly
what the hegumen had said and he was afraid to ask him to
repeat it. Petr directed the cook to prepare some cabbage for
the hegumen. When the hegumen was served, he looked at
what was prepared for him and called for Petr. Petr came and
the hegumen arose, went over to him and said:

"Did I ask you to serve me that kind of cabbage?" Without even waiting for an answer, he then struck Petr across the
cheek so hard he almost tottered off his feet. The hegumen
forcefully drove him beyond the threshold of his cell yelling
behind him:

"Out, you good-for-nothing!"

Petr, trembling with fear, returned to his own cell. He
thought that if the hegumen had been so cruel to him for such
an insignificant error, what then would he do about something
really serious? The hegumen's cell servant, who shared the
cell with Petr, also angered the hegumen over something.
Word had been spread that the hegumen was praising himself
to someone for dealing with the two novices as he thought fit.
The monks, who all were well disposed toward Petr, told him
what they had overheard from the hegumen. The cell servant
was quite familiar with the ways of the hegumen so he decided
to flee from the monastery and he invited Petr to come along.
Petr expected no good for himself from such a hegumen, so
he agreed to leave. During Palm Week of the Great Fast,
the appropriate time to flee presented itself. During the night,
while the monks were asleep, the fugitives, after praying together, quietly stole away from the monastery. They went

down to the banks of the Dnieper where guards were out on patrol. When they saw a big enough break between the guards they began to make their way across the river, trembling at the possibility of being caught. They made their way successfully though to the opposite bank. Since the morning would soon dawn, and because they decided not to take some unknown route, they settled in a comfortable place for the remainder of the dark hours to preserve their strength for the forthcoming journey.

CHAPTER II

Wanderings in the Ukraine

At the break of dawn the fugitives found a route, and soon they arrived in a village. After resting and eating a bit there, they continued on their way southward. They passed through huge dense forests and stopped in small villages to spend the nights, or simply slept in the forests beneath the open sky. Within several days they came to the Pripet River across which they saw the city of Chernobyl. They were hesitant to cross because the ice on the river looked quite hopeless. While they stood on the bank deliberating, several men came to the river and bravely crossed on the ice to the other side. Our travelers then followed behind, but not without fear because the ice in many places was broken. After crossing half way, they noticed before them a deep cleft, almost an *arshen* wide. They stepped over the cleft fearing inevitable death, but the rest of the way presented no difficulties. They walked onto the opposite bank of the river and sat down to rest. No sooner had they begun to relax when they began to hear a loud cracking noise, as of a falling tree. Before their eyes the ice cracked and broke along the whole visible length and width of the river. Ice-floes, like high walls, pressed against each other, floating down river. Greatly shocked by the sight before them, Petr and his partner tearfully thanked God, who led them across the ice one moment before it broke.

Chernobyl was not surrounded by any demarcation lines or barriers nor were there any guards patrolling the entrance to the city. Petr and his companion entered the city with ease and there they found a calm haven for themselves.

It was Lazarus Saturday. On the morning of the next day, while Petr and his friend were walking through the city, some-

one called out Petr's full name. Petr was frightened as he
turned and looked around. Then he noticed a fellow Poltavan,
son of an elder townsman, who greeted Petr with exuberance
and invited both wayfarers into his home. He told Petr how
he was in the city on an assignment from Colonel Kochubei
of Poltava for the purchase of forest land. He also told Petr,
however, how his mother was grieving over him and how her
neighbors in Poltava were sharing in her sadness. He tried
convincing Petr to return to his mother but Petr was still so
unwonted by the unexpected meeting that he could not utter
a word. Petr had only one thought in his mind: that this
acquaintance could detain him and return him to his homeland.
They continued to converse affably as the host led Petr into
his home and ordered that he be served lunch. Petr, however,
was so afraid that he lost his appetite. After lunch, the host,
seeing off his two guests, invited them to come more often,
and being aware of Petr's flight from home he admired him
for his determination to retreat from the world. He went on
to say how he himself lived in Poltava, until Petr's arrival
at Liubech, at the parochial school near the Dormition Church
and that he remembers quite clearly Petr's mother and relatives as well as Petr himself. But he said that he could not
conceive of Petr hiding in the Liubechskii Monastery.

Such praise and friendly reminiscence were painfully
distressing for Petr. He could see that he was not very successful at concealing himself from other people. Fearing therefore
a return to Poltava, Petr decided that day to leave Chernobyl.
He went to the nearest parochial school, wasting no spare
moments to find out whether or not anybody was departing for
the Ukraine. Petr found such a person, a monk who was leaving
that very day for the south. After Petr's pleading for him and
his companion to be taken along, the monk at last overcame
a certain reluctance and gave in, ordering them to come along
in a hurry. Petr hurried back to his room to get his friend but
he was not around. Petr waited for some time, but his friend
never appeared so he left alone without him for fear of
losing his ride. By the time Petr had returned the monk was
already on his way and Petr caught up with him down the

road. They rode through nothing but forests for several days before they reached the Ukraine.

At this time the right bank of the Ukraine was in a very sad state. It was suffering very much due to the religious fanaticism of the Jesuits and Uniates. Archbishop Filaret of Chernigov described this persecution in his history of the Church:

It is difficult to imagine all the cruelties and torments endured by the Orthodox at this time. Orthodox priests were tied to stakes and scourged with whips, thrown into prison, refused food, dismembered of their fingers, and their arms and legs were broken. Any survivors of such tortures who still refused the *Unia* were driven from their homes. From day to day, monasteries were attacked, plundered and burned, and the monks were tortured and often times killed. Rural dwellers, merchants and tradesmen were subjected to tortures in order to force them into the *Unia*. Like sheep, the Orthodox were driven into the Uniate Church. On one occasion a henchman walked into an Orthodox Church during the Gospel reading and began beating the people there with a whip, driving them out like cattle. Many people suffered the destruction of their homes and death itself in the battles. In Kiev, the religious center of the country, vehement protests were expressed everyday by south-western Ukrainians who were coerced into the *Unia*. Those village clergy and laity alike who were driven out from their parishes, deprived of their very own blood and possessions and cruelly assaulted and mutilated, traveled to Kiev to reverence the holy shrines, confident in the protection promised them by the metropolitan, and in spite of the orders of the political authorities and the nearby Polish military cordons. The crowds of pilgrims were filled with horror over what they had heard about the suffering that was endured in their homeland for their faithfulness to Orthodoxy. Cossack insurgents rose in the defense of their faith and nation. At the beginning of the eighteenth century such an insurgency movement was in full force and it continued to grow in intensity until the middle of that century. The Polish government sent troops to capture the Cossack insurgents and to quiet the rebellion. These forces proved to be a tremendous burden for the people, all the more increasing the discord.

One of the most powerful of such insurrections occurred in 1734, about five or six years before Paisii Velichkovskii began his wanderings. In this country, amid such troubled surroundings, the young searcher of true monasticism had to accomplish his journey.

After several days of wandering Petr was struck by trouble. Because of the unusually long journeying on foot, to which Petr was not accustomed, his left leg swelled up from the heel of his foot to his knee. Moving became more and more difficult for him so that he was forced to stop for rest quite frequently. Several times the monk with whom Petr was traveling threatened to leave him behind, but Petr's tearful entreaties prevented that from happening. They were handicapped for many days since Petr's aching leg felt no improvement. Soon they arrived at a small skete called Rzhishchev, overlooking the Dnieper River south of Kiev. Here Petr was struck by another sickness. Whatever small amount of food he would eat would cause serve vomiting. Within a month, he lost so much weight and grew so weak that he could not even walk. He prayed with burning ardour to God that he be saved from death.

During that time three traveling monks who were living in the skete decided to go to Moldavia. Petr asked to go along. Because he was so weak the monks did not want to take him but at last they conceded to his undeclinable requests. Petr had difficulty leaving the skete, but as soon as he got up into the mountains, in the fresh air and open spaces, he felt immediately healthier. On that same day they were caught in a violent thunderstorm. The monks ran ahead in search of shelter or some place for lodging, and feeble Petr trailed along behind, caught in the downpour and turbulence of the storm. Along with the heavy rain, walnut-size hailstones fell and covered the ground a fourth of an *arshen* deep. Soaked to his skin, Petr made his way into the village late at night and took shelter.

After spending the night in a village hut, Petr arose and searched for his friends. He found them staying in the school near the home of the village cantor. They felt relieved when they saw that Petr was safe and sound. In the meantime, they were inquiring of the cantor about how to go to Moldavia. When the cantor heard their question he said:

Holy Fathers, I advise you not to go there. Soldiers are patrolling the roads everywhere in search of thieves and brigands. If you should fall into their hands, they will assault you cruelly out of their hatred for our Orthodox faith.

There was one such assault recently in our village. The cantor who preceded me here was afraid of denunciation by the persecutors of Orthodoxy. While reading the Creed during the Divine Liturgy he read the eighth article in the folowing way: "And in the Holy Spirit, the Lord and Giver of life, Who truly proceeds from the Father"; and for some time he was deceiving the Uniates in this way.* Before long, however, he was reported to the landlord for not reciting the Creed according to the Uniate practice. Upon hearing this, the landlord went into a rage. He called a soldier and together they entered the church just before the Creed was to have been read. When that blessed cantor had stepped out into the center of the church and began reading the Creed, the landlord drew near to him and listened to every single word attentively. The cantor knew why the landlord was present so he read especially loudly, slowly and triumphantly, and when he came to the words "And in the Holy Spirit," he, himself being filled with the Holy Spirit, exclaimed loudly and distinctly: "And in the Holy Spirit, the Lord and

---

* There is a play on words here. The Uniates wanted the cantor to say the Creed with the *filioque* which in Russian is *i syna*. The word "truly," which the cantor used in its place, is *istinno*. Pronounced quickly, it would be hard to distinguish the two.

Giver of life, Who proceeds from the Father," omitting
the world "truly" which he used to add to the text because of his fear. The landlord screamed out like a wild
animal and, seizing the cantor by his hair, threw him
down onto the church floor and began kicking him. He
had the cantor dragged out from the church and cruelly
beaten with rods. While he was being beaten someone
in the crowd rushed to fetch the mother of the cantor.
She ran to her son and with tears in her eyes encouraged
him not to lose his staunch spirit but to give up his life
for his faith.

'Do not fear such fleeting suffering,' she said, 'but
endure it unto death that you may be worthy to receive
the crown of martyrdom from Christ in Heaven.'

'Have no doubts about me, dear mother,' the martyr
said, 'for I am ready to endure not only these wounds
for my faith but a thousand times more. This is the sure
hope of my salvation.' Upon hearing such words, the
mother of the cantor greatly rejoiced in her soul and
she thanked Christ for allowing her to be the mother
of a martyr for the faith. When the landlord saw and
heard what was happening between the cantor and his
mother, he ordered the soldiers to beat the martyr even
more fiercely. Under the heavy blows the martyr finally
delivered his soul into the hands of God.

The story frightened our wayfarers; so they heeded the
advice of the cantor and decided not to go to Moldavia. Instead they followed a route along the Dnieper River and
visited the Orthodox monasteries that were located along the
way. In one of the villages that they passed along the way
they met a hieromonk who told them about a certain pious
hermit named Isikhii. The hermit was on a nearby isolated
island in the middle of the river where he was striving toward
his salvation. Petr, extremely captivated by what the wandering hieromonk had just told them about the hermit, remained
behind while his traveling companions went ahead on the
journey. Petr wanted not only to visit this hermit but he hoped
for the good fortune to be able to live with him. Petr felt

then that this was what his soul was desiring. He asked the hieromonk to lead him to the hermit Isikhii. When they had arrived on the island the hermit came out to meet them. Then the hieromonk departed, leaving Petr on the island with the hermit. Petr was filled with happiness because he at last had found the kind of person that he needed.

The hermit Isikhii was truly a servant of God, who was diligently fulfilling all His commandments and who possessed a great love for the Sacred Scriptures. He labored zealously and unremittingly in making copies of patristic texts. The following incident shows how ardently he attended to this task lying before him.

Once he heard about a certain rare and very useful book that was in a distant monastery of the Diocese of Chernigov. The hermit had no reservations about going by boat to that monastery, so he went and asked the hegumen and monks of the monastery if he could have the book. They gave the book to him, he returned to his cell with it, and immediately sat down to make a copy of it. He worked carefully and meticulously and, as soon as he finished, he returned the book and thanked the monks for the kindness that they had extended to him. Such was his love for books.

Petr, noticing the lofty spiritual heights of this hermit, desired greatly to remain with him, and so he was greatly disheartened when the hermit refused to take him in as a disciple.

> Child, I am a sinful and unworthy man. I am not capable of directing even my own miserable soul in the way of Godliness. How, then, can I even dare to receive you under my direction? Such a task is not within my means. I beg you not to burden me by your request.

Thinking that the hermit was refusing out of humility, Petr implored him more persistently, even falling to his knees before him, but the hermit remained firm. Petr was so hurt and he wept so much that his face was swollen from his tears. The hermit was trying with his whole heart to console the boy, but he nevertheless remained obstinate in his refusal.

I beg you for the sake of the Lord, do not be so sad
just over my not accepting you. I am doing this not out
of malice for your salvation, but actually because of the
infirmity of my own soul. Put all your hope in the Lord.
He will never forsake you if you seek salvation for
your soul, but He will set you on the right path by
His grace!

Petr did not know what to do. He fell into a state of extreme despondency. The hieromonk who brought him to the
island was not returning and Petr, because of his innate
shyness, would not attempt to go away alone anywhere. To
stay near the hermit any longer was simply impossible. At
last the hieromonk returned and the hermit told him to take
Petr to some monastery. When the time had come for Petr
to finally part with the hermit, whom he loved very much,
he fell at the feet of the hermit and wept bitterly because he
could not live with him in holy obedience. Once again the
hermit tried to console Petr by advising him to put all his trust
in God who would one day grant him the kind of life he desired. After thanking the hermit for his love Petr bade him
farewell and departed with the hieromonk upon a new journey.
They visited several monasteries and then they came to the
St. Nikolai Monastery, also known as the Medvedovskii Monastery, which was under the jurisdiction of the metropolitan
of Kiev. Hieromonk Nikifor was the head priest, but he was
not the same Nikifor under whose guidance Petr entered the
Liubechskii Monastery.

Father Nikifor tenderly received Petr. He put him in a cell
with another novice and assigned him to the same general
obedience all the other monks were under. The monks gathered hay and Petr worked along with them. He also was
assigned to knead dough for bread, but when the monks
noticed how Petr kept cutting his fingers and his general inexperience he was transferred to the granary, where he was
to carry sheaves to the threshing floor. But here Petr was
again taken by misfortune. Not knowing how to drive oxen

he upset the wagon load, spilling the sheaves, and not knowing what to do then, he ended up sitting on the ground and crying. The monks gathered around him and reproached him for not knowing how to do anything. Finally they asked Petr to carry clay and water to the threshing floor. Even though this new task was beyond the capacity of Petr's physical strength, he nevertheless fulfilled it joyfully, working from morning into the late evening. Petr's obedience was not limited to this alone. The superior assigned him to sing with the choir, to cut bread and to serve food to the monks in the refectory, to wash the dishes and to sweep the refectory floor after meals. Petr did all of this willingly, rejoicing that he was able to serve his brothers.

When the Dormition Fast began, the superior told Petr, "On the feast of Transfiguration, I would like to tonsure you and your cellmate as riasophores. So, go to your spiritual father for confession and prepare yourself to receive the Holy Mysteries of Christ. Also, request Hieromonk Nikodim to be your sponsor at your tonsure." After prostrating at the superior's feet and receiving his blessing, Petr left the cell filled with joy and fear at being permitted to enter into the first rank of monastic life. He hurried to his father confessor and received his blessing to prepare for the Eucharist. When Petr requested Nikodim's sponsorship, Nikodim asked him if he was making the request on his own or if he was ordered to do so. After he found out that Petr came to him under instructions, he agreed to fulfill the boy's request. Nikodim told Petr to wash his hair on the evening before his forthcoming tonsure because months had passed since he had fled the Liubechskii Monastery and had had a chance to groom himself.

Petr was tonsured as a riasophore during the Hours on the feast of Transfiguration, receiving the name Porfirii while his friend took the name Platon. As all the monks were leaving the church after the Liturgy, several monks who could not hear the superior very well during the service switched the new names of the riasophores, calling Petr Platon and his friend, Porfirii. Petr was bothered by this, so he went to the superior.

"If the brothers exchanged your names," said the superior,

"then, so be it! From now on we shall call you Platon and your cellmate Porfirii. Be not the least bit offended by it. Such is God's will."

A few days after the tonsure, Platon was asked by a certain monk whether or not he served the hieromonk who had sponsored him at his tonsuring.

"No," answered Platon.

"How is that possible?" said the monk, "You are supposed to serve him in some way or other either by cutting firewood and building fires, carrying water or sweeping his cell and the like." Platon was grateful to the monk for his advice, and he went to his sponsor immediately. Bowing to the ground before Nikodim he excused himself for his ignorance thus far in not serving him.

"General obedience is enough to be expected from you," said Nikodim. "I don't need any service from you. Thanks to God, I'm still able to serve myself." Later on Platon met the monk again. The monk knew somehow that Nikodim was not requiring any extra duties from Platon.

"Go to Nikodim once more," said the monk, "and ask him to give you a cell-rule." Again Platon thanked the monk for the advice and he went to ask his starets, Nikodim, for a cell-rule.

"You, brother," said the starets, "are well trained. Therefore, I shall not submit you to any rule. Instead, as God himself will teach you, so keep a rule within your own cell." A week after their conversation, the Starets Nikodim left the Medvedovskii Monastery, not knowing where he was going, and Platon never saw him again. Reminiscing about this in his personal notes Starets Paissii writes the following:

> In such a way I was left to remain behind, as a stray sheep without a shepherd. Nowhere had I the possibility to live in obedience under the direction of a spiritual father. Even though the structure of my soul, during my youth, was inclined toward obedience, I was not worthy enough to be the recipient of such a divine gift.

Dissatisfied with the duties that were assigned to him, Platon took on certain additional responsibilities. On his own accord he helped the cook by bringing him water, cutting and bringing firewood and joyfully doing other helpful chores. At the same time he tried to discipline himself to sleep little.

When I was young, I was considering the principles of monasticism, and I decided in my heart that I would not lie down to sleep, but would instead spend the day in obedience and according to a rule. Only during the night would I allow myself to sleep—in a standing position. After a while my legs began to ache and then I was not able to walk about so easily. I found a box made of bast, cut a piece out from one of its sides and fell asleep sitting on it for a short time, that is, until the box overturned and I along with it. When I awoke I was afraid that I had slept through Matins. Once I saw that the church was closed I felt at ease and returned to my cell happy.

Another time Paisii wrote:

In my youth I once prayed to God for forty days in order to avoid sleeping too much and I learned from the Lord that three hours of sleep per day was sufficient for me. Now in my old age if I could only sleep for three hours I would consider it to be a great kindness from God. There are times when I am hardly able to sleep for an hour.

Platon's life was passing by peacefully and quietly in the Medvedovskii Monastery when suddenly a new storm was stirred by the Uniates. A certain functionary from the district headquarters arrived and gathered together all the monks in the superior's cell, attempting to convince them that they should join the *Unia*. When he noticed that the monks were decisively and firmly opposed to this, he was infuriated. He ran off to the monastery church, took an inventory of its contents, locked its doors and posted the government seal on them.

This produced great discontent among the monks and, after the church had remained locked for a month's time, the monks began to leave the monastery. Platon thought again about moving away to Orthodox Moldavia. Only his fear of the Polish police and the absence of an experienced person who was capable of leading the way made him hesitate. Then the monk Martirii, (Platon's spiritual adviser) and another monk, a former chorister from the Kievan Metropolitan Choir, decided to go to Kiev to enter the Kievan Lavra of the Crypts. Platon decided to join them. They prayed to God and departed on their journey. It was December, snow was falling, and it was freezing cold. Platon suffered severely because he did not have the proper clothing. Somehow the wayfarers went as far as the city of Vasil'kova where they were held by the Polish government for six weeks. But finally they were granted permission to cross the border and before long they arrived in Kiev.

CHAPTER III

The Kievan Lavra

Upon their arrival at the Kievan Lavra of the Crypts, our wandering friends submitted a request to the archimandrite of the lavra, Timofei Shcherbatskii, for their admittance into the monastic community. They were called before the administration and, after being examined, were admitted into the community. Martirii was assigned to assist the steward and his friend, the former singer from the Kievan Metropolitan Choir, was assigned to sing in the *kliros*. Platon, though, was assigned to a special obedience. It so happened that the archimandrite and Platon's late father were very close friends from the Kievan Brotherhood School. Their friendship was so intimate that they promised to maintain mutual love and loyalty for each other until their deaths.

After recognizing Platon as the son of his late friend, the archimandrite felt it his duty to extend his love for Platon's father to Platon himself. In order to keep Platon in the lavra for as long as possible, the archimandrite complicated any possibility of the boy's transferring to another monastery, assigning him to an obedience that was practiced in very few monasteries. Platon was assigned to an apprenticeship under Hieromonk Makarii to learn metal and wood icon engraving. Platon accepted his obedience in his usual joyful manner. Makarii loved his new pupil, especially so when he noticed his extraordinary modesty and silence and his peculiar habit of never repeating anything he had heard from conversations in Father Makarii's cell. Seeing such rare qualities in his pupil, Makarii was not afraid of counseling any visitors when Platon was around. Platon kept in his heart all that was good and useful from what he had heard. Daily, with the exceptions of Sundays and feasts, after the early Divine Liturgy, Platon would go directly to his teacher and would work for him from morning until Vespers, stopping only for lunch. When Platon came to the church for Vespers he would stand behind the right *kliros* just as he did at Matins. On one occasion before the Great Fast, while Platon was standing in his usual place, one of the singers walked up and told Platon that the ecclesiarch wanted him. Platon was terribly afraid. He walked over to the ecclesiarch, who then told him to go to the right *kliros*. Platon, still very much afraid, told the ecclesiarch that he did not know how to sing.

"All right," the ecclesiarch said, "if you do not know how to sing, you will read whatever will be assigned to you." From that day on, Platon remained on the right *kliros*, singing as he knew how and reading from the *Horologion* and the *Octoechos*. The Great Fast began and Platon went to the supervisor of the distant crypts, the Hieromonk Ioann, who was the confessor for all the monks, to confess all his sins. After reading the Prayer of Absolution the confessor, with tears in his eyes, said to Platon:

I can see from your confession that the Lord has preserved you from greatly burdensome sins. Had your life been spent in some secluded monastery under the direction of an experienced starets you perhaps might have been protected from any future sins. Because you have come instead to live with us sinners in this sacred lavra, in the middle of the world, I fear that here, in your youth, your soul might pass through extremely harmful trials. This can happen to you very easily if you begin to cultivate friendships with other men who are as young as yourself but who have no fear of God in their hearts. This is my advice to you in the name of God: never drink any intoxicating beverages. If you follow my advice, with the help of God you will be successful in avoiding the ruination of your soul. Tell me then, my child, can you do what I tell you?

The words of the good starets penetrated Platon deeply.

"From my birth I have never tasted any strong drink and my very body rejects it. And your words, which I accept as from the mouth of God himself, I shall strive with all my power to follow." Hearing such an answer, the starets was filled with joy.

> If [said the starets], you will keep your promise, I believe God will keep you from every spiritual harm. Know, though, that many will seek your friendship and will entice you to drink with them. When they meet with your refusal they will do their best to cause you grief. Endure all their temptations and do not surrender. Finally they will cease to approach you and your soul will be established in the most profound tranquility.

Everything which had been said that day by the starets came to pass.

Platon had to suffer many trials and tribulations that were inflicted upon him by those who sought to allure him into their company. Platon never forgot what had been told to him by the starets and he remained staunch. Many of the senior monks in the lavra took notice of Platon and loved him. The older Hieromonk Veniamin, the director of the printing press, was particularly favorably inclined toward Platon. Upon his arrival at the lavra in winter Platon had no other clothes but the summer clothing in which he began his journey. In church he would shiver from the chill, and he was too shy to request warmer clothes for himself. Fr. Veniamin noticed this so he supplied Platon with the necessary clothing and made sure that he was given whatever else he needed.

During the next summer Platon's sister-in-law, the wife of his deceased brother, the priest, arrived in Kiev with her brother and uncle for a pilgrimage. They met with Platon and went with him to his cell, where they told him what was happening to his mother.

> After your departure for Kiev, [they began], your mother reminisced and wept over you, but she never

ceased to feel that you would not abandon her. When
the news of your flight from Kiev and of your withdrawal to some unknown place reached her, she was
overcome by unbearable grief. She was in no condition
to bring herself to calm and peace so she went to Kiev
to search for you. In the severe cold of winter she
wandered among monasteries and sketes but all her
searching was in vain. She returned to her home exhausted, barely alive. At home she wept and wailed
without end and no one was able to console her. Her
soul was so severely overcome by such grief that she
refused to eat or drink for the rest of her days. Within
a few days, she was so weakened that her thoughts
became entirely confused. She lay on her bed, absolutely
strengthless, awaiting her quick death. All her kin
gathered around her and looked upon her with extremely deep pity. Suddenly, as though seeing a terri-
fying vision, she became afraid and then in a panic
she called for a prayer book. As soon as the book was
handed to her she began reading aloud an Akathist to
the Mother of God. After she finished reading the service once to the end she read through it a second time
and continued to repeat it. Her kin tried to take the
prayer book from her hands but she refused to give it
over. In such a way the entire day and night passed.
The ailing mother suddenly raised her eyes and gazed
upward immovably for some time and then shouted
out in a loud voice: 'If such is the will of God, then I
shall not grieve over my son any longer.' Her relatives
begged her to tell them what it was she had seen, but
all she could utter to them was a request for her father
confessor. When he had come he remained with her
alone while she told him everything that had happened
to her. Soon she regained consciousness. Her relatives
again asked about her vision, but she remained silent.
Thinking that she could perhaps not speak because of
her weakness, they poured a spoonful of water into
her mouth and then gave her some liquified food, the
kind used for feeding babies. Before long she was able

to take food for herself and to sit up in her bed.

'When I was absolutely strengthless because of hunger,' [she said], 'and had already begun to await the coming of death, I suddenly saw before me a mass of demons, gloomy, frightening and ready to fall upon me. That is when I became frightened and called out to you for my prayerbook. By reading the Akathist and putting my trust in the Mother of God, I was able to protect myself from those demons. When they heard these holy words, they trembled in fear and stood back, afraid to come near me. The day and night passed and then an ineffable ecstasy overtook me. I gazed upward toward Heaven and an angel of God, descending toward me like a bright lightning flash, stood near me and said: "Foolish woman! What are you doing to yourself? Instead of loving Christ your Lord above every creature, you prefer your son more, and, because of your senseless love for him, you have decided to destroy yourself. For that you fall to God's eternal judgment. Even had your son left home and occupied himself with thievery or some other corruption it would still not be proper for you to grieve so immeasurably. Everyone must answer before God for himself. Your son left home by God's will, however, and did not choose to follow corruption, but the monastic life. How could you grieve so despondently and destroy your soul? Know well that by God's grace your son will certainly become a monk. Instead of grieving over him you should emulate his example by fleeing the world. Such is the will of God, and if you oppose his will you will fall prey to the demons around you as an example to everyone not to love their own children or anything more than God himself."

'Having heard from the angel this message, I cried out loudly: If such is God's will, then no longer shall I grieve over my son. I hardly finished saying this, when the demons disappeared and the angel of the Lord rejoiced and went up to Heaven.'

Hearing this story from your mother, your relatives

were filled with fear and they glorified God who, by
such a wonder, had delivered your mother from her
destructive grief and self-willed death. Your mother
fully regained her health soon after. Although she cried
a little from time to time, she still kept God's answer
in her heart, restrained herself from falling into such
immeasurable grief, and then she prepared herself to
enter the Holy Virgin Protection Convent. To this
present day she lives there with your grandmother, the
abbess.

Consequently Platon was aware that his mother had at last
accepted the tonsure and that she and his grandmother were
living together with his aunt in the same cell. After living
in the convent for ten years, Platon's mother peacefully went
to the Lord.

At that time, while Platon was living in the Kievan Lavra
of the Crypts, a considerable number of remarkable ascetics
were there. The chief spiritual counselor and father confessor
of the lavra, Hieromonk Ioann, lived alone in seclusion for
many years. Hieroschema-monk Pavel was another remarkable
ascetic. On one occasion Platon came to him and asked what
constitutes meekness. The starets glared at Platon sternly and
drew back his hand as if he were about to strike him across
the face. Platon coiled back. Then Pavel said to him

God is with you my son, so do not be afraid. You asked
me what constitutes meekness. Had I explained it to
you in words you would have forgotten very soon.
Meekness is this: if someone strikes you across the
face, you not only do not become angered by him but
you offer him your other cheek as Christ says to do.

Another noteworthy ascetic was a certain schema-monk of
the distant crypts. For more than forty years he led a group
of devotees throughout the crypts. On his naked body he wore
a shirt made from coarse steel wire with the prickly side
turned inward against his flesh. When he slept he could not
recline but slept instead in a sitting posture. An assistant to

the lavra blacksmith also attracted attention to himself by bearing forty pounds of iron on his body.

One year had passed since Platon had arrived at the lavra and the slightest thought about leaving never occurred to him. He was all the more awed by a certain occurrence. One day the blacksmith's assistant saw Platon and called him over to his cell.

"I am very sorry for you," he said, "because you will not remain much longer here with us in this holy lavra, but you will leave for another place, where the Lord himself will lead you." Platon was strongly affected by the monk's prediction.

"Believe me, homest Father," Platon said, "I have no intention of leaving this lavra. With God's help, I intend to remain here until my last breath."

"Know certainly, brother," the starets said, "my words will come to pass very soon, and then you will see that I am speaking the truth."

A few days following this conversation, Aleksei Filevich, one of Platon's closest schoolmates, came to him and asked:

> Do you remember, the promise that we made to each other when we were still in school: not to be tonsured or to live in any affluent monasteries but instead to leave the world, to dedicate ourselves to wandering and to living in the wilderness in obedience to a starets, to feed and clothe ourselves by the work of our own hands, and finally not to abandon each other until the end? Now, I see you violated our oath by not living in the cloistered silence of the wilderness and by returning to your homeland to live in an affluent monastery.

"Indeed we kept in our hearts all the promises that you mention," said Platon, "but unfortunately not a single one of my friends came along with me when I left the world. Our friend Dimitrii remained with his mother rather than take my advice. Wandering all alone, I have not yet come upon a single pious starets who would agree to accept me unto himself in holy obedience, although I have asked many."

"So, I suppose then," said Aleksei, "that you have finally given up on the idea of settling together with a friend of the same mind in the wilderness under the direction of a starets?"

"Presently," said Platon, "I have not even the slightest intention of doing that, since I have found almost absolute peace for my soul here. I intend to remain here in this holy monastery until my last breath."

"If I were to propose that you and I together begin to wander and to live in the wilderness," asked Aleksei, "would you agree to join me?"

"My dear friend," Platon answered, "if you were to make such a suggestion I would be glad to go with you immediately."

Then Aleksei stood up from where he was sitting and said solemnly, "If you love me so, that you would be ready to leave even this holy place for my sake, then I humble myself before God and before you and I place my confidence in the grace of God. I am ready to remain with you until death." Deeply stirred by their decision the two friends prayed to God, tearfully begging for His help and blessings for their new life.

Platon remained alone in his cell for a while after. He could not cease to be awed and astonished by his unexpected and sudden change of mind and by the fulfillment of the monk's prediction. When Platon met the monk again, he was so ashamed that he could not even look into his eyes, knowing that he had told him the truth and that he himself had turned out to be a liar.

CHAPTER IV

An Unexpected Meeting

Aleksei Filevich turned to two student friends from the brotherhood school for help. These two friends were born across the border and therefore could easily secure passes from the Polish government into their homeland. The students arranged for a certain old monk who lived across the border to help Aleksei and Platon flee from Kiev. The monk did not offer to lead them across the border himself, but he did promise to find a reliable person who would take the travelers as far as the border where they would then be met by the monk himself. The coach driver planned to meet Aleksei and Platon at the Kirillov Monastery, in Kiev, from where he would take them to a certain place and leave them before reaching the border. They would then cross the border in different places, and come together again on the opposite side where they would meet the coachman with the old monk.

At the appointed time they met at the Kirillov Monastery and began their escape. Everything proceeded according to the plan. Soon they arrived at the place where they were to separate and the coachman explained to them how they should cross the border. The boys followed the guide's instructions, praying to God that they be spared from every harm. At last they came to the grounds of the brotherhood monastery which Aleksei knew well. They turned to the left and went through a forest for quite a long time in order to avoid crossing the monastery's property. When they turned back onto the road, they noticed that they still had not crossed over all the monastery's land. Suddenly some people appeared before them, obviously from the monastery, who asked them who they were and where they were going. The boys were so frightened that they confessed everything, but to their surprise the strangers commended their good intention and advised them to continue along the same road and not to turn off anywhere.

The deadness of night had set in. Suddenly they heard whistling ahead of them down the road. Aleksei ran ahead but quickly returned to Platon, very obviously in despair.

"We are in trouble," Aleksei cried out. "My cousin from across the border is up ahead, along with the old monk and the coach driver. He undoubtedly informed my mother who is on her way now, I am sure, to put an end to my wandering." When the cousin of Aleksei saw him weeping, he began to console him, praising him for his effort to zealously save his soul and even assuring him that he would not inform his mother about their meeting. After awhile Aleksei stopped weeping and calmed down. He and Platon went ahead on their journey leaving behind the old monk, the coach driver, and Aleksei's cousin. As they approached the border, two strangers whom they had met earlier appeared behind them, apparently planning to assault the two travelers. But not daring to attack the boys, they shouted out instead, with the intention of calling the attention of the border guard.

"Who are you? Where are you from? You are probably criminals fleeing across the border!" Hearing them shout, the cousin of Aleksei attacked them with a stick and they ran away in fear, shouting to the border guard for help.

Platon and Aleksei ran ahead to the river which separated Russia from Poland. Making their way across, they took refuge in the house of Aleksei's cousin, which was situated on the Polish side. The cousin of Aleksei sent a messenger to the boy's mother in Kiev that night telling her to come after her son quickly. He detained the boys in his home, extended hospitality to them, and promised to let them go in three days. When the monk learned where the boys were staying, he hid himself out of fear in some unknown place.

During that time, Aleksei's two friends from the Kievan Brotherhood School, who helped arrange the escape, came to visit Platon and Aleksei at the cousin's home. Before long the mother of Aleksei also arrived. As soon as she saw Platon, she decided that he was the culprit who had instigated her son's escape, so she showered him with reproaches and insults and even wanted to beat him. Only with considerable difficulty were they able to calm her. After the blame had been transferred to the old monk who had helped them cross the border, she calmed down. Platon and the two students from Kiev continued on the journey, glancing back occasionally at the friend they were leaving behind. But Aleksei refused to stay behind and ran off after his friends. When he caught up to them he cried and fell on the ground before them, smiting his breast and begging them to take him along. While this was going on, the cousin of Aleksei and some other people appeared in the distance, on horses. In spite of his tears and weeping, Aleksei's cousin took him back to his mother by force.

Platon and his companions soon reached the Matroninskii Monastery where the superior received them gladly. This was at the beginning of the Great Fast in 1792. Living in the monastery, Platon soon learned that Hieroschema-monk Mikhail, a starets of high spiritual repute, was temporarily in residence there. Starets Mikhail especially loved Platon and gave him spiritual literature to read. After learning that the permanent residence of the starets was in Moldo-Walachia, Platon told him that he had been hoping to go there for some time but that the opportunity had never presented itself and that he would be glad if the starets could take him along. The starets advised Platon to go there right away without even waiting for him and to settle in the Skete of Treistena which is located near the city of Fokshan. The superior there was a disciple of the starets. The starets promised to come as soon as conditions would permit. Platon accepted the advice of the starets and began to seek out a traveling partner for himself. He found three other monks in the Matroninskii Monastery who agreed to accompany him: Anthony, Jeropheus, and Theodulus. After the feast of Christ's Resurrection, Starets Mikhail permitted them to depart, but he summoned them to his cell before they left for a final discussion and prayer. Seeing that the starets was very loving, Platon asked him if he would accept his friend Aleksei into the Matroninskii Monastery and also bring him to Moldo-Walachia. Protected by the grace of God they successfully made their way through the Ukraine, crossed the Dniester, and entered into the outskirts of Moldo-Walachia.

CHAPTER V

Monasticism in the Eighteenth Century

Platon came to Moldo-Walachia with a feeling of deep awe and love for the country. This was one of the flourishing corners of the Orthodox world. In the Greek East, Orthodoxy was under the yoke of the Turks and therefore could not enjoy complete freedom. In Russia, monasticism was suffering from the oppressions of the government. Moldo-Walachia, ruled by pious gospodars, was in all aspects a comfortable place for the peaceful existence and blossoming of Orthodox monasticism. Monasteries had existed here from the remotest Christian times. Chronicles continually record how the pious gospodars, boyars and people from other social strata built monasteries. In return, these benefactors expected certain religious, ethical and pedagogical activities from the monastic communities. One gospodar, after building a monastery, threatened the monastery with anathema if they did not set aside their annual income for the poor, the sick, the serfs and the dowries of poor girls. The most valuable libraries were found in the monasteries which kept numerous chronicles, many of which were in Slavonic. These libraries had a peculiar method for increasing their collections. As penance father confessors assigned the penitent to copy by hand certain books for the monastery libraries. There were many highly educated monks in these monasteries. The monasteries conducted not only elementary schools but higher schools of poetics, mathematics, comparative linguistics and theology. The Moldo-Walachian monasteries maintained living contacts with the Orthodox East and Russia.

After crossing the Moldavian border, our wayfarers came to the St. Cyprian Skete, also called Kondritsa, where they were welcomed by the superior. Theodulus and Jeropheus remained here but Platon and Anthony went on further. They reached the Holy Archangels Skete, called Dolgoutsi, which was under the spiritual guidance of a certain Starets Vasilii. Platon liked the skete. Many great ascetics lived here, among them a Father Raphael, who was a copy-maker of patristic texts and a pious man filled with the fear of God. Another was the monk Dositheus, who lived at a distance from the skete with the Hieromonk Timothy. Dositheus was experienced in spiritual discernment and patristic exegesis. Platon and Anthony remained here for a short time and then continued on their way. At last they came to the St. Nicholas Skete, called Treistena, and the superior, Hieromonk Dometius, accepted them with open arms. It was here that Platon heard, for the first time, about the Athonite rule of prayer which was observed with great reverence and fear of God.

At the skete, about twenty monks lived together in a common dormitory and almost fifty lived as hermits in the vicinity, securing food and clothing by the work of their hands. Here, too, Platon was able to meet more remarkable ascetics. One of them was the Schema-monk Proterius, a Little Russian from Reshetilovka in Poltava. He enjoyed taking in wandering novices and offering them his hospitality. He had a great love for birds and he taught them to fly into his cell at certain times during the day. When Proterius went to church, the birds would follow him along the path to the very doors of the church, alighting on his head and shoulders and flying around him with joyful singing. When he entered into the church, the birds would fly to the church roof and perch there, waiting for him to come out. As soon as Proterius would appear, the birds would sweep down and surround him, leading him back to his cell. Another remarkable ascetic, a Great Russian by birth, had the practice of distributing handicrafts that he himself had made to the other monks during meal time. He also walked around washing their feet.

When Platon and Anthony arrived in Treistena, the monks were busy building cells. Even the superior of the skete worked along with the rest of the monks. But Platon, because of his weakness, was not taken along with the others to work in the woods and was assigned instead to obedience in the refectory. Platon noticed that each monk had a turn at preparing food and baking bread for the meal and he was frightened, because he would have to take his turn before long. Once, all the monks were called to work in the forest for several days. The superior told Platon that he would be responsible for feeding the monks. Platon, afraid of what he had to do, told the superior that he had never prepared food before and that he did not know what to do. The superior appointed another monk to look after Platon and to show him how to cook. But Platon, in all his nervousness and inexperience, confused the instructions of the monk. When the food began to boil, Platon went to move it from the fire but, in his clumsiness, he upset the kettle, spilling the food all over the floor and scalding his hands in addition. With sighs and tears, he again started to prepare some vegetables and he set a fresh kettle of water over the fire. In the meantime, the monks returned from the woods and when they discovered that their food was still not ready, they grew angry and prepared it themselves.

This happened more than once. When the superior noticed that Platon was finally learning to cook somewhat more successfully, he decided to teach him how to bake bread. One day, while the monks were away cutting wood in the forest again, one monk taught Platon how to do this. He gave his instructions to Platon in detail, poured water into a pot, showed him a washtub full of sifted flour and a pan of yeast and said, "When the water gets warm, add it to the flour and the yeast and mix everything together." When Platon began mixing, he noticed that there was less water and much more flour. Not guessing that he would have to add more water to the ingredients, Platon tried to knead the dough. It turned out to be so stiff that he could not even penetrate his fingers into it, and all this time, flour still remained in the washtub. Platon then cut his dough into portions, sprinkled the pieces with still more flour and pressed them with a rolling pin. He finally succeeded in getting all the flour out from the washtub. When he had finished kneading the dough, he put all of it back into the washtub and put the whole thing, with difficulty, into the oven in order for it to rise faster. One half hour passed and one of the monks came back from the forest to see if the bread was ready. Platon answered with a sigh that the dough was not even ready yet. When Platon told the monk how he had prepared the dough, the monk smiled and said:

"How stupid can you be! When you saw how little water there was, why didn't you either add more or else take out some of the flour? Then you could have kneaded it. Did you use any yeast?" With this question, Platon blushed from both shame and sadness. He had completely forgotten about the yeast.

"Do not be upset," said the monk. "We can fix everything." The monk heated some water, poured it into the washtub with the dough, added some yeast and began mixing. He told Platon what else had to be done and then he returned to the forest. Some time passed and Platon decided that the dough had risen enough. He removed the embers from the oven which by this time was so scorching hot that sparks were flying out. He put the bread in the oven, feeling certain that everything would be right at last. No sooner did he get the bread into the oven than it was scorched through from top to bottom. He pulled the burnt lump of dough out from the oven and began to await the fearful return of the monks. When they finally came, Platon, ashamed of himself, fell at their feet with tears and begged for their forgiveness. The superior and the other monks could not find it in themselves even to begin to reproach Platon. Instead, they picked up one loaf and cut it. It turned out to be only superficially burnt and not unsuitable for eating. Then they cooked some cornmeal and sat down to eat. From then on, Platon was no longer compelled to bake bread. Paisii Velichkovskii comments about this in his notes:

> I recounted all of this for one purpose: so that anyone who comes into our community will not be despondent because of his inexperience in anything, and so he will remember that the only real success comes from God's help.

Soon after this event, the monk Dositheus came to Treistena from the skete at Dolgoutsi. When he noticed Platon, he called him over to talk to him.

> I want to warn you that our Starets Vasilii had a disciple by the name of Paisii, who died three years ago. This Paisii was his pupil from childhood and he grew up in the presence of the starets. The starets loved him greatly and, since he needed a priest, he convinced Paisii, against his own will, to accept ordination to the priesthood much earlier than the established age for becoming a priest. When the disciple Paisii died, the starets grieved and lamented over him, partly because he had lost a favorite disciple and partly because he was deprived of a priest. Starets Vasilii will be coming here shortly to visit the monks. When he sees you, he will probably want to take you to live with him. Before long he will begin coercing you into becoming a priest. If you do as he wishes and become a priest, your conscience will never find peace for the rest of your life. If you want to remain faithful to the rules of the Church, you can transfer your residence and live with the starets but, if not, then withdraw to some other place until you are old enough to be ordained. Then you can return to the starets.

Platon thanked the monk Dositheus for his advice and expressed his intention never to become a priest because of his unworthiness.

Just as the monk Dositheus had said, Starets Vasilii arrived at the skete. Immediately his attention turned to Platon and he told the superior to persuade Platon to transfer his residence to be near him in the Polyano-Merulskii Skete. Platon, remembering the advice he received from Dositheus, refused to concede to the request of Starets Vasilii. Understanding why Platon refused, the starets informed him that there would be no compulsion for ordination to the priesthood before the proper time. Platon still refused, saying that he would never take upon himself such terrible and responsible service, even after coming of age. The starets at last ceased to insist upon his own request. This was the reason, writes Paisii, that he did not live with Starets Vasilii, even though he desired greatly to do so. News was received that the Hieroschema-monk Mikhail with his disciples were approaching the skete and that Aleksei, the friend of Platon, was coming with them.

After they had eaten together, Platon called Aleksei aside and asked him to relate in detail how he was able to leave his homeland. This is what Aleksei told Platon:

After we parted and mother took me home, I was overcome by such anxiety that I even became sick. As He himself knows, I prayed to God ceaselessly and tearfully to lead me out of the world. By providence, one of my friends, Aleksei Elis, hearing about my sickness, came to visit me. During our conversation, he told me that he himself hoped to become a monk. Taking his advice, I concealed my sadness from my mother. She began to take a liking to my friend, thinking that, under his influence, I had begun to forget about monasticism. With the arrival of spring, my friend found a wandering monk. After revealing our intentions to him, Aleksei asked him to help us. The monk advised us to leave and to buy a boat. He promised to lead us by boat as far as the Matroninskii Monastery. We bought a boat and some items that we would need for the journey. First we stopped to pray in the Church of St. Nicholas and then we departed on our journey. Our trip went well but, as we sailed through Tripol and saw some guards standing along the riverbank, we feared they might hold us back. As we approached the bank, the monk, looking up at the guards, told them quietly that we were friends. The guards obviously knew our monk. After greeting him, they asked him where he was going.

'I am on my way to the village which belongs to the Kirillov Monastery. I am being sent there by the hegumen to manage it.' The guards wanted to know who the people in the boat were.

'These are my clerks which the hegumen sent with

me.' The monk offered the guards some vodka which he had brought along in case such an event as this might occur. Then he offered them some bread, a few other rations and even some money. The guards were quite content with the bribes, so they let us go peacefully. With tears we gave thanks to God for having delivered us from this danger. Within a few days we came to the place where our journey would end. We sold our boat to some local villagers and then went to the Matroninskii Monastery which was not very far away. When Starets Mikhail saw us approaching, he rejoiced, and immediately took upon himself to care for our bodily and spiritual needs. With the help of God, we successfully completed our journey through the Ukraine, and arrived in a blessed country, coming to this Skete of St. Nicholas the Wonderworker, where I now share your company, my beloved friend, with indescribable joy. I thank God for leading me here to live together with you in this holy monastery.

After living together for awhile with Aleksei in the skete, Platon observed with amazement how his friend, who was almost always sickly and weak, suddenly began to grow in strength so that he could easily do any of the harvesting work. Aleksei was able to carry logs of such weight from the forest to the monastery that Platon would shudder at the sight of him. Since the arrival of Aleksei at the monastery, Platon waited for him to begin discussing the agreement which they made some time back to settle together in a monastic community and to encourage and support each other in their monastic strivings. Aleksei, though, did not utter a word about it, but, even though his silence angered and at the same time puzzled Platon, he refused to remind Aleksei about the subject. The Dormition Fast had begun. Starets Mikhail tonsured Aleksei Filevich and his friends as riasofores. Platon was happy that Aleksei finally received the first tonsure.

The superior of the skete assigned Platon to a new obedience. He was put in charge of guarding the monastery's vineyards. He was allowed to eat as many grapes as he wished but only on the condition that he had eaten some bread earlier. Platon was eating so many grapes for whole days at a time that he developed a passion for them. He could not eat anything else because, by the time meals came around, he was filled up with grapes. Platon gradually weakened in strength and his face grew pale. His cheeks became so sunken that he looked as though he had been overcome by some grave illness. When the grape harvest was finished, Platon was forced to resume a regular diet, eating in the refectory with the other monks. Very soon he was again as healthy as usual.

Before the beginning of the grape harvest, the superior transferred Platon to a new cell. One Sunday morning, Platon was so sound asleep in his new cell that he did not hear the bell for Matins. By the time he had come to church, the Gospel had been finished and the canon had begun. Out of shame Platon would not enter the church but returned instead to his cell, weeping. Platon did not return to the church even for the Liturgy but left his cell and went farther away from the monastery to a secluded place where he remained alone and cried. When the Divine Liturgy had been finished and the noon day meal was begun, the starets, the superior and the other monks, having noticed Platon's absence from both the Liturgy and the meal, began asking one another about him. As Platon had never missed a church service before, the brothers were quite worried about him.

"Fathers and brothers," said the starets, "I beseech you for the sake of our Lord, let us refrain from our meal for awhile until we find out what has happened to our brother Platon." Immediately the starets sent the monk Athanasius, a copier of patristic texts, to find Platon. After a difficult search, Athanasius found him sitting alone and weeping. Athanasius tried to give him courage but Platon nevertheless could not even begin to explain the cause of his grief. Athanasius tried to calm and console Platon. He asked the boy to return to the refectory because the other monks would not eat until they returned.

"How can I return to the holy fathers with such a face," said Platon, "or show myself to them after the great sin which I have committed before God and man!" Athanasius continued to console him and, at last, he persuaded Platon to come back with him to the refectory. With tear-covered cheeks, Platon went along. They entered the refectory and Platon saw the starets with the other monks seated at the tables awaiting his return. Platon fell on the floor, trembling in shame and wailing unconsolably. He was then told to sit down to the meal but, being so ashamed and sad, he could not eat anything. Only towards the end of the meal did Platon feel capable of eating—just a morsel of bread. When Platon left for his cell, Starets Mikhail began exhorting the other monks and the younger ones especially.

> See the devotion and ardor of our young brother! Let him be to all of you an example of painstaking observance of church discipline. He unwittingly missed prayer and was so saddened by this that he wept. Crushed by great affliction and because of his contrition of heart, he deprived himself of food and could not even bring himself to look upon the light of the sun. Pray God that He will grant you such fervent care and love for the Divine.

From then on, until the end of his sojourn at the skete, Platon never again laid down on his bed to sleep but, instead, took short naps while sitting upright on a bench.

The following October, the Schema-monk Onuphrius arrived in Treistena from the Archangel Michael Skete, also known as the Kiarnul Skete, situated in the mountains along the Buzeu River. He told everyone at the Treistena Skete about life in his mountain cloister, about the beauty of its surroundings and the purity of nature there. All of this made Platon want to live with Starets Onuphrius in his monastery. Platon and several other young monks decided then to return with Starets Onuphrius to Kiarnul. Starets Mikhail gave the monks his blessing and he provided them with a guide, his long-time disciple, Hieromonk Aleksei, who would remain with them throughout the forthcoming winter. The novices departed for Kiarnul and along the way passed through huge, dense forests, across high mountains and low valleys. At last, on the third day, they came to the Kiarnul Skete where they were lovingly received. The next day, the superior assigned each of the new novices to a separate cell. The regulations of this skete were patterned after those of sketes on Mount Athos. On Sundays and feast days, the monks assembled together for church services. After the Divine Liturgy, it was their rule to sit together for a common meal and, after the meal, to spend the the rest of the day in discussion about spirituality. Following Vespers, each monk retired to his own cell to fulfill his rule in solitude.

By now Platon and his companions had been living at the skete for some time. They would visit the Hieromonk Aleksei at assigned times to hear him read and explain patristic texts and sometimes simply to discuss subjects concerning their spiritual life. Hieromonk Aleksei was a humble, meek and loving man whose gift it was to be able to console the most sorrowful heart. Sometimes Aleksei went along with his novices to visit the hermit Onuphrius who lived in his secluded mountain cell, far from the skete. The pathway that led there went along the edge of a beautiful forest and mountain region. From the mountain tops they saw the surrounding valleys, other mountains in the distance and forested gorges in the valleys beneath. A very short distance from the hermit's cell, down the side of the mountain, there flowed a fresh and clear stream. The hermit Onuphrius always fetched water there.

Starets Onuphrius and Father Aleksei had long discussions with each other about psychic and fleshly passions and about the terrible and interminable mental struggle with demons, their crafty designs and deceits.

If Christ the Lover of men would not guard his people, [Starets Onuphrius would say], then even the saints would not be able to work for salvation. Whoever comes to Christ and falls down before Him in consolation, peace, joy and a burning love for God, in faith, in humility and tears, is granted ineffable joy. The proof of this is manifested in sincere tears out of great love, self-reproach, humility and endless gratitude to Christ. Man, therefore, out of his love for God,

becomes insensitive and mortified to the good things
of this world.

After hearing this, Platon was inspired with an even
greater love for the monastic life and entered into a much
deeper understanding of monasticism. He grew more serious
and quite strict with himself. Being immensely influenced by
all which had overtaken him, Platon withdrew to a secluded
place. There he fell to the ground, smote his breast, and with
tears beseeched Christ for help, offering to Him his vows.
In his cell, Platon devoted himself to ardent prayer and diligent daily reading of the Fathers. He searched and tested his
conscience continually, grieved over his sins and weaknesses.
He began each day by putting himself before God's judgment
for correction.

Summer was approaching and the Hieromonk Aleksei was
called back to the monastery by Starets Mikhail. Some of the
other novices, among whom were acquaintances of Platon,
returned to Treistena with Father Aleksei. Soon after that,
the brother of Starets Onuphrius, Bartholomew, was made the
superior of the skete. Bartholomew treated the monks with
care, building a large cell where the monks could gather for
common meals and theological discussions. That very spring,
Platon made a small kitchen garden where he planted beans
and onions. Though the onions never became ripe enough, the
beans ripened very well, only to be eaten by mice. Platon was
able to harvest no more than a basket-full. Platon himself
made all the tools which he needed for cultivating the meadow
lands and he gradually began to acquire a certain skill at such
handiwork. However, he did not busy himself much with such
crafts and there was no one encouraging him to do so. Having
lived at the skete the past winter in expectation of the coming
summer, Platon, with the blessing of the superior, again set
out on a new journey. Unfortunately, the personal handwritten notes of Starets Paisii are missing here.

Various passages in some of the letters of Starets Paisii
show that he evidently was at the Nativity of the Mother of
God Monastery in Moldavia and also in the Niamets Monastery. By 1746 he was surely intent upon going to Mount Athos.

What moved Platon to make such a decision? Platon attributes his decision to his apprehension of being coerced by
the Moldavian startsy to be ordained to the priesthood. It is
impossible not to see God's Providence working here. It was
the Lord's good pleasure to put the future great starets to
the difficult test of a calamitous and secluded life on Mount
Athos and to begin there the formation of his monastic community. Athonite influence was strongly felt in Moldavia. It
was there that Platon first experienced a liturgical life in
accordance with the Athonite practice and came into close
contact with wandering monks who had visited the Holy
Mountain. This great influence attracted Platon's soul with
exceeding force. Mount Athos, with its centuries-old legends,
its lofty examples of asceticism, its severe and majestic nature
and its storehouse of patristic literature was an attractive
place, where Platon could begin a new period in his life. The
biographer of Starets Paisii, taking into account everything
which has been written about him thus far, writes the following
concerning his move to Mount Athos:

> Who can comprehend the ways of the Lord? Who
> knows his counsel? By the Divine Providence of God,
> Paisii was led from his fatherland through many coun-
> tries, so that he might gather unto himself a great
> spiritual wealth. God finally led him to the Holy
> Mount Athos where, by continuing his spiritual harvest,
> he would make him an example of spirituality for all
> who were searching. The Lord made him another
> Venerable *Antonii*, who also was a Little Russian.
> Just as the Venerable *Antonii* was led by wandering
> and searching to the Holy Mountain, where he took
> upon himself the angelic image, became worthy of great
> spiritual gifts and was returned to his homeland to
> plant the seeds of monastic life and to increase its
> growth, so the Blessed Paisii, having increased in spiri-
> tual maturity and riches, returned to Moldavia that
> he might regenerate a decrepit monastic order; revive
> it from its general state of moral degradation; implant
> in it a thrice-blessed obedience, by enlightening those

sitting in the darkness of ignorance with his teachings and by giving them understanding through his translations of patristic and theological literature from Greek.

Now let us turn to examine this most important period in the life of Starets Paisii.

Part Three

The Secluded Life of Starets Paisii on Mount Athos and the Beginning of His Monastic Community
(1746-1763)

CHAPTER I

Mount Athos

The emigration of Platon to Mount Athos marks the end of his novitiate and the beginning of his independent struggle in seclusion. Hieromonk Tryfon was Platon's fellow traveler during the journey to Athos. They departed on their journey having no more than a few coins in their possession, but their poverty did not disturb them. In Galati they boarded a small boat that took them to Constantinople and from there they journeyed to Mount Athos. On July 4, the eve of the feast of the Venerable Father Athanasius of Athos, they entered into his holy lavra. So many recollections from history, thoughts and feelings are summoned forth from the heart of an Orthodox Christian by the words of Emperor Alexis Comnenus, "The most royal and Divine Mountain which is more superb than all the mountains in the universe." Since ancient times, Athos has attracted Christian ascetics, becoming the center of spiritual enlightenment in the Orthodox East. Mount Athos is one of three peninsulas which together form the Salonica or Chalcidice peninsula that extends from the Greek mainland into the Aegean Sea. Athos is eighty kilometers wide. At the southernmost extremities of the mountains, an immense peak of white marble rises above the clouds and into the sky. Athos was so famous for this in pagan antiquity that the entire triple-peninsula was consequently named Athos. The highest mountain peak is about two kilometers above sealevel. Almost the entire mountain range except for the southern peaks, is covered with exotic plants, oranges, lemons, pears, chestnuts, and vineyards. The eastern slopes of Athos are especially well cultivated. Clear mountain streams supply Athos with fresh water. The winds that come off the sea keep down the intense summer heat. Snow seldom falls, but when it does it lasts for a very short time. There are few birds and almost no wild animals on Mount Athos. Amid all the beauty of Athos is an imprint of a certain sadness and even sternness. The mammoth mountains and deep precipices are astonishing in their magnitude, which makes any journey through Athos quite difficult. Especially majestic and inaccessible is the highest summit of the mountains on Athos, and pilgrims rarely go there. The climate changes on the mountains at various levels of ascent, and halfway up the pilgrims cannot find any lemon and orange trees, though, in the mountain ridges, they find firs and pines. The highest summit on Athos is completely barren of any vegetation — even bushes. Only the beauty of Athos, the so-called "unwilting little flower of the Mother of God," grows and pours out its fragrance in the cloud-covered heights. But from this summit one can behold a marvelous view encompassing all of Mount Athos. To the west is the magnificent Mount Olympus soaring aloft in all its beauty above Salonica Bay where the Venerable Joannicus the Great shone forth the light of his holy life. Further in the distance is the blue mountain chain of Macedonia. The long range of mountains on Athos extends toward the isthmus in the form of picturesque rolling waves of thick greenery. St. Athanasius of Athos noticed that the mountain ranges there actually formed a cross shape. The summit of Mount Athos itself is a plateau, covered almost entirely by a church which is dedicated to the memory of Christ's Transfiguration on Mount Tabor. The length of the church building, including the vestibule, does not exceed six meters. It is awesome, standing on the edge of a cliff at this head-spinning height, to look down at the boundless blue sea as it splashes at the foot of the mountain. The endless greenery of Mount Athos is studded with white stone monasteries, sketes, cloistered cells, and grottoes as the sky is studded with glistening stars. Sketes are smaller monastic communities or dormitories which are located on the grounds of a larger monastery and are dependent on them as appendages. Cloistered cells are simply individual little houses with attached chapels where monks live together in small groups under the jurisdiction of a larger monastery. Grottoes are merely little houses or huts, sometimes hollowed out in the side of a hill or a mountain, which have no attached chapel.

Monastic life began on Mount Athos in ancient times. The Queen of Heaven herself blessed Mount Athos by her presence. In the seventh century, when the Sixth Ecumenical Council decided that all monastics should move from the cities into the wilderness, Emperor Constantine IV (Pogonatus) granted the entire task of governing Mount Athos to the monks so that it would be a comfortable place to practice monasticism. The number of novices increased rapidly here so that by the tenth century, Athos had about one hundred and eighty monasteries and by the sixteenth century, more than eighteen thousand monks. This latter figure does not include the skete-dwellers about whom a certain narrator wrote that only God could calculate their number. From the time of its beginning as a monastic community, Athos was absolutely separated from the outside world. It remained unchanged, as it had been in the days of the Comnenus and Paleologus dynasties, as though it was forgotten in the wilderness of its own peninsula. One finds much that is strange and curious in such a peculiar world. There is a certain strict adherence to canons and traditions and yet one finds an almost absolute independence, the quality of which can hardly be matched anywhere else. Athos, remaining true to its task, functioned almost always as a higher school for monastic discipline and as a protector of the purity of the faith and of piety for the entire Orthodox East. Men came here from all the Orthodox countries of the world to take on the monastic way of life and to grow and mature in the wisdom of Christianity. The activity of the Athonite monks consisted not only of ascetic exercises such as fasting, prayer, in working toward spiritual perfection, but in a very special devotion to Christian scholarship and theology. Under local conditions the Athonite monks pursued theological scholarship with considerable success. Athos became the center of theological scholarship for Christian Byzantium. The arrival of Slavic monks gave impetus to the translating activities on Athos. The monks collected Greek manuscripts, translated them into Slavonic, and made numerous additional copies with which they supplied the libraries not only of the Athonite monasteries but of Bulgaria, Moldavia, Russia, Serbia, and Walachia. A well-known traveler throughout the Christian East in the middle of the eighteenth century, Vasilii Grigorovich Barskii, saw the libraries of Athos and was amazed at the wealth of their rare collections. In one collection, he saw a highly valued and famous *Psalter* which the local monks ascribed to St. John Chrysostom. Why they did so, Barskii could not understand. Whether Chrysostom copied the text with his own hand or kept it for his own use could not be discovered. There were no signatures or markings which identified the book in any way.

The libraries of Athos presently contain more than ten thousand manuscripts of various works, not only of Christian but also of non-Christian epochs. The manuscripts have not been studied adequately. The high level of spirituality and ascetic life did not remain constant in Athos. During those years when Paisii was on Athos, it had degenerated considerably. Barskii attributes this to the oppression of the Turks. The Turkish regime tore monasticism asunder: they persecuted the monasteries so severely that the monks fell into unpayable debts, and were forced to depart from their cloisters. The flourishing monasteries were left to the mercy of fate. A reason for the difficulties which burdened the Slavic novices was the hostile attitude of the Greeks toward them. Barskii wrote that the Greeks actually compelled the Slavs to leave so that they had to wander about the mountains, and being despised by all, they had to feed and shelter themselves by the labor of their own hands. The foxes and birds had nests but the Russians had nowhere to lay their heads in a cloistered place so perfectly conducive to monastic life.

CHAPTER II

Monastic Life

After several days of rest in the St. Athanasius Lavra, Platon and his fellow travelers moved northward to the Pantokratoros Monastery near which the Slavic monks were living. The rocky and mountainous route to the monastery was extremely difficult to traverse. The heat was so intense that their clothes were saturated with perspiration, so they stopped for a rest in the cool forest. There they sat down on the cool stones and drank cold water from the streams. On the same day, they became ill with a severe case of Athos fever. They moved along, feverish, to the Pantokratoros Monastery. When the wayfarers arrived, their countrymen rejoiced at the sight of them and at first did not note that they were sick. The monks thought that the wanderers were ill from swimming in the sea, but once they discovered that they became ill while journeying on Athos, they were terror-stricken by the possibility that their disease could be fatal. The monks immediately began massaging the sick travelers with hot alcohol, and they worked so long on some that they hardly had any strength left when they came to Platon. They were not able to save the life of Hieromonk Tryfon who died three days after his arrival. Platon had to be forced to take some food and wine, because he refused to break his habit of not drinking alcoholic beverages. Nevertheless he was forced again and again to drink wine until finally his vomiting saved him. In a few days he was completely well again and he then settled down in a cell near the monastery.

Platon became acquainted with his new neighbors gradually. He went around visiting the monks and hermits, hoping that he would find for himself a spiritual guide who was well informed about patristic literature and who was living in silence and poverty. Platon, however, could not find such a guide for himself so he had to live in loneliness. This is when the most difficult time in Platon's life began. He lived through extreme poverty, helplessness, turbulent spiritual struggles and many tears. He lived in such a way for four long years, and those years transformed a shy and timid boy into an experienced and strong man. Platon spent his time in avid reading, chanting Psalms, study of Scripture and the writings of the Fathers, and in sincere prayer. He struggled to cultivate within himself deep humility, continual self-re-proach, contrition of heart, an abundance of tears, love for God and his neighbors alike, and a continual remembrance of death. This is what he himself wrote about those times:

> When I came from my Orthodox homeland to the Holy Mountain I was so poor that I could not pay back a debt of even three half kopecks to my traveling partner. In my bodily weakness I was able to support myself by charity only. If the holy monks and my countrymen who lived on the Holy Mountain had not supported me, I never could have existed here. Very often I went about in the winter almost naked, shirtless and barefooted. My existence continued in this manner for four years. Whenever I had to crawl back to my cell either from the lavra or the Khilandar carrying all the handouts that were given to me, or out of the forest with firewood, or from doing any other kind of heavy work, I would have to lie in bed like a paralytic for four days in order to recuperate.

Whenever Platon left his cell he never closed his door nor was there any need to do so. The only contents in his cell were the patristic texts which he acquired from Bulgarian and Serbian monasteries.

In the beginning of the year 1750, Starets Vasilii, the Moldavian schema-monk with whom we are well acquainted by now, came to Mount Athos. His arrival on the Holy Mountain was of special importance for Platon. Starets Vasilii explained to him the danger of silence and solitude and the necessity of a community life for beginning ascetics. Starets Vasilii explained that all of monastic society is divided into three types. The first type, cenobitic monasticism, is community monasticism whereby many monks, living together in a community, share a common routine life. The second type, semi-eremitic monasticism, is the sharing of a common life by two or three monks who settle together and live in obedience to each other out of their love and fear of God. Any property, such as food or clothing, is shared by them. They themselves live by exchanging their handicrafts for goods. They live in concern for one another and remain detached from their individual personal wills. Eremitic monasticism is the third type, and only holy and perfect men are suitable for it. Such monks, called eremites, live a life of silence and seclusion in which they devote themselves to prayer of the heart or *hesychasm*. Presently, some monks opposing the directions of the Fathers choose a fourth form of monasticism for themselves. Each monk builds his own grotto where he lives alone and independently from others. Each monk prefers the dictates of his own will to a life of obedience beneath the direction of a spiritual guide. Although such monks may seem similar to the eremites, they actually are quite arbitrary in their existence. They actually hinder their own salvation because they follow a path of life for which they are spiritually inadequate. After a careful reading of St. Gregory the Sinaite, one will discover that what is referred to as arbitrariness is actually such a cloistered self-determined uncommunal way of life. It is far better for one to live together with one's brothers, to acknowledge one's own faults, to repent daily, and thereby to be cleansed by Christ than to carry on in one's own vanity and evil and to try to cover such faults by a cloistered existence. Such people, says St. John Climacus, cannot see any indications of their passionateness. St. Barsanuphius says that premature silence is the cause of high-mindedness. At the request of Platon, Starets Vasilii tonsured him to the rank of mantiya-bearer and then changed his name to Paisii.

Three months after Paisii's tonsure, a young monk from Moldo-Walachia, Vissarion, came to him and begged him

with tears to give him guidance for the salvation of his soul
and to find him a counselor who was well experienced in the
spiritual life. At first Paisii could only weep and sigh, but then
he became silent and while remaining so for a considerable
length of time, he prayed within himself. He then responded
to Vissarion.

My brother, you are forcing me to speak about
something very sad and you are inflicting my heart with
pain. I myself, just as you are now doing, went through
great effort to find a spiritual guide for myself, but
nowhere was I able to find one. Therefore I was and
still am afflicted with great sorrow. But seeing you
overcome by such sorrow I sympathize with you and
therefore I shall give you a little advice from my very
insufficient wisdom. This salvation of the soul about
which you are inquiring cannot be achieved without the
help of a true spiritual guide, who himself lives according to the commandments of God and in obedience
to the words of Christ, who commands us to teach and
to set an example. How is it possible to lead semeone
along a certain way which one himself has not traveled?
You have to battle against all the passions of the soul
and body until blood flows, to conquer lust and anger
with the help of Christ, and to subdue voluptuousness,
vainglory, cupidity and all other evil passions. In such
struggles, the only real leader and guide is Jesus Christ.
When Christ was led out into the wilderness to be
tempted, He repelled Satan by fasting, humility, poverty, vigilance, prayer, and the Sacred Scripture, and
thus He crowned our nature with the crown of victory,
teaching and granting us power over the devil. Whoever follows his Lord with love and humility in all
things, to him will be granted the task of healing other
souls and setting them aright according to the commandments of the Lord, and to be victorious over passions. Once this has been accomplished in such a person
by the grace of God, then he will be radiant with the
gifts of the Holy Spirit and thus will be able to reveal to

his disciples, indeed without any illusion, all the commandments of Christ and the virtues of humility, meekness, and the poverty of Christ, patience in all things,
mercy above all, fervent love for God and a sincere
love for one's neighbors. From all of these comes a
true spiritual sensibility. Such a true guide will instruct
his disciples to put all their trust in the will of the
Lord. The disciple, having seen and heard all this in
his guide, and following his example in faith and love
can, with the help of God and following the advice of
his guide, succeed in fulfilling Christ's commandments
and achieve salvation. That is the kind of guide we
should seek, my brother. But alas, we are living in disastrous times which were foreseen by our God-bearing
Fathers by the power of the Holy Spirit. They took pity
on us by warning and encouraging us in their writings.
St. Symeon the New Theologian says:

'There are very few, especially in our times, who
are capable of leading a flock and who are able
to heal understanding souls. Some can still keep
fasts and vigils and maintain an internal piety,
but of those who can attain to humility, continual
mourning, freedom from passions and acquisition
of virtues there are very few.'

In conjunction with this, St. Symeon refers to the Holy
Fathers who said:

'Whoever desires to be freed from his passions
will be freed from them by lamentation, and whoever wishes to acquire virtues will acquire them
by weeping.'

It is therefore evident that the monk who neither la-
ments daily, detaches himself from his passions, nor
acquires virtues cannot be a participant in any graces.
For there are virtues and there are graces.

The same was said by one Father, who is very close

to us, a certain Russian luminary, Venerable Nil of the
Sora, who, having carefully studied the Sacred Scripture, and having observed the calamitous situation and
the human carelessness of his time, wrote the following
advice to his disciples:

> 'It is essential that one laboriously search for a
> knowledgeable guide, but if there is no such man,
> then the Holy Fathers order us to learn from the
> Sacred Scriptures and the teachings of the God-
> bearing Fathers, according to the very teaching of
> Our Saviour Himself who said: 'Search the Scrip-
> tures, for in them ye think ye have eternal life.'

Although St. Nil of the Sora says this in reference to
mental prayer, the need to have an experienced guide
while battling against evil passions in striving to fulfill God's will is nonetheless felt here as well. Therefore, my brother, all that I have called to mind thus far
reveals to us the absolute necessity to study the Scriptures and the writings of the Fathers in compunction
day and night with people who are of the same mind
as we are. It is necessary for us to emulate the good
example of the saints and so learn to do God's will.
Only by the cooperation of our personal efforts with
the grace of God can we achieve salvation.

Vissarion fell to the ground at Paisii's feet and tearfully
implored him to accept him as a disciple. Paisii was troubled
deeply by Vissarion's request for he himself desired to become
a disciple if only he could find an experienced guide. Persistently, for three days, Vissarion implored Paisii to accept him
as a disciple. Paisii, moved at last by Vissarion's incessant
tearful pleas, conceded and agreed to take him in, but only
as a friend and not as a disciple. They would live together
in semi-eremetic monasticism, revealing the will of God to
each other, inducing each other to fulfill the will of God,
enlightening each other by the understanding of Scripture,
submitting themselves one to another obediently in all that is

useful to the soul, maintaining in themselves oneness of spirit in all things. Paisii's desire to live together with a monk of the same mind in mutual love and obedience at last was fulfilled. They had the Sacred Scriptures and the teachings of the holy and God-bearing Fathers as their guides. So they began their common life together, living in profound peace, aflame with spirit and beginning their spiritual growth anew each day.

Within four years, Paisii and Vissarion were joined by more monks, who wanted to live under the spiritual direction of Paisii. Paisii, feeling that only the perfect and passionless were capable of spiritually guiding others and that he himself was quite imperfect and passionate, refused to accept them at first. Only after their persistent requests, as well as the requests by Vissarion, whom Paisii loved very much, on their behalf did Paisii agree to accept the monks, quite contrary to his own will. Paisii put all his hope in the all-powerful providence of God. When Paisii was joined by Parthenius and Coesarius living in their single cell became cramped for the four of them together. They were forced to buy another cell which was not far from where they were living. When their number increased to eight, they bought St. Constantine Skete and its attached chapel which was about two stone-throws from their first cell.

Paisii's first disciples were from Moldo-Walachia and they practiced the rule of prayer in Wallachian. When they moved into the St. Constantine Skete, the Slavic monks began to come for prayer offices so that in all there were twelve monks—seven Wallachians and five Slavs. They chanted and read the traditional prayer offices in Wallachian and Slavonic. Their life was quite difficult, as Paisii writes.

> Winter had come but we had no shelter because we did not have enough cells. We ourselves began to build five cells at the St. Constantine Skete. Who could even imagine the hardships that we endured during the next four months? We had insufficient clothing, we were shoeless, and in such a state we labored all winter long building our cells, hauling soil and heavy stones. On Sundays and feast days, in addition to being able to

rest somewhat, we had the opportunity to visit the
larger monasteries and ask for food. Our clothes were
so worn-out that we were almost naked as we shivered
in the cold. At times we were so exhausted from our
work that some of our monks collapsed on the ground
as though dead. Because the times were so hard and
we were so weak, we fell behind in fulfilling our prayer
offices. Instead of Compline, we read 'Psalm Fifty'
and then went to sleep. We did not omit Matins but
we fulfilled the office as well as we were able to, reading
three Kathismata and sometimes more. Sometimes instead of the Hours, we read a Parakleisis to the Theotokos. What else could we do? We were so completely
exhausted that we often fell asleep during prayer. Had
our most merciful Lord Jesus Christ not strengthened
us in humility, patience, and love for God and each
other, we never would have been able to surmount our
trials.

Before long the little community found itself in need of
a priest and father confessor. The monks took counsel among
themselves and consequently agreed to implore Paisii to become their priest and confessor. Paisii refused even to hear
about it, telling the monks how he had fled Moldo-Walachia
for that very same reason. The more Paisii refused, the more
his monks pleaded with him, falling prostrate before him and
giving him all the reasons for their entreaty. They especially
indicated to him how when confessing to other confessors
they would often receive counseling which was contrary to
that of Paisii, and because of this their souls would be filled
with discordance. Many other fathers who were living on
the Holy Mountain gave their support to the monks' cause
by persuading Paisii not to refuse since the task could be
imputed to him as a duty in any case. At last Paisii surrendered
himself to the common entreaty of the monks, considering
it to be the will of God. Paisii Velichkovskii was ordained
to the priesthood in the year 1758, at age thirty-six.

Conditions in the St. Constantine Skete became increasingly
crowded for the growing community. After a general council

and agreement among the monks, Father Paisii asked the Pantocratoros Monastery for the use of the old and empty Prophet Elijah Skete. Relying on their own manual labor, with the assistance of several benefactors, Father Paisii and his monks set about renovating the Prophet Elijah Skete. They built a church, a courtyard, a refectory, a bakery shop, a kitchen, a guest house and sixteen cells—all from bricks. A brook flowed into the skete. Father Paisii limited the residence to sixteen monks. It was a half-hour walk from the St. Constantine Skete to the Prophet Elijah Skete and about an hour from there to the Pantocratoros Monastery. The new Prophet Elijah Skete, far away from any big roads, was situated in peace and silence. The air was always fresh and healthy. The soil was fertile and the warm climate made possible the cultivation of fruit orchards. The vineyards yielded abundant harvests and the wine made from the grapes was excellent. Starets Paisii and his monks hoped to settle down at last, but their wish was never fully granted them.

A rumor about the good life of the ascetics was spreading. all over Mount Athos, and curious monks came from all parts of the Holy Mountain to see the skete, its good organization, the humble, reverent and God-fearing disposition of the monks in church, the tranquility of the liturgical singing and reading, the restrained use of words, the beauty of the church services, the humility and silence in which the monks went about their duties, the customary sincere peace that reigned over the monks, the mutual love and detachment from self-will, the obedience to their starets in faith and love, the paternal mercy of the starets to his spiritual children, his wise perception of the capabilities of each monk, his sincere compassion and love for all the monks in all their spiritual infirmities and bodily needs. The visiting monks soon began to feel a desire to be united to the community. With ardent tears they prayed the starets not to separate them from himself. Even though their plea was again contrary to the will of Starets Paisii he accepted them nevertheless and even rejoiced over their zeal for salvation. He put all his hope in Divine Providence. Because the facilities at Starets Paisii's skete were inadequate to be able to accommodate all the newly-

accepted monks, the monks lived by twos and threes in the cells
and they constructed additional smaller cells, attaching them
to the skete like swallows building their nests against the stone
walls of some building, and they were happy because the starets did not exclude them from his community. All the monks
diligently busied themselves with their duties and handicrafts.
The starets himself labored over the manufacturing of spoons,
but he spent the nights reading and translating patristic literature, usually sleeping no more than three hours.

In such a way this monastic community grew and solidified
under the direction of Starets Paisii. His good influence and
fame soon spread all around the Holy Mountain. But at the
same time Paisii was gaining many enemies who were jealous
of his fame and suspicious of his observance of ecclesiastical
regulations, even accusing him of violating them. Starets
Athanasius and his disciples from the Kapsokalivya Skete
were among the enemies of Starets Paisii. Aathanasius, a pious
zealot of the faith who was considerably uninformed about
the teachings and life of Starets Paisii, accused Starets Paisii
of abbreviating and therefore violating the rule of prayer
which was established by the Church for the monastics, of
incorrectly interpreting the teachings of St. Gregory the
Sinaite, of incorrectly addressing his spiritual father, of acting
like the Roman pope, who acknowledges the commandments
of God in word but violates them in deed, of replacing the
rule of prayer life of the Church with his own rule of prayer,
of having no humility, of credulously referring to Greek
books, of preferring philosophy to repentance and lamentation, of refusing to condemn heretics, and finally of replacing
the prayer of the Church by the Prayer of Jesus. Starets Athanasius expounded upon all these accusations in an extensive
letter, which he sent to Starets Paisii. He asked Paisii to repent
and not to digress from the common tradition of the Holy
Mountain. Paisii read the letter aloud before all the monks
and he even showed it to his father confessor, who later went
with Paisii to the older cathedral clergy. After examining the
letter they directed Paisii to write an answer to Athanasius
and to expose his unjust accusations. If Athanasius would

not admit his error and repent, they agreed to expose him pub-
lically before a Sobor of the Holy Mountain.

Starets Paisii did what the elder clergy told him to do. He
wrote a letter to Athanasius which consisted of fourteen chapters, wherein he refuted each one of the accusations which
Athanasius had directed against him:

> I implore you, fathers, to cease your vain and use-
> less rejection of the writings of the Fathers. I highly
> esteem your life, I bless your great accomplishments,
> and I greatly value your presence. So that your labors
> be not in vain, intelligence and reasoning are essential
> for your accomplishments. Therefore, if you wish to
> save yourselves and to reveal the 'Way to the Kingdom'
> to your disciples, which is fulfilling the commandments
> of Christ, then avidly adhere to reading books. This
> and the exegesis by experienced spiritual fathers will
> be a true guide for you and your disciples, setting you
> on the way to salvation. There is no other way to save
> yourself. St. John Chrysostom says that it is impossible
> for a man to save another if he himself does not de-
> light in reading spiritual literature. St. Basil the Great
> says that a starets should instruct his disciples in the
> wisdom of the Sacred Scripture, and that if he does not,
> he will be a false witness to God and the holy Fathers.
> The great Anastasius the Sinaite teaches that we must
> have the support of Sacred Scripture in all that we say
> and do, for otherwise we are deceived by human actions
> and motivations and then we fall from the true way
> into the abyss of destruction. Furthermore, when study-
> ing Sacred Scripture, we have to fear and love God and
> to imbue ourselves and others with the remembrance
> of the word of God. This is what the saints teach
> us, and they inspire us to read the Sacred Scriptures
> with zeal and diligence. Do not say, fathers, that it is
> enough to read one or two books on spirituality in order
> to be fit to provide spiritual guidance. A bee does not
> collect honey from one or two flowers, but only from
> many flowers. So it is with one who reads the writings

of the Fathers: he will be guided in faith and wisdom
by one Father, in silence and prayer by another, in obedience, humility, and patience by another, and in self-
reproach and love for God and one's neighbors by yet
another. One is taught how to live the evangelic life
by reading many Fathers.

Paisii, in telling about the extreme difficulties encountered
by his first community, accounted for his abbreviated rule
of prayer. At one time he was bed-ridden for three days and
being unable to move, like a paralytic, he was in no condition to observe the rule of prayer as it was established for
monastics:

> I confess all these things to my spiritual father and to
> all the other elder clergy. Since I was not able to ob-
> serve the rule of prayer because of my extreme weak-
> ness my thoughts told me to return to Russia. Then my
> spiritual father encouraged me and told me not to leave
> the Holy Mountain to where I had been led by God
> Himself. He advised me to be patient, to observe the
> rule of prayer as well as I could, and to always thank
> God because my very thanksgiving, in all my weakness
> and need, would benefit me far more than any rule of
> prayer could. So I followed his instructions and kept
> my rule of prayer, lived in my infirmity, rejoicing in
> the Lord and thanking Him, praying for loving-kind-
> ness and that He would strengthen me until the very
> end of my life here on Mount Athos.

Starets Paisii gave detailed answers in response to all the other
accusations which were brought against him. Paisii's letter
made such a great impression upon Athanasius that he
acknowledged his own error, repented, and begged Starets
Paisii for forgiveness. At last peace was established between
them.

CHAPTER III

Spiritual Bases of Paisii's Monastery

Let us now become acquainted with the patristic principles upon which Starets Paisii developed his monastic community on Mount Athos. One possible source for such information is a letter of the starets to his friend and disciple, the priest Dimitri, which he wrote in May, 1766.

My beloved friend,

Know that the Holy Spirit, through the Holy Fathers, divided monastic life into three ranks: eremitic or solitary monasticism, semi-eremitic or semi-solitary monasticism and cenobitic or communal monasticism. The eremite requires complete withdrawal from society into solitude. He entrusts all earthly cares about food, clothing, bodily needs and care for the soul to God alone. During his battles with bodily and spiritual infirmities, he must have God alone for his helper and comforter. He must shun every consolation of the world for the love of God. Semi-eremites live together with one or two other like-minded monks and they must live under the close guidance of a starets who is knowledgeable in Sacred Scripture and experienced in spiritual life. The semi-eremites, who are his disciples, must be obedient and dutiful to their starets in all bodily and spiritual matters. The cenobites live in a common community of many monks which, according to St. Basil the Great, begins with a simple common life together, as was that of Christ and his twelve apostles. Such a small group of people sharing a common life can grow into a large community made up of several generations

and personality types but finding at the same time their
ultimate value in a singleness of mind, heart, spirit
and desire in Jesus Christ through the fulfillment of
His divine commandments. The cenobites must carry
each other's burdens and be obedient to each other in
the fear of God. They have to live as a community
under the direction of a superior who is their spiritual
father and guide. The superior must be experienced in
the exegesis of Sacred Scripture and capable of guiding
the community by his own actions as well as words.
The cenobites are obliged to be obedient to their superior as to the Lord himself and they must detach themselves absolutely from the will and reasoning of their
ego. They must not oppose the dictates of the superior
unless they are contrary to the commandments of Christ
and to the teachings of the Holy Fathers. In each of
these forms of monastic life, which were established
by the Holy Spirit, many Holy Fathers attained perfection and pleased God, shining forth rays of spiritual
light like the sun and leaving us with a high example
for emulation. The three forms of monastic life are
given clear testimony by the Sacred Scriptures. Which
form, though, should one choose over the others?
St. John Climacus, a great guide of monastic life, advises those who leave the world and enter the monastic
life not to choose either of the extreme forms, eremitic or cenobitic, but to begin with the moderate, semi-
eremitic form. The solitary seclusion of eremetic monasticism demands an angelic strength, which the novice
does not have. The novice is so prone to spiritual passions such as anger, vainglory, envy, self-conceit, and
lacks to such an extent the boldness for such a her-
mitic existence, that he can fall very easily into mental
frenzy. At the same time, St. John Climacus advises the
novice not to enter cenobitic monasticism, not because
it would be useless to him but because it also demands
a special kind of endurance. The semi-eremitic way,
practiced in the company of a small group of like-minded monks who are under the close spiritual direction

of their starets, is best for the beginner. It does not require of the novice the great endurance that would be required of him by the cenobitic rule and it is much more gratifying than the eremitic rule. According to the semi-eremitic rule, the monks must be obedient to their starets and to each other. The cenobitic rule requires obedience of a monk not only to his starets but to every single person in the community. He must be able to endure their annoying reproaches, abuses and profanations, to suffer all kinds of temptations, to be as dirt beneath everyone's feet, to be like a purchased slave, to serve everyone with humility and the fear of God without utterance or complaint. He must be able to endure extreme need, hunger, nakedness, poverty and all the ailments which are peculiar to the community.

A combination of various aspects from the three different forms of monastic life and a premature conversion to eremitism inevitably leads to the saddest consequences. Whoever rejects the order which was established by God and instead leaves a community in order to train himself in holy and blessed obedience through which he can acquire true humility and which could lead him to a liberation from his passions or whoever ventures into the wilderness, choosing for himself a silent and secluded life, is actually exposing himself to the wrath of God. Such an inexperienced warrior dees not know how to handle this kind of personal and internal invisible warfare, which confronts the eremite because he comes from the totally opposite experience of the cenobitic life. He is not able, because of ignorance to arm himself with spiritual weapons. Having had the audacity to separate himself from the experienced warriors of Christ and to enter alone into battle with his demonic foes, God tolerates him to suffer defeat. He falls before his enemies, and soon is absolutely stifled by them. All this befalls him because he violates God's order, which Jesus Christ Himself adhered to by His most pure life in the flesh.

Such a monk, instead of suffering with Christ in the monastic community, is infringing, out of his own pride, upon the Cross of Christ. He is actually not an eremite, but an arbitrarily self-appointed monk and therefore not a manifestation of the good but only of the charm of the devil. The history of monasticism is filled with such examples, from ancient times down to the present, of self-appointed novices who fell into their own destruction. Under the charm of the devil, they lost their faculties of reasoning, were mentally bemuddled and consequently did away with themselves by some of the most horrifying methods of murder, from which may God by His grace save us.

The life of those who submissively and firmly adhere to the divinely entabled rule of monasticism is absolutely different. At the foundation of this true rule is obedience, the true tree of life. By tasting of its fruits, a feeble novice achieves self-denial and detachment from his own will and reasoning and so he escapes death and every other charm of the devil, which is inevitable for the self-appointed monk. For His pupils here in the world, Jesus Christ established a common community based on obedience and such a community is the root of monastic life. The Twelve Apostles who were obedient to Christ's divine commandments constitute a living example of such a community. Divine obedience is the chief virtue of the angels and was revealed in Paradise as the basis of the blessedness of the first people there. Consequently, when the first people lost this obedience, the Son of God, out of his great loving kindness for men, took it upon Himself to renew and regenerate obedience within Himself, by being obedient to His heavenly Father even to His death on the Cross. By His obedience Christ healed our disobedience and to all who truly believe in Him and are obedient to His commandments, He opened the doors of His heavenly Kingdom.

In the early Church, eight thousand Christians, emulating the example of Christ, lived communally, not claiming any private ownership but sharing all things. Because of such a life they were worthy enough to attain to a unity of heart and spirit.

Our venerable and ancient fathers lived just such a common life in lavras and monasteries everywhere, guiding themselves according to the regulations which were formulated by St. Basil the Great and shining with the brilliance of the sun. No manner of living other than the cenobitic type with obedience can bring such success to man. Due to humility, which is born of blessed obedience, man is led back to his original purity, the likeness of God is renewed and restored in him as is that gift which he received from God in baptism. In addition, the true novice is granted other blessings of which he becomes a partaker by his humility through the grace of God, and which he can experience repeatedly with his spiritual sensibility. Such a cenobitic community of monks, who have gathered together in Christ's name from all parts of the world, is held together by such a strong bond of mutual love that all the monks actually constitute one body, each monk being a member of the rest with Jesus Christ as their head. The members of this body of Christ burn with love for God and for each other. They are one in spirit and in mind, having one and the same purpose: to fulfill God's will. They encourage each other in their purpose by adhering to God's commandments, by being obedient to each other, by bearing each other's burdens and by being masters of themselves and servants of each other. In the name of this holy and true love, with one mind, the monks become emulators of the very life of Christ Himself and of His twelve apostles—by being obedient to their spiritual father in all things; by confessing all the secrets of their heart to Him; by accepting His teachings and commandments as if from the mouth of God Himself; by despising their own will and reasoning, which are contrary to the wisdom of their spiritual father, like unclean clothing, and by condemning, casting off and

escaping them like the fires of gehenna while ceaselessly praying God to deliver them from this burden
and to help them return to Him, their Father, with
their whole hearts they pray like children to their
mother, to follow Him in all things like sheep follow
their shepherd and to obey Him like the artifact obeys
its artificer, never digressing in anything on their own
accord. This divine obedience, the root and basis of all
forms of monastic life, is as intimately connected with
cenobitic monasticism as the soul is to the body. One
cannot exist without the other. Obedience is the short-
est and most direct ladder to Heaven for it has but
one rung: detachment from the ego. By ascending to
this first step one quickly ascends to Heaven. Whoever falls away from obedience at the same time falls
away from God and from Heaven. Our holy and God-
bearing Fathers witness to this clearly.

These are the patristic principles upon which Starets Paisii
founded his cenobitic monastic community. They can be reduced to the virtues of absolute voluntary poverty and obedience. To what degree, however, were these principles
established in his monastery? In response to this question, we
find the following answer in the same letter of Starets Paisii.

No monk in our monastery owns anything personally, to such an extent that no one even dreams of
acquiring something for himself alone. The monks are
convinced that such is the way of Judas the Betrayer.
Everyone who is received into the monastery must present his personal possessions, if he has any, including
the smallest trinkets, at the feet of the starets and all
the other monks. He must surrender all his material
possessions as well as his soul and body to the Lord.
He must submit himself to holy obedience, even unto
death.

One may not enter the monastery on any other
terms. The second indispensable condition for being
allowed entrance into the monastery is one's denial

of one's ego and one's strict adherence to obedience in all things. By firmly maintaining these two principles as the basis of our community, we attempt precisely to observe all other regulations of the cenobitic rule. Denying themselves of all the blessings of this world out of their love for Christ, the monks take up their crosses and follow Him. They try to bear each others' burdens, to encourage each other to do good works, to keep a unity of mind and spirit and to surpass each other in faith and love for their starets. My soul rejoices at the sight of this, and I thank God tearfully that He has made me worthy to behold how His servants dwell together with one another. I am comforted by their countenance. It is a fact that everyone who lives in our monastery has not yet attained the same level of spiritual growth, but this cannot be otherwise. Some have succeeded in mortifying their egos through obedience, patiently suffering insults, abuses, reproaches and various forms of temptations and this they do with such joy as if they had already been assumed into the fullness of God's great mercy. In the depths of their hearts they are filled with self-reproach and they consider themselves the chief and foremost of all sinners. There are those monks too who fall and rise, transgress and repent. They are able to tolerate reproaches and temptations only with great difficulty but they mature in spiritual strength. They do not remain separated from the monks of the first category but rather join with them in ardorous tearful prayer to God for His help. Finally, there are those monks who are still too immature to be fed solid food, as the Bible states it. In simple terms, they are not able to patiently endure reproaches, abuses and temptations. They must still be fed the milk of human love and condescension, until they spiritually mature into the patience that is demanded of them. They try to replace their faults and weaknesses with continual self-reproachment and sincere desire for salvation. In spite of their varying levels of spiritual maturity, all the monks are equally penetrated by the desire to keep God's commandments firmly because they are mutually united in that indissoluble bond of His love. For the sake of this love and their eternal salvation, they whole-heartedly and with gratitude toward God, suffer constant poverty in all things. They place all their hope in their one Saviour who is God.

The lofty temper of Paisii's monastic community would have been impossible to maintain had he himself not projected such an image and concretely actualized his own boundless love. In this same letter Paisii writes the following:

I suffer endlessly from spiritual grief and affliction and as such shall stand before the dread tribunal at the terrible Last Judgment to render an account for all the souls of those many monks who submitted themselves to me in obedience, as inadequate as I am to fulfill the demands of my responsibilities. Even though I stand unworthy before God and the Theotokos, I nevertheless hope for salvation and despair not that God will have mercy on my soul because of the prayers of my brethren. Blessed be God if I will not be condemned to eternal torment by my own deeds since such is my due reward for violating his commandments. I pray Him always to grant me but one wish—that, in His great loving kindness, He make me worthy as the rich man in the bosom of Abraham to see my spiritual children, true servants and sufferers for Christ, in His Heavenly Kingdom. That would be sufficient for me, instead of any reward.

CHAPTER IV

Literary Activities of Starets Paisii on Mount Athos

In his teachings on monastic life and in his organization of a monastic community, Starets Paisii was guided by the writings of the Holy Fathers. From the very start, he diligently, but unsuccessfully, searched for a spiritual counselor for himself.

When I left the world, [Paisii writes], having an ardent desire to strive toward God by following the monastic way of life, I was not privileged to have been given the slightest bit of spiritual advice that agreed with what the Fathers taught about how a novice should embark upon monasticism. After settling in a certain quite secluded monastery, where by the grace of God I was actually able to begin to pursue my monastic calling, I was never even given an explanation of obedience and its purpose for the novice. Neither the monastery superior nor my starets gave me any guidance in these matters. They tonsured me before I had had any previous experience of monasticism and they permitted me to live in their monastery without having any guide for my spiritual direction. My sponsor, who left the monastery for some unknown place just one week after my tonsure, told me in parting: 'Brother, you are an educated person and therefore, as God teaches us to live, so live!'

Left like a lamb without a shepherd, [writes Paisii], I took to wandering, from time to time dwelling in sketes, here and there, trying to find direction and peace for my soul, struggling to gain control of my senses. With the exceptions of the blessed Startsy Vasilii and Mikhail, who gave me their spiritual guidance and were of great spiritual benefit to me—but with whom I could no longer remain out of fear of compulsive ordination to the priesthood—I found no one. Finally I came to the calm and quiet haven of the Holy Mountain, hoping to receive some consolation for my soul. There, I came upon some monks from our Russian homeland who were literate and well-read in the Holy Scriptures. Still, I did not find the guide that my soul desired. I settled there alone for awhile in a secluded cell and, putting all my trust and confidence in God's will, I began to read a little, but with careful attention, from the writings of the Fathers which were given to me as gifts from the Serbian and Bulgarian monasteries. By reading these books, I was able to discover, as though I were looking into a mirror, how I should begin my impoverished monastic life and what great bliss I was depriving myself of by not living in obedience under an experienced spiritual guide. I understood that my so-called silence was inadequate without the guidance of a spiritual director and that it was an activity for which only the perfect and passionless were fit. Bewildered about what I should do and to whom I should surrender myself in obedience, I grieved and wept like a child over its dead mother.

From that time on, Paisii read the writings of the Fathers with particular zeal. True, he had also loved to read the Fathers in his childhood, but then his reading did not involve total personal submergence into the subtle details of their meaning. Whatever meaning spontaneously came to his mind and sensibility then satisfied him. After his meticulous and continual study of the Fathers' writings in his search for his own edification and for direction about how to live the monastic life, Paisii noticed innumerable errors in the Slavonic translations of these texts. Suddenly he was confronted with a new and extremely important task: the correction of the inaccurate translations and obscured passages of the patristic texts. Paisii himself writes the following about his new responsibility to Archimandrite Theodosius of the St. Sofronius Monastery.

While I was still living on Mount Athos, I became well aware of the teachings and commandments of our God-bearing Fathers as to how the director of a monastic community should guide or teach his monks, not on the basis of his own mentality and reasoning but rather, via his adherence to the true and correct teachings of the Holy Scriptures, the Fathers, ecumenical teachers and instructors in monasticism, who were enlightened by the Holy Spirit. At the same time, being well aware of my own small-mindedness and apprehensive of my own inexperience, afraid of falling like a blind man into a pit and bringing down along with myself others as well, I decided to adopt the Old and New Testaments, and the Sacred Tradition of the Church (the teachings of our God-bearing Fathers, the ecumenical teachers and instructors of monastic life, the rules of apostolic councils and of our Holy Fathers which are kept by the Holy Catholic and Apostolic Church of the East) and all their commandments and regulations as the unshakable foundation for monastic life. I adopted all this as guidance for myself and for my brethren in order that, living together and benefiting from this by the co-operation and instruction of Divine Grace itself, we might not digress from the true, pure and wholesome catholic mentality of the Holy Orthodox Church. I began by diligently acquiring, not without great difficulty and expense, patristic texts on obedience, sobriety, vigilance and prayer. I copied several of them with my own hand. Others I purchased for the money which I had earned by working and by continually depriving myself of food and clothing. We bought all the above-mentioned patristic texts in their Slavonic language editions and guarded them like a sacred trea-

sure sent to us by God Himself. While avidly reading
them during the course of many years, I noticed a great
number of ambiguous passages and, in many places,
absolute ignorance of grammatical rules. Even though
I read and reread these texts endlessly, with great effort
and discernment, only God knew what grief filled my
soul. Being confused about what to do, I felt that the
Slavonic texts could probably be salvaged at least partially by a comparison with other Slavonic editions of
the same texts. I started by copying with my own hand
the books of St. Isichius, Presbyter of Jerusalem, St. Philotheus the Sinaite and St. Theodore of Edessa from
four different Slavonic editions, hoping that after I had
compared them, I would be able to discern some kind
of grammatical continuity and meaning. But all my
efforts were useless because the comparison revealed
nothing that I had hoped to find. After about six weeks
of work—day and night—I managed to correct the book
of St. Isaac the Syrian by comparing it with another
edition which, I had been told, corresponded with the
original Greek. But that work turned out to be useless
as well and I discovered that I had ruined my best book
by adjusting it according to the worst. After such bitter
experiences, I came to realize what a vain task I had
taken upon myself in attempting to correct Slavonic
texts according to other Slavonic texts. Then I began
an assiduous investigation of the possible causes for
such textual ambiguities and grammatical negligence
in the Slavonic books. I eventually concluded my investigation with two possibilities. The first was a lack of
skill on the part of earlier translators to render Hellenic Greek into Slavonic and the second was their
inexperience and linguistic ignorance. Being convinced
of these two facts, I lost all hope of finding any translations among Slavonic texts that would be as correct
and accurate in meaning as the Hellenic Greek originals. After spending a few years on Mount Athos and
becoming comfortable with at least simple, colloquial
Greek, I attempted to locate original Greek texts in

order to compare them with their Slavonic versions. No matter where I searched, I was unsuccessful. I went to the St. Anna Skete of the Great Lavra, to the Sketes of Kapsokaliva, to the St. Demetrius Skete of Vatopedi and to many other lavras and monasteries, questioning knowledgeable people, experienced spiritual fathers and pious novices, but nowhere was I able to find even one such book. Not only did I receive the same negative reply from all whom I asked, but I also discovered that they were not even familiar with the names of the compilers. I was absolutely bewildered and wonder-struck that in such a holy place, where so many great saints lived, not only was I unable to locate their great ascetical writings but their names were not even known. This saddened me tremendously. Nevertheless my hope in God was not destroyed and I prayed to Him to help me find the precious sources. My gentle and merciful God answered my fervent prayer. I finally found the books for which I was searching and some I even obtained as personal possessions. My good fortune happened in the following way. On one occasion I was travelling with two monks from the St. Athanasius Lavra to the St. Anna Skete and I was passing near the high hill of the Prophet Elias Skete which was the same height as the third highest peak of Holy Athos. At the top of this hill was St. Basil the Great Monastery which had been just recently built by monks who had left Caesarea Cappadocia. The skete was located in a most barren locale where—aside from rain—there was no water source. There were no vineyards, no olive or fig trees. We wanted to stop by, partly to give our regards and partly to look around since we had never been in this particular skete. We entered and sat near the church. A novice noticed us and immediately invited us to his cell. He went to find some food to give us after our journey. As I stood at the open window of his cell I noticed an open book on his little table. It was obviously the transcription of some monk. I examined it more closely and discovered that it was a

text by St. Peter the Damascene. Ineffable joy flooded
my soul. I felt that I had found a heavenly treasure on
earth. When the novice returned, I asked him how such
a precious book had ended up in his cell. He replied
that he had still another book by the same saint. In reply
to my further inquiries, the novice disclosed where I
could find other ascetical books: the works of St. Anthony the Great, St. Gregory the Sinaite, St. Philotheus,
St. Hesychius, St. Diodochus, St. Thalassius, St. Symeon
the New Theologian, St. Nicephorus, St. Isaiah and
others. When I asked him why I had been unable to
locate any of these books, he answered that no one was
able to read them. They were written in pure Hellenic
Greek which none but educated Greeks could read.
Thus, these books were almost completely forgotten.
The novices who has just arrived from Caesarea Cappadocia came to Athos when they heard about these
books. They learned not only colloquial Greek but ancient Greek as well in order to copy these books and
to study them as best they could. Filled with joy over
the news I had heard, I begged the novice to make
copies of his books for me and promised to pay whatever sum he would require. The novice was so over-
burdened with copywork at the time, however, that he
was forced to refuse and directed me to another copier
instead. When I asked the second, also a novice, I
promised him triple the price that was usually requested
by the first novice. But, seeing my burning desire to
have the books, he refused the triple sum and promised
to copy the books with the help of God for the regular
price.

This is how Starets Paisii finally acquired his long desired
treasure. He could now begin to correct the Slavonic patristic
texts from their ancient Greek originals. This happened only
two years before his departure from Mount Athos to Moldo-
Walachia. By that time, the novice who had agreed to copy
the books was able to finish transcribing only a portion of
what Starets Paisii had requested. Nevertheless Starets Paisii

accepted them as a gift from God and carried them away with him to Moldo-Walachia where he used them for his correction work. We shall discuss the literary works of Starets Paisii when we describe his Moldavian period.

Meanwhile, the number of monks at the Prophet Elijah Skete continued to increase and, by this time, exceeded fifty persons. Starets Paisii did not know how he would accommodate them all when there was hardly enough room for his original group. Nevertheless more disciples were arriving in spite of his warnings that there was no room and that the little community lacked sufficient material resources. The more Starets Paisii meekly refused them entrance, the more they came to him, tearfully imploring him not to turn them away. He surrendered to their tearful supplications, accepted them and put all his hope in God's help. Noticing the difficult position of Starets Paisii, several highly respected novices of his community, among whom was Patriarch Seraphim, advised the starets to transfer his community to the St. Simon-Peter Monastery, which had much more space and was abandoned by its former community on account of their debts. Starets Paisii submitted the request to the Sobor of the Holy Mountain and it was granted. The starets made the move taking half of his monks with him. They had been living in their new monastery only three months when the Turkish creditors, having learned of the monastery's new occupants, arrived and demanded repayment of the debt which the previous community had incurred. They forcefully took 700 levs from the starets. Fearing similar reactions by other creditors, Starets Paisii made haste to abandon the monastery and return to the Prophet Elijah Skete.

The situation of Starets Paisii's community worsened, and there was no possible escape from their material plight in sight. The tight living quarters, the meagerness of the resources, a continual danger of taxation and the impossibility to turn away the ever-increasing group of newcomers desiring to live a monastic life under the guidance of an experienced starets provoked Starets Paisii to seek out a new home for his monastic community. But where could he settle with so many monks? There were no available places on Mount Athos.

He had to consider another country and the only one that could even be considered then was Moldo-Walachia. Starets Paisii had been acquainted with the country for a long time and had strong spiritual ties with it as it was the homeland of half of his original monastic community. The Orthodox faith and the monastic life were flourishing there and its many pious ecclesiastical and secular rulers undoubtedly knew about and highly respected him. They were able to provide him and his community with the proper refuge. In Moldo-Walachia, Starets Paisii's monastic community was able to exist peacefully, to realize its own potential and to develop more fully.

After considerable time spent on contemplation and perhaps even preliminary communications with influential personalities in Moldo-Walachia, Starets Paisii and his community of monks decided to leave Mount Athos and to settle there. In his letter to the Priest Demetrius, Starets Paisii writes about the reasons for his move away from Mount Athos.

> The very location, so cruel and difficult, was hardly conducive to life on Mount Athos, since two or three monks living together could hardly meet their bodily needs even with bloody sweat and hard labor. What made life even more difficult was the great number of monks. Beside that, the Turkish rulers would demand tributes from our impoverished community similar to those paid to them by the other monasteries of Athos which, as I was told, were obligatory and fixed. For these reasons and others, about which I have already written to you, we feared that our community, created by much labor and effort, would be broken apart and meet its end. I therefore put all my hope in Almighty God, who is praised in all places of His dominion, and decided to leave with my community from the Holy Mountain for the Orthodox land, Moldo-Walachia.

The accomplishments of Starets Paisii during his seventeen years on Mount Athos were by no means useless for those monks who lived elsewhere on the Holy Mountain. The Prophet Elijah Skete which he founded was the basis for today's highly structured monastic community there and the precepts of the starets have come to fruition in the lives and accomplishments of the most recent Athonite startsy. Starets Paisii's move to Moldo-Walachia ended the third period of his life. At the time, he was forty-one years old. He had completed the first half of his life's accomplishments. Having gathered tremendous spiritual wealth, he strengthened and increased it by his own internal, independent achievements. By prayer and the study of the Fathers' writings, he attained such a high level of spiritual maturity that he was able to become the guide for others who pursued that spiritual life which he manifested by founding and organizing his very own monastic community on Athos. To complete the second half of his life's work was the only task left before him now: sharing with others the great spiritual wealth which he had gathered, expanding and affirming the monastic way of life which he had established, renewing and deepening the spirituality of Orthodox monasticism by his own example and influence. Starets Paisii's fulfillment of this second half of his life's accomplishments corresponds with that last period of his "career" which can be called his "Instructorship" or *starchestvo*, continuing until his death. Let us now turn to an examination of this last period in the life of our starets.

Part Four

The Flowering of Starets Paisii's Brotherhood in Moldavia: Dragomirna, Sekul, Niamets. Last Days and Death of the Starets (1763-1794)

"And the multitude of them that believed were of one heart and of one soul: neither said any of them that ought of the things which he possessed was his own; but they had all things in common, and distribution was made unto every man according as he had need."

Acts of the Apostles 4:32,35

CHAPTER I

Organization of the Brotherhood

The migration of Starets Paisii and his brotherhood to Moldavia turned out to be quite useful for their work. Had the starets remained on Athos, first, the growth of his monastic community would have been stifled because of inadequate accommodations as well as insufficient means for existence and, second, he would not have so immensely influenced the spirituality of Orthodox monasticism in Moldavia and Russia. The life of his monastic community on Athos can be compared to the life of a sapling in a small, crowded garden, which grows so fast that food cannot be produced fast enough to feed it. It needs to be transplanted to a more spacious and comfortable place in order for it to grow. Paisii's monastic community found such a place in Moldo-Walachia. The change of location inevitably provoked some discord in the life of the monastic brotherhood but it was only temporary because the community overcame it quickly and flourished in strength and fullness.

In preparation for their departure, Starets Paisii rented two boats. One, he himself boarded along with the Slavic monks, while the other was boarded by Father Vissarion and the Moldavian monks. There were sixty-four persons on both boats and they voyaged first to Constantinople and then to Galati, from where the starets had set off seventeen years earlier when he first came to Athos. In Moldo-Walachia the starets and his monks were first placed in the Varzareshti Skete and then were allowed entrance to the Monastery of the Holy Spirit in Dragomirna, Bukovina, a territory liberated from tributes by the famous Governor Gregory. The monastery was in poor condition when it was offered to Starets Paisii: five cells, a roofless

131

refectory, five books, and six oxen in the cattle yard. The monastery occupied a wide land expanse in a quiet and secluded place. There were great possibilities to organize the new community here and Starets Paisii and his monks were satisfied. Before long, generous donations began coming in from many benefactors who wished to help the starets. The pious governor built new cells and guest houses. The generosity of the governor was an example to the boyars who offered cattle, sheep, grapes, wine, wheat and clothing. Such general compassion and generosity touched the starets and his monks deeply and they thanked God for His mercy with tears of joy.

The Monastery of the Holy Spirit in Dragomirna is close to Sochava, a city located between Bukovina and Moldavia, and the settlement of Itskan. It is situated in the Carpathian Mountain valleys. Seeing the monastery from without, one would think it a fortress because of the high wall and towers surrounding it. The residents of Sochava used to take shelter there during raids by the Zaporozhian Cossacks and Tatar Horde. Its founder and date of founding are not known exactly, but people commonly date it 1602 and attribute it to Bishop Anastasii Krymka of Radauti. But this is not correct. When Bukovina was joined to Austria at the end of the eighteenth century, the Austrian government seized and incorporated the monasteries' real estate into the diocesan land reserves. A special commission was assigned to take account of the properties. It was discovered that Governor Peter VII (Chromiy) issued two charters (March 28 and October 21, 1584) by which Dragomirna was granted perpetual and irrevocable claims to all arable lands near the settlement of Kostin in the Sochava district. This proves that the monastery existed already at the end of the sixteenth century. Perhaps then, it fell into depression and was rehabilitated by Bishop Anastasii Krymka. In any case, his participation in the organization of the monastery is indubitable. In 1602 Bishop Anastasii added a church to the monastery and dedicated it to the Holy Spirit. In one of the towers above the monastery gate he erected a chapel in honor of St. Nicholas the Wonderworker and, in the monastery garden, another church to the memory of the Prophets Enoch and Elijah and the Apostle John.

Soon after settling in Dragomirna, Starets Paisii submitted a report concerning the founding of his monastery and its regulations to the Metropolitan Synod of Moldavia.

(1) The first rule and practice persistently observed by all in our monastery is that no monk may possess even the smallest object as his own personal property. All things are shared by all the monks. In order to preserve this practice, the monastery superior must discern the material needs of his monks, as a father discerns the needs of his children, giving what is necessary to any monk who is in need, not on the basis of his own personal preference or dislike for him. Such is the obedience of the superior. Being founded upon this principle, the monastic community will grow in genuine love for God and man, humility, meekness, peace, singleness of mind and self-detachment. The monks are subjected to obedience not for the sake of temporary abstinence, glory, honor, carnal tranquility or human consideration, but solely for their salvation. The result of this is a unity of heart and mind so that worldly envy, hatred, pride, hostility and other evils have no place to lay their heads. Personal and private property in the community gives birth to every evil and violation of God's commandments. Emphasizing this rule, we make it known to every new monk according to the Sacred Scripture, that he may not have any personal possessions in any form or manner unto his very last breath. All the monks unanimously obey this rule.

(2) Obedience is what we consider to be absolutely essential to the whole of monastic life. This means to scorn and turn away from one's own will, reasoning and arbitrariness; to strive wholeheartedly toward fulfilling the will, reasoning and commandments of God and to serve one's brethren as the Lord Himself, in agreement with the teachings of Sacred Scripture, in fear of God and humility, until death.

(3) What are the obligations and responsibilities of a superior? He must study Sacred Scriptures and the teachings of the Spiritual Fathers. Besides witnessing to these things, he must not transmit any of his own teachings and commandments to his brethren but must continually direct them accord-

ing to the will of God. He must direct any obedience which he assigns according to the Sacred Scripture, always remembering that the Word of God was given to him and his brethren as a teacher and guide to salvation. He must be an example of humility, harmony and single-minded unity of spiritual love in all things. He may begin no action without the advice of the brethren who are experienced in spirituality and searching the Scriptures. If something happens which must be announced before an entire sobor of the community, the whole sobor acts upon it with common knowledge and consensus. In such a way, peace, unity of mind and an indestructible bond of love are maintained among the brethren.

(4) The cathedral rule is the basis for liturgical life, i.e., Vespers, Compline, the Midnight Office, Matins, Hours and the Divine Liturgy for all cycles of feasts of the Lord, the Theotokos, and the Great Saints with vigils and special festal lectionaries; on all minor feasts, the polieleion and doxology with readings, as for all other liturgical offices. The cathedral rule must always be kept by our community, as we observed it on Mount Athos, without haste and in its proper time. According to the liturgical prescription of the Holy Church, all founders and benefactors, the living and the departed, must be commemorated at the services. According to the cathedral rule, the superior and all the brethren must dress in the garb of their rank, that is, in *mantiia, riasa* and *klobuk*. This rule is never to be violated except in cases of illness and obedience. If any from among the brethren does not observe the rule, the superior must summon him to the refectory for investigation before the entire community. If he does not warrant a blessing, then the superior must assign a fitting dispensation which he must fulfill during the course of his deprivation from food in place of his usual verbal instruction.

(5) The brethren must gather together daily with their superior in the refectory, observing the common regulations and dispensations of the monastery. In the refectory, each monk must dress according to his rank in *mantiia, riasa,* and *klobuk*. The brethren must be attentive in absolute silence and in the fear of God to the reading of the day, be it from the Lives of the Saints, patristic writings or books of instruction

in the regulations of the Church. The Panagia must be observed without fail on all Sundays and feasts of the Lord, great feasts, feasts of the saints and, if possible, everyday. The entire refectory rite in our monastery must be observed according to the rite of the Holy Mountain. Under no conditions, except for illness and extreme old age, may the superior and brethren eat in their cells. The type of food prepared must be the same for all the brethren. Only the sick, according to the Fathers, may have special foods that are good for them and, even then, according to the discretion of the superior. However they too must eat in the refectory and not in their cells.

(6) The brethren must live in their cells with the fear of God. According to the tradition of the Holy Fathers, they must prefer mental prayer over any other ascetical labor, as God's love, the source of virtue, is fulfilled in the heart by the mind. This is the teaching of many God-bearing Fathers. Besides prayer, they have psalmody and guided reading of the Old and New Testaments and of instructive patristic writings. Not only in their cells but in all places, and during any activity, the brethren must remember death and their sins, the dread Judgment of Christ, eternal torments, the Kingdom of Heaven and self-reproach. The brethren must exercise themselves in the arts or handicrafts designated to them by their superior. Idleness is not permitted, for it is the source of every evil. Premature departure from one's cell and useless conversation must be avoided and fled from as one flees from poison. On mental prayer, the following Holy Fathers must be read: John Chrysostom, Patriarch Callistus II of Constantinople, Metropolitan Symeon of Thessalonica, Bishop Diodochus of Cotica, Hesychius of Jerusalem, Nilus of Sinai, John Climacus, Maximus the Confessor, Peter the Damascene, Symeon the New Theologian, and Gregory the Sinaite.

(7) For the purpose of testing humility, obedience, and self-detachment from will and reasoning in all things, which is the very ladder leading to the Kingdom of Heaven, it is not improper for the superior to assign the brethren to obedience in the kitchen, bakery, cell-chamber, refectory and to other jobs in the monastery. Ever looking to Christ as their example of obedience and humility, the brethren must not refuse any

obedience, they must fulfill it, believing that if they serve each other not as man but as the Lord Himself, with humility and the fear of God, they will attain the Kingdom of Heaven.

(8) The superior must have the same love for all the brethren. He must carefully observe that the brethren live in a relationship of sincere and real love for each other as a sign of their discipleship in Christ. Individual personal loves and isolated friendships are sources of envy and are destructive to real love. They should be eradicated by all means. The superior must suffer patiently and with paternal love all the falls and weaknesses of his spiritual children in hope of their correction and true repentance. He must correct them by word in the spirit of meekness. Such brethren should not be estranged or removed from the body of the community, especially if they cause no harm to the rest of the community. The superior must not, however, endure the arbitrariness of those brethren who, by following the dictates of their own will and reasoning, refuse the blessed yoke of obedience and thereby cause harm to the rest of their brethren. But after sufficient admonition and private persuasion, in the presence of two or three brethren, and before the assembly of brethren, they should be separated and expelled from the community, even with many tears, regrets, and with spiritual malady, so that others would not catch their fatal disease in turn. And those who come to their senses and turn to repentance ought to be welcomed back with joy and granted every charity, sympathy and forgiveness of sins by the superior, while he rejoices with the whole community.

(9) The superior should have, for the administration of monastery lands and laborers and all external monastery business, an experienced brother who would be capable, without violating God's commandments and ruining himself spiritually, of administering this external business well. This is necessary so that, being free to do as he sees fit, he may with greater facility look after the spiritual salvation of the brethren and after the maintenance of propriety in church and community. Likewise, in the brother's spiritual care there should be as an assistant, a brother clever in mind, whom he can leave behind with the brethren during any periods of his

absence, for the sake of their spiritual edification. Should the superior wish to depart anywhere he should gather the entire assembly of brethren by bell-ringing into the church and, having venerated the holy icons and having received the traveler's prayer from a priest, should announce his intention to the whole community and humbly ask it to pray to God that he return successfully and in health. After asking everyone's forgiveness and giving his blessing, he should depart on his journey. Upon his return he should not go directly to his cell, but instead gather all the brethren and go first to church, where all should render thanks to God. He should also thank the brethren for their prayers, and, having expounded to the brethren on God's mercy which had manifested itself in the common benefits for which the journey had been undertaken, he should withdraw to his cell.

(10) This concerns the acceptance of brethren into the monastic community, the infirmary, various crafts, and the hostel. A brother who is led by God into monasticism should first be examined in private by the superior, who should explain to him in scriptural terms the power of monastic communal living, of obedience according to God, and of the self-detachment of will and reasoning unto death.

Should the superior find in him a sincere, unpretentious desire for monasticism and a zeal for God, he will admit him to the communal life, after once again revealing to him the power of communal living, and obedience in the presence of the entire sobor of the brethren. He should not be tonsured immediately, but after a period of time determined by regulations. One should be kept in lay clothing for six months, and another for three years, depending on the fruits of obedience and self-detachment. Tonsured to wear the *riasa* or the *mantiia,* he should then join the brethren. If, however, at the end of the trial period the superior finds neither true obedience nor true self-detachment in him even after three years, he should not tonsure him but release him into the world, so that he would not serve as a temptation to the communal life.

(11) If anyone entering monasticism from the outside world brings any possessions with him into the monastery, the superior must keep these possessions intact in the mon-

astery storehouse until the brother's tonsure. Upon the latter's tonsure the superior can use these possessions for the monastery's general needs. Should the brother wish to leave the monastery prior to his tonsure, then all the possessions which he had brought into the monastery should be returned to him intact, to avoid any embarrassment both for the brother and for the monastery.

(12) An infirmary should be established inside the monastery as a matter of course, so that any ill brethren would receive special consideration in food, drink, and all manner of repose. An experienced brother should be placed in it, so that he may serve the sick in spiritual wisdom. If anyone even partially familiar with medicine should be found, he should then be placed there.

(13) The superior should also see to it that various crafts be practiced at the monastery, especially those necessary for human communal living, and that brethren be appointed for this. The unskilled should be taught skills so that in this manner the brethren themselves, in learning various skills for the common benefit, would enable the community of the brethren to satisfy its needs without going to any trouble. And there would be no need to go out into the world because of them, thus avoiding spiritual harm.

(14) Two hostels should be established, one inside the monastery, for visiting clergy and laity, and another outside the monastery. Let visitors to the monastery find tranquility both for themselves inside the monastery and for their livestock outside it. And the superior should place over these services experienced brethren who would be able to serve their brethren in spiritual wisdom. As he must have spiritual love for his spiritual brethren he should likewise show a similar love for all beggars and sick or homeless visitors to the monastery. He should receive some with love into the hostel, others into the infirmary, and care after their bodily needs as much as possible. Having provided them with all the necessities, he should let them depart in peace. As we observed these and other regulations of community life on Holy Mount Athos to our best abilities, so here, too, we observe them to the greatest possible degree. But we still do not have enough prepared

hostels or cells for the brethren, so we are very crowded. We hope, however, that the Lord will grant us all our necessities, so that any brother, having performed tasks in observance of the rule of the church and of various forms of obedience, and for the sake of the works of the mind and bodily feats, would also, for his tranquility, have his own special little cell as a quiet and placid harbor. Thus there would be a better spiritual atmosphere and better spiritual progress among the brethren.

(15) We appeal to Your Grace that the female sex be enjoined from entering the monastery, with the exception of extreme necessity during war and flight. Likewise, let the skete dedicated to Ss. Enoch, Elijah, and John never be separated from the monastery. Let its brethren be appointed from the monastery by the superior, and a prescribed observed order and statute be received from the entire assembly of brethren. All their necessities of life should come from the community. Wandering monks and those seeking special benefits shall not stay there under any circumstances. And by the prescription of the assembly of brethren let church rules be observed there and the Divine Liturgy performed for the sake of the commemoration of founders and benefactors.

(16) Included is the rule stipulating the transfer of monastery laborers to the village and the establishment there of a church with a non-monastic priest, so that the monastery would remain free of any embarrassment.

(17) Concerning the election of superiors, let not one be brought in from the outside upon the death of an incumbent. He should be chosen from the community through unanimous election by the entire assembly of brethren and with the recommendation of the dying superior and the blessing of his eminence the metropolitan. He would have to surpass all in spiritual wisdom and in the knowledge of the Holy Scriptures and the community statutes, as well as in obedience, self-detachment, love, humility, meekness and all virtues which can serve as a good example, honored by the priestly rank, to the brethren by word or deed. And since three languages—Greek, Slavonic, and Moldavian—are used in our community, he should know them well, or at least he should know Slavonic and Moldavian. If such a leader will be placed from the out-

side and not from the assembly of brethren, and if by his very deeds he does not seek obedience and self-detachment of will and reasoning, not having undergone in community life the trials of reproach and dishonor, ignorant of the power of the Scriptures and community statutes, and, in addition, having his own particular possessions and accepting the leadership not for the goal of laying down his soul for the brethren but for the goal of the attainment of comfort and the enlargement of his estate—how can such a man direct satisfactorily a flock of God's sheep? And how could the sobor of brethren submit to such an instructor? And if something like this should ever occur (i.e. the appointment of a leader over the brethren without an election by the assembly) it could only be followed by a final and complete dissipation of the brethren and destruction of community life. The only exception to this would occur if it would be impossible to find in the assembly of the brethren anyone capable, through word and deed, of leading the brethren to salvation. But even in such a case one taken from the outside due to such an extreme necessity should be appointed with the voluntary consent of all the brethren, with the promise to God in the presence of all the brethren not to possess or acquire any personal belongings to his very death, and to have the same needs as the brethren. Only under such conditions can the life of the community avoid desolation.

(18) This monastery shall not be venerated in any place nor at any time, for we have made a solemn oath to this effect to the blessed memory of this monastery's founder. Otherwise there would be final destruction of community life. A monastery nowhere venerated can exist by the Grace of God, and the community life of its brethren can remain secure and steadfast.

The brotherhood regulations presented by Starets Paisii were approved and confirmed by the supreme Moldavian Church authorities. The starets and his brethren could quietly begin arranging their life at the new location. Soon after moving to Dragomirna Starets Paisii took the schema. His long-time friend and instructor, the hieromonk Aleksei, who was living at the Merlopoliansk Skete in Walachia with the Starets Vasilii, heard about the arrival of the starets to Dragomirna. He came to Dragomirna and spent the whole winter with the starets. At Paisii's request, Hieromonk Aleksei bestowed the schema upon him, preserving his previous name of Paisii. This event brought great joy to the entire brotherhood. Father Aleksei stayed at Dragomirna until Easter of 1764 and returned to his *skete* to the great regret of both the starets and the brethren, for he attracted the hearts of all with his unusual kindness. At the death of schema-monk Vasilii, Aleksei became the head and starets of his *skete*.

Arranging his life in Dragomirna, Starets Paisii first of all turned his attention to the order of divine services, which forms the basis of any church community. The divine services at Dragomirna were performed strictly according to the prescriptions of the Holy Mountain. Singing was done in Slavonic from the right *Klyros* and in Moldavian from the left one. Community regulations were observed just as strictly. None of the brethren even dared to call something his own or someone else's, but had to consider everything as if it was sent by God to be the common property of the brotherhood, receiving from the starets all personal necessities. The meals were served communally, except for the sick and the aged or infirm. All forms of obedience within the monastery—in the kitchen, the bakery, etc.—were performed by the brethren. They also performed various crafts by themselves, such as shoemaking, carpentry, metalwork, tailoring, etc. Each performed his obedience readily and enthusiastically, and as conscientiously as possible for the sake of God. There was no room in the brotherhood for disobedience, self-will, and contradiction. The brethren themselves worked both in the gardens and in the fields, and took care of the livestock. During work there was supposed to be silence upon everyone's lips and secret prayer within everyone's hearts. The starets himself often came out with the brethren for the general obedience and worked together with the others, in order to serve as an example. During the bread harvest the brethren sometimes spent up to several days in the fields. Due to the Church's Rule and other church needs a spiritual father carrying the Divine Gifts would accompany the brethren into the fields. The starets would often summon a physician as well, while occasionally he would come himself, spending three or four days with the brethren, which would be cause for great celebration among the brethren. The starets would bless their labor, rejoice at their diligence, and converse with them. Whenever the starets would leave, the brethren would see him off with love, ask for his blessing and prayers, kiss his hands, and return to work, rejoicing at having seen their starets and at having listened to his conversation and exhortations. Whenever the starets would not be able to visit the harvesters, he would send them a written greeting. He would teach them how they ought to treat each other, care for and love one another. He wrote to them:

> Beware of envy. Wherever there is envy, God's spirit does not exist. Control the tongue, so that it will not utter empty words. Whoever preserves his tongue, preserves his soul from grief. Life and death both come from the tongue. The old should teach the young and the inexperienced. Everyone should have humility, kindness, and love. It is necessary to strengthen oneself by the fear of God and by the memory of death and eternal sufferings. One's thoughts should be conferred to the starets every day. The Jesus Prayer is to be repeated constantly. Offer a pure, undefiled, and sweet-smelling sacrifice to God, according to your Christian promises. Offer your labors and your bloody sweat as a burnt sacrifice. Let sunburn be for you as the endurance of the martyrs.

In concluding the letter the starets prays that God will save those who labor from all spiritual and bodily harm and protect them from the wiles of the devil. Such letters, permeated with love and concern, encouraged and inspired the brethren and made their burdensome and exhausting labor easy and joyful.

The starets demanded that in the cells each brother fulfill his calling with complete consciousness and diligence, that he be a monk not only according to dress but also according to spirit. He required that in the cells the brethren would read the writings of the Fathers, perform mental prayer, and prostrate themselves with tears as often as possible. Each evening the brethren, beginners in particular, would come to their starets to confess their thoughts. The starets considered the confession of thoughts to be the basis of spiritual life and saw in it the hope for salvation of the soul which sincerely repents of its sins. If there was a misunderstanding among the brethren, a reconciliation was to follow without fail, according to the words of the Scriptures: "Let not the sun go down on your wrath" (Eph. 4:26). And if any brother was so hardened as to wish to remain unreconciled, he was to be placed under suspension by the starets, being forbidden from even setting foot on the church's threshold and from reciting the Lord's Prayer till he humbled himself. For obedience outside the monastery the starets would send brethren who would not tempt the worldly in any way and whose own souls would not be harmed. And if the performance of any task involved the violation of any commandment, the starets would order the cessation of that task, saying that it would be better for the task to remain unfulfilled rather than for a divine commandment to be broken and for the brethren to undergo eternal condemnation. The sick, the infirmed, and the aged were housed in the infirmary and were placed under the care of brother Onorii, who was somewhat familiar with medicine and was known for his love-abounding heart and ability to console any suffering person with spiritual conversation. The starets loved and valued Onorii greatly. He alone was allowed to take as much money as he needed from the cell of the starets for the needs of the sick. On his part, Onorii was totally devoted to the starets and outlived him only by one year. Little by little a warm church was set up in the monastery, cells and an *archondaric*, etc., were put up.

The starets would devote whole days to the brethren, and the doors to his cell would remain open at times till nine o'clock. Some would leave, while others would come in to discuss spiritual or domestic matters. Some he would console, with others he would rejoice, but domestic misfortunes never upset him—he only grieved over spiritual misfortunes. "I lived thirteen years with him," writes his biographer, "and I never saw him grieving over material needs. The only time he would grieve intensely was whenever he saw the violation of God's commandments." In spite of his constant solicitude for the brotherhood Starets Paisii found time for his favorite literary endeavors as well. He devoted whole nights to them. Having supplied himself on Mount Athos with patristic books in the original Greek, the starets examined and corrected Slavonic translations in Dragomirna. He gives a detailed description of his work on the books in a letter to Archimandrite Feodosii:

When we settled at the holy Dragomirna Monastery I started thinking of various ways in which I could approach the correction of Slavonic patristic books, or even better, the translation of patristic writings from Greek. However, I encountered a number of obstacles in this undertaking. The first obstacle was that the translator of the books had to be fully informed, not only in grammar, spelling, and in the peculiarities of either language, but also in the higher fields of knowledge, such as rhetoric and philosophy, and, finally, he had to have, so to say, more than a passing knowledge of theology. Although I had spent four years in Kievan academies during my youth, I only gained a partial knowledge of Latin grammar there, since my further education was hampered by my desire to enter monasticism. However, even that meager knowledge which I gained during that period was totally lost by the passing of time, so that it was with fear and trembling that I approached such a great undertaking as the correction or translation of patristic books with such weak knowledge. The second obstacle was my poor knowledge in orthography, i.e. spelling. Anyone poor in spelling who dares write sacred books, although believing in the truth with his heart and confessing salvation with his lips, in my opinion, commits a sacrilege with his hand as a result of his incompetence. This is why, being at the time still a poor speller, I was terrified at undertaking such a great matter. The third obstacle was that I did not have the necessary lexicons. To translate the books without lexicons is tantamount to practicing any kind of trade without having the tools necessary for it. The fourth obstacle was that I knew very few Greek words then, and actually did not know that language at all. The fifth obstacle was that Greek surpassed all other languages in its universal wisdom, beauty, depth, and its abundance and richness of expressions, so that even native Greeks themselves can hardly comprehend its depth. How could I, then, being so little informed, dare to undertake the matter of correction or translation of the books from a language of such great wisdom? The sixth obstacle was that I also had insufficient knowledge of our own glorious Slavonic language, which in my opinion surpasses many languages in its beauty, depth, and abundance of expression and is closest to Greek. Keeping in mind all of these circumstances, and also the fact that I was too greatly burdened by numerous spiritual and bodily, internal and external concerns, I almost lost hope in ever undertaking this attractive task. But seeing in our brotherhood a great hunger for God's Word from which the brethren's souls languished along with my own soul, and having placed all my hope in God, who makes the blind wise, I decided, trusting in my brethren's prayers, to approach this undertaking with great caution. I firmly resolved that my work, being imperfect in all respects, would remain without exception in our brotherhood until, with God's help, it was completely corrected. This was done in the realization that I would not immediately be able to complete the task of correcting and translating the books which I had begun to such a degree of perfection as to allow my corrections and translations to be sent to other monasteries right away for copying or printing, and that it might be found necessary to examine and correct them once again. I saw, as in a mirror, that not once but many more times, (to the extent to which I should acquire the necessary lexicons and perfect my knowledge of both Greek and Slavonic) the need will arise to examine the revised books once again and submit them to a new correction either by myself, if God extends my life on earth, or by other brethren experienced in this task upon my death. I commenced my work in the following manner. In view of the lack of lexicons, and also due to my inexperience, I took as a guideline the translation of patristic books from Greek into Moldavian which had been done by our beloved brethren Hieromonk Makarii and Didascal Ilarion, both of whom were learned and experienced in the translation of books. Part of this translation was done by brother Makarii when he was still on Mount Athos, while another part was done in Dragomirna, while Father Ilarion worked on his translation in our brotherhood. Having accepted their translation as undoubtedly correct in all respects, I began using their translation as a guide, and referring to the Greek original, revising the Slavonic texts. In this manner I revised the writings of the following patristic authors: Hesychius, Diadochus, Macarius (Second Letter), Philotheos, Nilus (*On Prayer*), Thalasius, Gregory the Sinaite, Symeon the New Theologian (*Sermon on Attentiveness and Prayer*), Cassian the Roman (*On the Eight Thoughts*), and others, holding to the above-mentioned Moldavian translation as a blind man holds on to a railing and thus completing the first revision of the above-named books. After a period of time, as I gradually began to acquire better knowledge of my task, I noticed a great number of errors in my first revisions. Then I revised some of these books again. Still later, having noticed new errors in the books, I made a third revision. Actually, some of the books remained in their initially revised form, since I had no time to revise them a second time. I must say, however, that the books I corrected were far from being perfect, since those very Greek books which had been copied on Mount Athos turned out to be not quite correct in places. Revising old Slavonic books and not yet having at my disposal a single lexicon, I nevertheless translated from Greek books the writings of the following saints: Anthony the Great, Isaiah the Recluse, and Peter Damascene (*Book 2*), but these translations, as a result of my inability, include so many errors that I am afraid to even think about the subject. There is no possibility of correcting them properly without the correct Greek texts. At the same time I translated the book of St. Theodore the Studite from contemporary Greek, because of the crying need for it, not having been privileged to see it in the original Greek to this very day. Incidentally, in this translation of mine there are also a great many errors, for the indicated reasons. I spent a whole year correcting the book of St. Isaac the Syrian in its Old Slavonic translation, comparing it with the original printed Greek text, as well as with the Moldavian translation. But I see to my great sorrow that this book too is far from being perfect, and if only the Lord in his mercy extends my life and gives me, already partially blind, the necessary sight, I will have to work again on its correction.

Elsewhere, Starets Paisii tells also of the following details of his corrections of the Slavonic texts of this book:

When I was living among the still small number of brethren on Mount Athos, I had a book by St. Issac the Syrian, part of which I copied back in the days of my youth at the Kievo-Pechersk Lavra, the rest being completed by an enthusiast on Mount Athos at my request. I have this book even now. Reading this book on Mount Athos carefully many times, I could not make sense out of many passages . . . I made special notations of such passages in the margins hoping that by finding a better version, I could correct them. Somewhat later I met a hieromonk who turned out to have a book of St. Isaac, seemingly similar in all ways to the Bulgarian version, which had been written over 400 years before and seemingly similar to the Greek version. Believing such an assertion and wishing to correct my book, I persuaded the hieromonk to let me have the book and spent six weeks correcting my book according to it day and night. But it turned out that the ambiguous passages of my book remained ambiguous, for they were written in the book given to me in the same way as in mine. My wish to obtain St. Isaac's book in the original Greek remained unfulfilled both during my stay at Mount Athos and during the first years of my residence at Dragomirna. Many years later, when I had already lost any hope of obtaining this book, Almighty God, through his grace, induced the Jerusalem Patriarch Ephraim to print this book, and the patriarch assigned this task to the most-wise hierodidaskalos Nikifor, who was later to become bishop of Astrakhan, and was at that time living in Constantinople. Upon discovering this, one of the brethren from our community who was also in Constantinople started begging both Patriarch Ephraim and the hierodidaskalos Nikifor to give their blessings and to send this book to me at Dragomirna as soon as it comes out in print. With the patriarch's blessing Father Nikifor informed our brother that "as soon as this book gets printed I will send it to your starets as a sign of my love for him." All this took place in 1768. When our brother, upon returning to the monastery, told us about this, my soul was filled with the greatest joy and I awaited the fulfillment of the promise with hope ... In 1770 during Advent the hierodidaskalos Nikifor fulfilled his promise and sent me the priceless gift of the printed Greek version of St. Isaac's book, which I accepted with inexpressible joy. I immediately started reading my Slavonic version, comparing it word by word with the printed Greek one, with the intention of making corrections in those passages of the Slavonic version which made no grammatical sense, but certainly not of making a new translation of the book, for I did not have sufficient knowledge of Greek or the necessary books at that time. And this is why my work of that time can in no way be called a translation, but only a certain revision of the Slavonic version . . . When St. Isaac's Greek book was translated into Moldavian, I compared this translation with my Slavonic version, making in it certain additional necessary corrections. And since the Slavonic version in certain places turned out to be richer in word than the Greek one, and these words, in my view, were authentic, I did not eliminate them from the Slavonic version, but simply marked them. My whole work on the correction of the Slavonic version of St. Isaac's book began in 1770 and was completed in 1771.

As regards Paisii's translation of St. Isaac's book from Greek into Slavonic, it was not done until 1787, when the starets was already living at the Niamets Monastery, and we will speak of this translation elsewhere. In 1774 a Greek monk named Constantius come from the holy mountain to Dragomirna and brought with him a Greek book, written by his hand and consisting of numerous patristic books. It turned out that in it were included books which Paisii had not yet seen in Slavonic. At Paisii's urgent request the monk copied these books for him. But since he totally lacked any knowledge of grammar, he brought numerous errors both into his own book and into his copy, "so that there resulted a treasure of holy words, wallowing in the mud of illiteracy, from which even the well educated, not having at hand reliable Greek originals, could hardly have purified this treasure."

Out of the books which the monk Constantius copied the starets translated into Slavonic 300 chapters of St. Mark and St. Nicetas Stethatos. From the same books of the monk Constantius he also translated the book of St. Theodore of Edessa. But all of these books not only were unfit for printing, but for copying on the side, for they required thorough preliminary correction according to reliable originals. Starets Paisii writes further:

What can I say about the book of St. Callistus, patriarch of Constantinople, and of St. Ignatius, about whom the blessed Symeon, archbishop of Thessalonica, witnesses? I greatly wished to at least have seen this book during my lifetime, but God arranged it so that I not only saw it but even managed to translate it into Slavonic as well. But this book, too, although it turned out to be better-written than the others, is not free of such errors. Even the most skillful of all translators of Greek books into Moldavian, Father Ilarion, could not make any real sense out of certain passages and had to translate in such a way as it seemed correct to him. I also adhered to his view in my translation. This is why this book is also difficult to print and to circulate anywhere on the side. I have to say the same about St. Callistus the Kataphigiote's second book. Although I translated it into Slavonic, it, too, contains many errors. The life of St. Gregory the Sinaite, written by his pupil the most-holy Callistus, patriarch of Constantinople, was brought by the schema-monk Sava from the holy mountain to our common father and starets Vasilii, and we, taking advantage of this, copied it for ourselves. We had only one book by St. Maximus the Confessor—400 chapters on love, printed in Moscow, as well as a sermon on fasting in question and answer form which I had copied back in the days of my youth in our fatherland with numerous errors and omissions. I have not yet seen its original Greek text, in spite of all my desire to do so. The books of St. Nil Sorskii do not exist in Greek at all, but only in Slavonic, and back in the days of my youth I copied it with numerous spelling errors which I still have not had time to correct.

Such is starets Paisii's own tale of his literary activity at Dragomirna.

We see from this tale that here, as well as at Mount Athos, the starets worked mostly on the correction of Slavonic translations, but while at Mount Athos he made his corrections according to Slavonic copies, while at Dragomirna he made them according to Greek originals. It was here in Dragomirna that we see the beginning of the starets' translation activity, which reached its full development at the Niamets Monastery. While working on the correction and translation of the books of the Holy Fathers, Starets Paisii shared the results of his work with his brethren, and for this the following procedure was established in his monastery: as winter would approach along with Advent, and the brethren would come in from their outside work into the monastery, the starets, using the corrected books, would continue from the beginning of Advent to Lazarus Saturday. Every day, except for Sundays and feast days, the brethren would gather at the refectory in the evenings, candles would be lit, the starets would come, and sitting at his usual place, would read the books of either Basil the Great, John Climacus, Dorotheus, Theodore the Studite, Symeon the New Theologian, or another of the God-bearing Fathers. One evening the reading and instruction would be carried on in Slavonic, on the next it would be in Moldavian. When the reading would be in Slavonic, the Moldavians would read compline and vice-versa. While reading the books, the starets would immediately explain the readings, quoting passages from the Holy Scriptures and patristic books.

Here is a sample of his discussions:

Brethren and fathers, we should perform works with a contrite heart, as the divine Fathers teach us, for, as John Climacus says, 'Even if we lead a superior life but do not acquire a pained heart, then all this is pretentious and vain.' And Gregory the Sinaite tells us that 'pain of the heart, humility and works of obedience according to the strength of each, along with rightness of heart, fulfills the work of the truth.' And again he says: 'Any bodily or spiritual activity which does not involve the work of the heart will not bring fruit to the one who performs it, for the Kingdom of God is attained through effort, and those who make an effort attain it, as the Lord said. For even if anyone worked on works painlessly for many years, but did not bother to perform works of repentance with burning zeal of heart, he is a stranger to purity and cannot participate in the Holy Spirit. And furthermore, whosoever

works carelessly and lazily, even if it seems that he
works a lot, will not obtain and bear fruit, for those
taking the painless way fall from despair into useless
cares and become darkened.' We hear the same from
Symeon the New Theologian: 'Whosoever does not
imitate Christ's Passion with repentance, tears, humility,
obedience, and patience, and especially with poverty
and sorrowing, while receiving abuse and cursing,
and does not participate in his humiliating death, cannot be a participant in his spiritual resurrection here
and cannot receive the grace of the Holy Spirit. For,
as the divine Paul says, "If we suffer, we shall also
reign with him" (2 Tim. 2:12). If we are ashamed to
imitate his suffering, which he endured for us, and
if there abides in us a worldly justification of the flesh
to avoid this passion, it is clear that neither can we
participate in his glory. For without repentance and
tears, as we said, nothing from the aforesaid can exist
and will not exist, either in us or in others.' Elsewhere
he says 'No one can prove from the Divine Scriptures,
that without tears and constant tenderness of heart he
could be purified of his passions, could receive the Holy
Spirit, be able to see God or to feel him within himself
in his heart without preliminary repentance and tenderness of heart, for only to the extent of tears of
sorrow and repentance can all this create the divine
fire of tenderness.' And again he says, 'Beware that
you do not lose Christ's presence within yourself and
that you do not leave this life with empty hands, at
which time you will cry out and wail.'

Referring to these words of the Holy Fathers the starets exhorted the brethren with tears to obey Christ's commandments
and to acquire a humble and contrite heart. His exhortations,
his cares, and his troubled heart were all directed to the
keeping of God's commandments by the brethren with total
unanimity and with their whole hearts and souls, so that they
would not spend the time God gave them for repentance
fruitlessly and carelessly. He would exhort the brethren to

perform diligently the reading of patristic books and to strictly observe Christ's commandments, without which their community life itself could not last. He would say,

> Let none of you say that it is impossible to weep each day, for those who say this also say that it is impossible to repent each day. First of all, with an unquestionably firm faith and warm love, you ought to approach God and decidedly renounce this world with all its beauties and pleasures and your will and reasoning, and resolve to be poor in spirit and body. And then through Christ's grace a holy zeal will be kindled in perfected souls. With the passing of time and to the degree of effort, tears and weeping will come forth, along with a slight hope for the soul's comfort. Hunger and thirst after righteousness shall appear, that is, a fiery effort to behave in everything according to his commandments and to achieve humility, patience, mercy and love for everyone, particularly for those who mourn, who are ill, who suffer from evil, and for the aged. All of these are the fruits of the spirit according to the words of the divine apostle. There will appear a zeal to bear the infirmity of one's neighbor, to lay down one's soul for one's brother, to endure various types of temptations, offenses, abuse, and reproaches, to forgive each other from the heart for causing each other unhappiness, to love your enemies, to bless those who curse you, to do good to those who hate you, and to pray for those who hurt and persecute you, as Christ demands. In addition to all this, to endure with fortitude and thankfulness various kinds of bodily afflictions, infirmities, fierce and bitter maladies, and temporary suffering for the sake of the eternal salvation of your souls. In this way you will attain perfect manhood, to the extent of your spiritual growth in Christ. And if you remain steadfast in such efforts, then your brotherhood will also last as long as it pleases God. And if you step away from attention to yourselves and from the reading of patristic books, you will fall away

also from Christ's world, from his love, and from the fulfillment of his commandments. Then there will be instilled among us disorder, bustle, disarray, spiritual confusion, wavering and hopelessness, complaints against one another, and mutual accusations, and as a result of the multiplication of all this the love of many, and perhaps, of all, shall wear itself out. And then your community will disintegrate, first spiritually and then bodily as well.

The daily reading by the starets of patristic books had a tremendous educational significance for the brethren. Later on, when the life of the brethren began to fall into decline, the brethren were to admit to themselves that one of the principal causes of this decline was the cessation of the starets' daily discussions. The starets had such a gift of persuasion that he could console even the most sorrowful person with his words and could inspire the most despondent. And where necessary, he would admonish, prohibit, plead, excommunicate, endure at great length, and when unsuccessful, would send an offender away. And he would impose prohibitions only against the most hardened and self-willed offenders, threatening them with God's anger. No one would leave him unhealed, and every day all would be ready to stand before him, simply to enjoy his conversation. Once, one of the brethren said to the starets, "Father, my thoughts tell me that you bear hatred toward me, since you often rebuke me angrily in the brethren's presence." The starets answered,

My beloved brother, to become angry and irritated is alien to the life of the Gospel. If the divine Gospel commands us both to love our enemies and to do good to them, then how can I possibly hate my spiritual children? And if I rebuke you angrily, then let God give you such anger as well. I force myself to appear angered, although through God's grace I never have anger or hate.

The brother fell to the starets' feet with tears, asking for forgiveness. The starets would often tell the brethren, "I do not wish for anyone of you to fear me as a stern ruler, but for all of you to love me as a father, just as I love you as my spiritual children."

As established by the starets each spiritual father would inform the starets about any brother to whom he could not reconcile himself, as well as about the cause of his confusion. And whenever such a sorrowful brother would enter the starets' cell, the starets would already see the reason for his visit, and having given the brother his blessing, before letting him say anything, he would start the discussion with him himself and with his sweet and consoling words would take his thoughts away from the sorrows that had befallen him. The starets would lead his discussion by adapting to the situation, the behavior, the intelligence, and the obedience of the brother. With the more intelligent ones he had the habit of speaking about higher subjects, explaining his words by referring to the Holy Scriptures, and he would amaze and console the brother to such an extent, that the latter, as a result of his spiritual joy, would become prepared to turn everything to nought—all of the world's glory, joy, and sorrows. But with the more simple brethren the starets would speak in a simpler fashion, giving them examples either from their craft or their works of obedience, and by his own words he would bring them into such a state, that they would be prepared to rebuke both themselves and their very sorrow, because of which they had come to the starets. Listening to the starets speak, the brethren would look within themselves and forget the reason for their visit to the starets, and having accepted the blessing, would leave him, rejoicing and thanking God. The starets told the brethren more than once that when he sees his spiritual children working zealously for the keeping of God's commandments and undergoing holy obedience with humility, he experiences such ineffable joy, that he does not wish to have greater joy even in the Heavenly Kingdom. On the other hand, when he sees them not caring about God's commandments, going about without the fear of God, and despising all obedience, then such sorrow overtakes his heart,

that even hell cannot match its depth. There once came a
brother to the starets and said that various thoughts often
keep bothering him. Smiling, the starets said,

> Why are you so stupid? Do as I do. I argue with you
> all day, and with some I weep, with others I rejoice
> and do other things. When I throw you out of my cell
> I throw out all my thoughts with you. Then I take
> a book into my hands and I hear nothing, as if I am
> keeping silence in the Jordanian Desert.

His biographer explains the fact that the starets' word
was strong and potent by his fulfillment of God's commandments from his childhood days. He read holy books with the
greatest attentiveness, from attentiveness would arise understanding, from understanding desire, from desire zeal. Once
read, everything remained in his memory forever. Once there
was a discussion about books in the starets' cell. One of the
participants in the discussion was a brother who knew New
Testament Greek. When asked how to translate a given Greek
sentence, he answered, "This was explained to us by our
teacher, but I cannot remember right now." Upon hearing this
the starets said with a smile, "And I, if I read something once,
will not forget it till my death."

Sensing themselves to be enveloped on all sides by the
starets' love and care, and listening to his discussions, the
brethren increasingly progressed in their love for God and
in Christ-like patience, although not in uniformity. The starets
would rejoice and instill in them even more diligence, saying
"Do not despair, for now is a good time, now is the day of
salvation." Then, in the biographer's words, life in Dragomirna seemed like a heaven on earth. People who renounced
their wills for the sake of God's love became dead to this
world. The secret feats, contrition of heart, profound humility,
fear of God, attentiveness, silence, and continuous prayer of
the heart are impossible to convey in words, and through them
the following words of St. Isaac were fufilled: "The council
of the humble is as pleasing to God as the council of the
Seraphim." The view of the essence of the monastic feat

existing in starets Paisii's brotherhood found its expression in the "Instructions Upon the Taking of Monastic Vows," attributed by some to the starets himself (Collection 485, the Academia Romana Manuscript. See Appendix 2).

This quiet, peaceful, and joyful life of the brethren was darkened by one sorrowful event.

Around 1766 Father Vissarion died. He was starets Paisii's first pupil at Mount Athos, and his like-minded friend and closest assistant. Having wept bitterly over the departed, the starets established the yearly commemoration of his memory and a yearly memorial meal for the brethren, which was observed till the starets' very death. In the first years of his presence at Dragomirna the starets was obliged to come out in defense of the Jesus Prayer, i.e. the internal existence with Christ in the prayer of the heart, as the principal means of overcoming evil thoughts and of the attainment of purity of heart. In the Moshen Mountains in the Ukraine there appeared a certain monk who rejected mental prayer as a heresy and a delusion. This monk acquired such an influence upon his brethren, that some of them, having listened to him speak, collected all the patristic books which taught about mental prayer, and tying rocks to them, drowned them in the river. Upon finding out about this, Starets Paisii wrote a work on mental prayer in six chapters which he sent to the erring monks. This work will be reproduced later.

CHAPTER II

The Teaching of Starets Paisii on the Jesus Prayer

"Sweet are the pure and constant memory of Jesus abiding in one's heart and the ineffable illumination resulting from it".
—St. Mark, Bishop of Ephesus

The teaching of starets Paisii on the Jesus Prayer, like his teaching on monasticism, is closely connected with the teaching of his instructor and friend, the schema-monk Vasilii, on this subject. We will therefore first give a brief account of Starets Vasilii's teaching on the Jesus Prayer, which he sets forth in his prefaces to the books of St. Gregory of Sinai, the Blessed Philotheos of Sinai, and the Blessed Hesychius of Jerusalem.

Starets Vasilii begins his preface to St. Gregory's book by indicating the incorrectness of the view of those who think that mental activity is appropriate only to those who are perfect and who have attained passionlessness and holiness. Those who think in this manner limit their worship to a mere performance of psalm chanting, troparia, and canons, without realizing that such external worship is prescribed to us by the Holy Fathers only as temporary, in light of the feebleness and childishness of our minds. This is done so that gradually perfecting ourselves, we can ascend the step of mental activity and will in no case be content with just external worship. According to St. Gregory, only to infants is it natural to think that while they perform external worship with their lips they are performing something great, and being content with the amount being read, foster in themselves an internal Pharisee. According to St. Symeon the New Theologian, whoever limits himself to external works of prayer cannot attain internal peace and excel in virtues, for he is like one who struggles with his enemies in the darkness of the night. He hears the enemies' voices, receives wounds from them, but does not see clearly who they are, where they came from, and how and for what reason they are struggling with him. According to St. Issac the Syrian and the venerable Nil Sorskii, if anyone, disregarding mental prayer, wishes to repel the enemy's advance and to resist any passion or evil intention only by external worship and external feelings, he will end up defeated many times. For the devils, overtaking him in struggle and voluntarily submitting to him anew as if defeated, make fun of him and dispose him toward vanity and self-dependence, proclaiming him to be a teacher and shepherd to his sheep. From the aforesaid we can see the power and intensity of both mental prayer and external worship. It is wrong to think that the Holy Fathers, in restraining us from excessive external worship, and in turning us toward mental prayer devalue external prayers. Nothing of the sort! For, all of the rites of the Church are established in it by the Holy Spirit, and all of them express the mystery of the incarnation of the Word of God. And there is nothing human in Church rituals, but everything is the activity of God's grace, which does not grow as a result of our virtues and does not decrease as a result of our sins. But we are speaking here not of the statutes of the holy Church, but of the special rule and livelihood of each of the monks, i.e. of mental prayer as an activity which attracts the grace of the Holy Spirit through diligence and rightness of heart, and not merely through words being pronounced inattentively by the lips and tongue. And it is not only a perfect person who can wisely engage in such mental activity, but any passionate beginner who watches over his heart. And this is why St. Gregory the Sinaite, having, more than anyone and to the greatest degree of precision, analyzed and discussed the grace of the Holy Spirit abiding in him, as well as the lives, writings, and spiritual feats of all the Saints, bids us to make every effort toward mental prayer.

"St. Symeon of Thessalonica also bids and advises bishops, priests, monks, and laymen to utter this holy prayer at every season and every hour and to breathe by it, as it were, for neither on earth nor in heaven is there a stronger weapon, he says together with the holy apostle, as the name of Jesus Christ. Know also, O good laborer in this holy activity, that not only in the desert or in solitary asceticism have there been teachers and numerous performers of this holy activity, but in the greatest lavras and even in cities. For instance, the holy Patriarch Photius, having been elevated from a senatorial positions and not being a monk, learned mental activity while already in his high position and excelled in it to such a degree, that, according to St. Symeon of Thessalonica, his face shined with the grace of the Holy Spirit as in a second Moses. According to the same St. Symeon, Patriarch Photius wrote a remarkable book on mental activity as well. He also says that St. John Chrysostom, St. Ignatius, and St. Callistus, while being patriarchs of the same Constantinople, all wrote their own books about this mental activity. Thus, if you, in speaking against mental prayer, will tell me that you are not a desert dweller to engage in this activity, you will be refuted by Patriarch Callistus, who learned mental activity while serving as a cook at the Great Lavra on Mount Athos, and Patriarch Photius, who while already a patriarch learned the art of being attentive to the heart. If you are too lazy to engage in the sobering of the mind, using works of obedience as an excuse, you especially deserve rebuke, for according to St. Gregory the Sinaite, neither the desert nor solitude are as conducive to this activity, as is wise obedience. If you know that you do not have an instructor to teach you this activity, the Lord Himself commands you to learn from the Holy Scriptures, saying, 'Search the scriptures; for in them ye think ye have eternal life' (John 5:39). If you become disturbed at not finding a silent spot, you are refuted by St. Peter Damascene, who says 'The beginning of man's salvation consists of the abandonment of his wishes and reasoning, and then nowhere in the world will there be an object or place which

could hinder his salvation.' If you are disturbed by the words
of St. Gregory the Sinaite, which speak often of the deception
accompanying such activity, then this very same holy Father
corrects you, saying 'We should be neither afraid nor doubtful
when calling upon God.' For even if some have gone astray
as a result of being harmed by their minds, know that this
has been caused by their arbitrariness and conceit. If one should
seek God in compliance to the spirit of inquiry and humility,
he will never undergo harm to Christ's grace. For he who
lives in a righteous and undefiled manner and avoids self-
gratification and conceit is not able to incur evil, even if the
whole army of devils would raise innumerable temptations
against him, according to the words of the Fathers. Only those
who act presumptuously and according to their own dictates
fall into deception. Those who upon stumbling on the rock
of the Holy Scriptures turn away from mental activity out
of fear of fascination, turn white into black and black into
white. For it is not to prohibit us from mental activity that
the Fathers teach us about the causes of deception which takes
place, but to protect us from this deception. Thus Gregory
the Sinaite, in commanding those learning to pray not to be
afraid and experience doubt, indicates also the causes of fascination—conceit and arbitrariness. Wishing us not to be harmed
by them, the Fathers bid us to study the Holy Scriptures and
to be guided by them, taking a brother as a good advisor, according to Peter Damascene. If you are afraid to approach
mental activity out of reverence and simplicity of heart, then I,
too, am prepared to be afraid along with you. But one should
not fear empty fables, as the proverb says, 'To fear the wolf
means staying out of the forest.' God, too, should be feared,
but one should not run from him or renounce him.

"Not the least of obstacles to the performance of mental
prayer for some is their bodily infirmity. Being incapable of
undergoing the kinds of labors and fasting that the saints
underwent, they think that without this it is impossible for
them to begin mental activity. Correcting their error, St. Basil
the Great tells us that 'abstinence is determined by each person
according to his bodily strength,' and I think that there is a
danger that a person can make his body inactive and incapable

of good deeds by destroying the strength of his body through excessive abstinence. Had it been good for us to be with weakened bodies and to lie as if dead, barely breathing, God would have created us like that. But if he did not create us like that, then those who do not preserve God's beautiful creation as it was created are the ones who sin. The ascetic should concern himself with only one thing—is there indolence concealed in his soul, have sobriety and earnest direction of the mind to God grown weak, have his spiritual sanctification and the resulting enlightenment of the soul become darkened? For if all of the above virtues keep growing within him, there will be no time for the bodily passions to arise within him, when his soul is busy with the heavenly and does not leave the body any time for the arousal of passions. If the soul is thus conditioned the person who takes no food does not differ from the one who takes it. And he has completed not only the fast, but total abstinence from food as well and is to be praised for his special concern for his body, for moderate living does not arouse the inflammation of lust. And St. Isaac says in agreement: 'If you exert a weak body beyond its strength, you will create a double disturbance in it.' And St. John Climacus says 'I saw this enemy (the womb) being given rest and giving vigilance to the mind.' And elsewhere: 'I saw it withering away through fasting and arousing lust, in order that we may depend not on ourselves, but on the Living God.' Such also is the lesson of the story recalled by the venerable Nikon: 'In our time a starets was discovered in the desert who had not seen a single person for thirty years, did not eat bread, eating only roots, and he admitted that all these years he had been fought by the devil of adultery. And the Fathers decided that the cause of this struggle with adultery was not pride or food, but the fact that the starets was not taught mental sobriety and resistance to the wiles of the enemy.' It is for this reason that Maximus the Confessor says: 'Give to the body according to its strength, and direct all your effort to mental activity.' And also St. Diadochus: 'Fasting obtains praise in itself, not through God. Its aim is to lead those who wish it to chastity.' So it therefore does not behoove pious spiritual warriors to be highminded about it, but to await the outcome of our condition in God's faith. In no art do the artists judge the result of their work by the tools they use, but they await the work's completion and by it judge the art. Adopting such a practice with regard to food, not placing all your hope on fasting, but fasting moderately and according to the amount of your strength, strive toward mental activity. In this way you can avoid pride and will not spurn God's good works, sending up praises to God for everything.

"Mental prayer is a powerful weapon by which the spiritual warrior conquers his invisible enemies. Some of the Fathers stipulate that monastics, along with the execution of Christ's commandments, should perform lengthy psalmodies, troparia, and canons. Other Fathers, having studied the most subtle activity of the spiritual mind, find it insufficient for beginners to undergo bodily instruction alone, but, teaching moderate chanting and reading along with the execution of Christ's commandments, they establish, instead of lengthy psalmodies and canons, the performance of mental prayer. And they add, that should the Holy Spirit come down through the performance of the prayer of the heart, then, without the least amount of doubt, the external rule should be abandoned, for it is fulfilled through the internal prayer. A third group of Fathers, having much experience and knowledge of the saints' lives and of the Holy Scriptures, being especially enlightened by the activity and wisdom of the Holy Spirit, establish for beginners a general, non-partial instruction in the performance of mental prayer, dividing it into two types—active and visual. These Fathers stipulate that all care should be given to mental activity, devoting a little time to chanting only in times of despair, for according to them, church services and chants are granted to all Christians in general, not to those who wish to keep silence. Actually, one can make progress through lengthy psalmodies and the reading of canons and troparia as well, albeit very slowly and with great difficulties. The second path is more convenient and simpler, while the third is the quickest and is accompanied with the comfort and frequent visitation of the Holy Spirit, confirming and preserving the heart, especially if there is diligent effort and good intent. Insofar as holy mental prayer is combined with the observance of God's commandments and expels demons and passions, so does the one who, on the contrary, ignores the commandments and is not concerned with mental prayer, but occupies himself only with chanting, become drawn by passions.

"The transgression of God's commandments is regarded similarly in everyone, but manifests itself variously. For example, someone makes it a rule not to transgress a commandment, not to succumb to passion, but if, through some circumstance or confusion, or through the wiles of the enemy, it should happen that he offend or condemn someone, fall into anger, be vanquished by vanity, argue and try to justify himself, indulge in idle talk, utter lies, or drink too much, have an evil thought, or do something of the kind, sensing himself guilty before God, he starts reproaching himself right away and falling down before God in repentance with a mental prayer from the heart, so that God would forgive him and would grant him help in not falling into such sins any more. In such a way he commences the observance of commandments and the protection of his heart from evil wiles in prayer, fearing and trembling lest the Heavenly Kingdom be lost because of them. Another one lives simply, not caring whether he falls or stands, and thinking that presently there is no one who keeps commandments and is afraid of transgressing them, and that anyone, willingly or unwillingly, sins before God and becomes guilty of various subtle sins and passions. Thus neither does he wish to beware of them, considering this to be impossible. Considering himself responsible only for adultery and fornication, murder and theft, poisoning and similar mortal sins, and abstaining from them, he deems himself as standing. The following words of the Fathers apply to such a case: 'The one who falls and rises is better than the one who stands and is unrepentant.' We can only wonder how both of these people, guilty of the same common sin, appear to be different before God and, I would think, before spiritual people also. One does not know falling and rising at all, although it is he who is possessed by passions, while the other falls and rises, gets vanquished and triumphs, makes a committment and works hard, and does not return evil for evil. But he does not practice abstention due to habit, he tries not to say anything malicious, grieves when offended, but reproaches himself for grieving and repents for it, or, if he does not mourn over the received offense, neither does he rejoice. Anyone in such a condition sets himself in opposition to passion and does not wish to submit to it, grieving and struggling. For, as the Fathers said, any object which the soul does not desire is short-lived.

"I wish to speak also of people who uproot passions. There are those who rejoice when offended, but because they hope to have a reward. Such a person uproots passions, but not wisely. Another rejoices when offended and feels that the offense was deserved, since he provoked it himself. Such a person uproots passion wisely. Finally, there is such a person who not only rejoices when offended and considers himself blameworthy, but also grieves over his offender's embarrassment. May God lead us into such a condition of the soul! For a clearer understanding of each of these ways of life let us also say the following: the first one, submitting himself to the law, performs only his chanting, while the second motivates himself toward mental activity and always has with himself the name of Jesus Christ for the destruction of the enemy and the passions. One rejoices if he only completes his chanting, while the other thanks God if he performs prayer in silence, without being disturbed by evil thoughts. One desires quantity, while the other—quality. One, as he rushes to fulfill the proper amount of chanting, soon develops a joyful conceit, on which he depends to nurture and grow an internal pharisee within himself, if he does not hearken to himself. The other, in attaching great value to the quality of the prayer, has an understanding of his weakness and God's help. While praying, or rather while calling upon the Lord Jesus against the wiles of the enemy, the passions, and evil thoughts, he sees their destruction by Christ's awesome name and comprehends God's strength and help. On the other hand, being constrained and confused by evil thoughts, he understands his weakness, for he cannot withstand them by virtue of his strength alone. And it is this which comprises his whole rule and whole life. And although the enemy can suggest joyous conceit and pharisaic thoughts to him as well, he encounters in this spiritual warrior a readiness to call upon Christ against all evil thoughts, and in this way he does not attain success in his wiles. But someone will say that the first person can call upon Christ against the wiles of the enemy. Yes, this is possible, but everyone knows from experience that at present the performers of the external rule are not accustomed to learn the prayer against evil thoughts. They especially do not wish to accept uttered or written words on internal concentration, which contains the art of praying against evil thoughts. And not only do they not accept them, but they resist them and, casting out their instructors, insist that the Fathers did not prescribe mental prayer for beginners, but only psalmodies, troparia, and canons performed by lips and tongue. And although they say and teach this incorrectly, everyone listens to them, since such worship does not require instruction or renunciation of earthly desires, but anyone, should he so wish, can pray in this manner, be he monk or layman. Holy mental activity, being a glorious and God-pleasing art of arts, and, demanding not only renunciation of the world with its desires, but also much instruction and study, does not find performers among monks. In addition to all this, one should beware of deviations to the right or left, i.e. despair and self-dependence. Noticing that those learning mental activity experience accidentally, not intentionally, an unwilling fall into what the Fathers call everyday sins, one should not become doubtful as a result, for according to the ability of each there are both progressions and downfalls from the good to its opposite. On the other hand, hearing of God's great mercy toward us sinners, we must not be self-dependent and approach this holy mental activity fearlessly without great humility and the fulfillment of commandments to the greatest possible degree. Realizing that both self-dependence and despair are inspired by the enemy, we should flee both.

In this way, with much examination of the Holy Scriptures and utilizing the advice of the experienced, one should be instructed in this activity with humility. The Fathers, who teach the conquest of passions and purification of heart through

Christ's commandments alone, direct spiritual warriors to have two strong weapons—the fear of God and the memory of God's omnipresence, as it is said: 'By the fear of the Lord depart from evil' (Pr. 3:7), and 'I have set the Lord always before me: ... I shall not be moved' (Ps. 16:8). In addition, they advise them to have the memory of the heart and of Gehenna, and also to read the Holy Scriptures. All this is good for good and reverent men, but to the insensitive and hardened, even if Gehenna itself or God himself would become manifest in visible shape, no fear would appear. Moreover, in beginning monks the mind itself becomes dull to the memory of such things and flees from them, as a bee from the burning of smoke. But although the indicated memory can be good and beneficial in the hour of battle, the most spiritual and experienced Fathers have indicated, in addition to this virtue, an even greater and incomparable virtue, which can help even the very weak.

"The first of these methods can be compared to the grinding of grain with millstones manually, using one's own strength, while the second is like grinding at a mill with water and various devices. As water moves the wheels and millstone by itself, so does the most sweet name of Jesus, along with the memory of God wholly abiding in Jesus, move the mind to prayer. About this, the great theologian Hesychius says: 'The soul which is benefitted by and delights in Jesus with joy, love, and confession sends up glory to the Benefactor, thanking him and calling upon him with gladness,' and elsewhere, 'Just as it is impossible for the soul to attain anything spiritual and pleasing to God or to free one's mind from sin without mental watchfulness, even if one would force himself not to sin out of fear of tortures.' And again, 'The Jesus Prayer, uttered out of the depth of the heart, can cast out thoughts which penetrate into our hearts, if we do not want them, and make us firm and show resistance.' Although progress is achieved through the first of the above methods without mental activity, this happens very slowly and with difficulty. But through the second method the doer draws near to God rapidly and easily. For in the former there is only external worship and instruction and the performance of commandments, while the latter includes both external and internal watchfulness. When a beginning monk, having renounced this world and the action of great and deadly sins, promises before God to abstain not only from the lesser everyday and forgivable sins, but from the action of the most passionate and evil thoughts, and having penetrated his heart with his mind, starts to call upon Lord Jesus against every attack or evil thought; or, if due to his weakness he yields to the wiles of the enemy and violates the Lord's commandments, falls down before the Lord with a sincere prayer in repentance and self-condemnation and will remain in this condition to his death, falling and rising, being vanquished and vanquishing, and asking his rival for retribution day and night—will there not be hope of salvation for him? For, as experience shows us, it is impossible for even the greatest of men to be totally preserved from everyday sins not leading to death, which are caused by words, thought, ignorance, forgetfulness, bondage, freedom, and chance, and which are forgiven by Christ's everyday grace, according to St. Cassian. If anyone, being faint-hearted, should say that by 'those who are purified through Christ's grace' St. Cassian means only the saints, not passionate beginners, let there be room for such a view as well. But keep in mind mainly the discussions and decisions on such matters in the holy writings, according to which any passionate beginner is condemned through these everyday sins and can again obtain forgiveness through Christ's grace, as did all the saints, through frequent repentance and confession to God. For, as St. Dorotheus says, there is the one who serves passions and the one who resists passions. The one who serves passions, upon hearing a single word, loses his composure, or says five or ten words in response to one and starts quarelling, becomes disconcerted; and even later, when already calmed from his agitation, does not cease to bear evil to the one who said that word to him, regrets not having said more to him, thinks up even angrier words to say to him, and says constantly, 'Why did I not say this to him?' And furthermore, 'I'll say this and that,' constantly displaying anger. This is a situation in which an angry condition is usual. Another person, upon hearing a word, likewise loses com-

posure, likewise says in return five or ten words, likewise
regrets not having said three more offensive words, grieves,
and remembers evil, but a few days go by and he calms down.
Still another remains in such a state for a week, while another
quiets down in a day, and yet another gives offense, quarrels,
makes himself and others uncomfortable, and quiets down
right away. This is how many different states there are, and
they are all liable to judgment, so long as they remain in force.
Thus we can judge in all the other instances as well as to why
a passionate person cannot be purified by Christ's Grace from
the everyday sins which seem minor to him.

"Let us now examine the situation when such sins are forgivable to passionate beginners. The same St. Dorotheus says,
'It happens that someone, upon hearing a word, grieves inside
himself, not about having been offended but about not having
overcome his impatience. This person is in the state of resisting
passion, while another struggles, labors, and gets vanquished
by passion. Another does not wish to return evil for evil, but
succumbs to habit. Another tries not to say anything evil,
but grieves that he was offended, reproaches himself for
grieving, but neither does he rejoice. They are all resisting
passion, for they do not wish to serve passion, and then they
grieve and persevere in spiritual struggle. Such people, are
passionate, but through Christ's grace they can receive forgiveness for their everyday sins, committed unwillingly and without intention, and which the Lord instructed St. Peter to forgive daily unto seven times seventy.' St. Anastasius the Sinaite
says the same: 'It is our view that for those who receive the
holy sacraments of the Body and Blood of the Lord and have
various lesser and forgivable sins caused by their tongues,
ears, eyes, vanity, sorrow, irritability, or anything similar,
but condemn themselves and confess their sins to God and
thus receive Communion, such Communion is unto the clean-
sing of their sins.' Since we spoke before of the well-skilled
overcoming of passions through mental prayer and commandments, let us now indicate more clearly the very route of
mental prayer and commandments in the struggle with passions. Whether the wiles of the enemy come upon us in the form
of some kind of passion or through evil thoughts, the per-

former of prayers calls upon Christ against them, and the devil perishes along with his wiles. Whether one should fall through weakness of thought or word, through irritability, or through fleshly desire, he prays to Christ, confessing to him and repenting. Should he be in the throes of despair and sorrow, which hinder his mind and heart, he takes hold of the memory of the heart, Gehenna, and God's omnipresence, and having exerted himself a little with their help, again begs Christ to be merciful to him for his sins, both voluntary and involuntary. In a word, at the hour of spiritual strife and peace he runs to Christ, and Christ becomes for him all in all, both in good and bad circumstances. Such a person does not get carried away with conceit, as if he fulfills something by praying or by pleasing God. For the significance of external prayer is different from that of internal prayer. One person, performing a certain amount of chanting sets his hopes on satisfying God in this manner, but condemns himself upon leaving him. But the other, being reproached by his conscience for his constant sins and enduring the attack of the enemy's wiles, always cries out to Christ, keeping in mind the words, 'Even if you ascend the whole ladder of perfection, pray for the forgiveness of your sins.' And again, 'I would rather speak five words with my mind than ten thousand in a tongue,' (1 Cor. 14:19) and in this way without any doubt he fulfills the resistance to passions indicated by St. Dorotheus.

"If anyone should say that it is possible to be cleansed of sins through Christ's grace by repenting without mental activity, we give the following response: place Christ's commandments on one side and on the other the constant prayer—Forgive us our transgressions. Give me also a true resolve not to violate a single commandment, i.e. not to abide in lust, show anger, judge, slander, lie, or speak idly, but to love my enemies, do good to those who hate me, pray for those who offend me, and to avoid voluptuousness, love of money, adulterous thoughts, sorrow, vanity, pride—in a word, all sins and evil thoughts. And with such resolve commence the learning of mental activity and pay close attention to how many times a day, in spite of your resolve, you will violate the commandments and will be pierced by evil thoughts. Take example from that widow who pleaded before the judge day and night, and start crying out to Christ every hour for every commandment that you violate, and for every passion or evil thought by which you may be vanquished. Add to this the good counselor—the Holy Scriptures—and having spent some time in this way, come and teach me what you will have seen in your heart. You will hardly refrain from admitting to yourself that it is impossible for all this to find room in external worship, but only in mental activity. For it teaches its practitioner all these mysteries and confirms to his soul that, in abandoning lengthy psalmodies, canons and troparia and directing all his concern toward mental prayer, he not only does not destroy his rule, but rather increases it. As the Old Testamental law had power and volition in the goal of bringing everyone to Christ, although it seemed that the Law itself was reduced by this, so does much chanting send away its performer to mental prayer, rather than expanding over the whole monastic life. For such a person learns by his very experience, when, while praying, he notices as it were, a certain barrier between himself and God, a sort of brass wall, according to the prophet. This wall does not allow his mind to look toward God clearly during prayer or to hearken to his heart, which contains all of his spiritual powers and is the source of his thoughts, both good and evil.

"Mental activity undoubtedly requires fear and trembling, contrition and humility, and much experiencing of the Holy Scriptures and consultation with like-minded brethren, but in no case does it require escape and denial, nor arrogance and arbitrariness. The arrogant and self-reliant person, in striving for that which is higher than his merits and his nature, hastens to external prayer with pride. In the grip of the vain wish to ascend to a high degree of perfection, and being permeated by a satanic, insincere desire, such a person easily gets caught in the snare of the devil. And why should we strive toward great progress in mental and holy prayer, which according to St. Isaac is the privilege of one out of ten thousand? It is sufficient, quite sufficient, for us who are passionate and weak, to see at least a trace of mental silence, i.e. active mental prayer, which casts the enemy's wiles and evil thoughts out of our hearts. In this lies the main concern of beginning and passionate monks, and through it the performance of visual and spiritual prayer can be achieved, if God so wills. We should not fall into despair from the fact that not many have the privilege of performing visual prayer, for there is no falsehood in God. But let us not be lazy in pursuing the way leading to this holy prayer, i.e. let us through mental prayer resist wiles and evil thoughts. Following the way of the saints, we will be made worthy of their lot, albeit not here on earth, as Isaac and many other saints tell us.

"Mental prayer is accompanied by various bodily sensations, from among which we should distinguish between correct and incorrect ones, as well as between those given by grace, the natural ones, and those coming about through deception. It is cause for horror and amazement that some people, knowing the Holy Scriptures, do not try to grasp them. And others, not knowing them and not asking the experienced, rely on their own minds and dare to approach mental concentration, saying, moreover, that concentration and prayer should be conducted in a certain preferred area—this, they say, is the area of the womb and heart. Such is the first and self-induced deception. Not only should prayers and concentration not be conducted in this area, but the very warmth which arises at the hour of prayer from the area of desire in the heart should not be accepted in any case.

"According to St. Gregory the Sinaite much effort is needed in order to comprehend clearly and to preserve oneself in purity from that which is opposed to grace, for the devil has the habit of demonstrating his deceptiveness to beginners under the guise of truth, presenting evil to them as something spiritual, showing wishfully one instead of the other in his arbitrariness, arousing his burning instead of warmth, and instead of gladness, bringing senseless joy and sensual pleasure. Actually, it is beneficial to the performer of mental prayer to know also that burning or warmth sometimes ascend from the loins to the heart by themselves in a natural manner, if they are not accompanied by tempestuous thoughts. And this, according to Patriarch Callistus, arises not from deception but from nature. Should someone take this natural warmth for

a gift of grace, then this will already undoubtedly be deception. For this reason the spiritual warrior should not rest his
attention upon it, but should fight it off. Sometimes, the devil,
having joined his burning with our desires, entices our minds
into adulterous thoughts. And this is unquestionable deception.
Now if the whole body becomes enflamed, while the mind
remains clean and passionless and, as it were, attached and
immersed in the depth of the heart, beginning and ending
prayer in the heart, this undoubtedly comes from grace, not
from deception."

Elsewhere, Starets Vasilii says the following about bodily
sensations during mental prayer: "First of all, according to the
holy Patriarch Callistus, warmth comes from the kidneys, as
if girding them, and it seems to be deception, but this is not
so. This warmth comes not from deception but from nature,
and is the consequence of the exercise of prayer. Now if one
should consider this warmth as coming from grace, not from
nature, then this is undoubtedly deception. But no matter how
pleasant this warmth may be, the spiritual warrior should
not receive it, but reject it. Another type of warmth also appears. It is from the heart, and if in experiencing it the mind
falls into adulterous thoughts, it unquestionably becomes
deception. But if the whole body is being warmed by the heart,
while the mind remains pure and passionless, and, as it were,
attached to the most profound depth of the heart, then this
is undoubtedly from grace and not from deception. Knowing
all this, it is essential from the very beginning to train one's
mind to stand above the heart and to contemplate its interior
during the hour of prayer, not at the halfway point along
the sides or at the end below. This is necessary because when
the mind stands above the heart and performs prayer within
it, then like a king sitting on high it freely observes the evil
thoughts seething below and dashes them against the rock of
Christ's name, as if they were the little ones of Babylon. In
addition, being sufficiently removed from the loins, it can
easily avoid the lustful burning which became inherent to our
nature through Adam's transgression. If anyone concentrates
on prayer half-heartedly, then either due to the impoverishment
of the heart's warmth, or as a result of the weakening of the

mind and of the hindering of concentration in the frequent performance of prayer, and also being under the influence of the struggle brought on by the enemy, the mind itself descends to the loins and merges unwillingly with bodily desire. Certain people, at least due to their want of sense or, rather, ignorance, commence performance of prayer from the end below, where the loins are, and in this way, touching with their mind part of the heart and part of the loins, themselves call forth deception, as a charmer calls forth a snake. Others, suffering from total foolishness, do not even know the very place of the heart, and thinking that it is found in the midst of the womb, dare to perform their prayer with the mind there. Woe to their deception!

"And in the warmth that comes with prayer it is also necessary to distinguish which type is a natural gift, poured forth into the heart as sweet-smelling myrrh through holy baptism, which type comes to us from the forefather's transgression, and which type is aroused by the devil. The first type starts with prayer in the heart alone and concludes this prayer in the heart, giving comfort and spiritual fruit to the soul. The second type has its origin in the kidneys and terminates prayer on the physical level, giving the soul coarseness, frigidity, and anxiety. The third one, arising out of a blending with lustful burning, excites the members and the heart with adulterous voluptuousness, captivates the mind with wretched thoughts, and draws one toward bodily copulation. The attentive person soon discerns all this and makes note of it—time, experience and feeling make everything clear to him. The Holy Scriptures say: 'Sir, did you not sow good seed in your field? How then has it weeds?' (Matt. 13:27). It is impossible for evil not to creep into the good—thus deception becomes entwined with sacred mental activity as a tree becomes entwined with ivy. From conceit and arbitrariness, there arises deception, the remedy for which is found in humility, examination of the Scriptures, and spiritual counsel, but not in avoidance of instruction in mental activity. For according to St. Gregory the Sinaite we should neither be afraid nor experience doubt when calling upon God, for even if some have strayed from the path, having been harmed by the mind, know that this came about as a result of arbitrariness and conceit. One cause of conceit is reckless and unchecked fasting, when the faster thinks that he is performing a virtuous deed, rather than fasting for the sake of chastity, while the other cause is solitary living. Removing the former cause, St. Dorotheus says: 'He who maintains silence must always hold to the royal way, for excess in anything is easily accompanied by conceit, which is followed by deception.' And destroying the second, he says: 'It befits only the strong and perfect to engage in single combat with the demons and to unsheathe against them the sword which is the Word of God.'

"The actual method and action of deception consist of: the enemy's participation in the lust of the internal loins, and specters and daydreaming. Cautioning against the former, the holy father says that although the enemy seemingly transforms the natural movement of the loins into a spiritual one, by arousing its burning instead of spiritual warmth, bringing senseless joy instead of gladness, and by forcing the acceptance of his deception as the action of grace, time, experience, and feeling, he exposes his guile. Pointing to the latter danger, the holy father teaches that during silence in no case should anything perceived through sensory or mental means, internally or externally, be accepted, be it the image of Christ, of angels, or of a saint, or a light fire, and so forth. At this point the antagonist will come alive again and will accuse mental activity of deception. For they think that deception does not enter into external chanting. However, let it be known that in anything, be it in chanting or in prayer, deception plays the same part if the performer lacks skill. As St. John Climacus says, 'Let us test, observe, and gauge which sweetness in singing comes to us from the demon of adultery and which comes from the grace and strength abiding in us.' And elsewhere, 'As you sing and pray, observe the approaching sweetness, no matter how much it is found to be diluted by bitter poisons.' Thus, you see that deception can equally strike both those who chant and those who practice prayer. But those unfamiliar with mental activity are only concerned with the fulfillment of the chanting rule and do not inquire into evil thoughts and into the seething of lust. Therefore, they cannot tell when the lustful part boils up by itself and when it is aroused through the enemy's participation, and they do not know how to avoid all this. They hear battles and receive wounds, but they do not know who their enemies are and what they are fighting for. Having understood from the aforesaid that it is not mental activity which is the cause of deception, but only our arbitrariness and conceit, we should not run from mental prayer. Not only does it not lead us into deception, but on the contrary it opens up to us the mental vision for its knowledge and comprehension."

Having familiarized ourselves with Starets Vasilii's teaching on mental prayer, let us now turn to Paisii Velichkovskii's teaching on the same subject. As was already stated, Starets Paisii was compelled to come out with his treatise in order to caution his brethren against the attacks on mental prayer which were widespread at that time, although he acknowledged that the task went beyond the power of his understanding.

"The rumor has reached me," he writes, "that certain persons of monastic calling, basing themselves simply on the sands of their false wisdom, dare to blaspheme Christ's divine prayer, which is performed in the heart for sanctification. They are armed for this, I dare say, by the enemy, so that their tongues, being their own weapons, would discredit this divine undertaking and would darken this spiritual sun with the blindness of their minds. Fearing, lest someone listening to their fables might fall into similar blasphemy, and would sin before God by blaspheming the teachings of so many God-bearing Fathers about this divine prayer; and being unable to take the arrogant words about this most undefiled activity, and also being persuaded by the fervent requests of the devotees of this prayer, I decided, having called to my aid my most sweet Lord Jesus, to write in rebuttal of the false philosophizing chatterers and in confirmation of the God-chosen flock gathered in our monastery a few words on mental divine prayer, basing myself on the Fathers for its steadfast, unshakable, and unquestionable confirmation. And thus, I, being ashes and dust, kneel mentally with my heart before the unapproachable greatness of your divine glory and implore you, the only begotten Son and Word of God who enlightened the man born blind, to also enlighten

my darkened mind. Let this effort be to the glory of your name
and to the benefit of those who wish to cleave to you with the
spirit through the mental performance of prayer and to always
bear you in the heart, and also to the correction of those who
through their extreme ignorance dared to blaspheme this
divine activity!" There follows an exposition of the teaching
on mental prayer in six chapters.

In the first chapter the starets writes that mental prayer was
the activity of the Ancient Fathers and defends it against the
blasphemers of this divine prayer. "Let it be known that this
divine activity was the constant occupation of our ancient
God-bearing Fathers and shone forth like the sun in many
places in the desert and cenobitic monasteries, such as Mount
Sinai, the Egyptian Skete, Mount Nitria, in Jerusalem and the
surrounding monasteries—in a word, in the whole East and
in Constantinople, and on Holy Mount Athos, and on the
islands of the sea, and most recently, in Great Russia as well.
Through this mental performance of holy prayer many of
our God-bearing Fathers, having been inflamed by the se-
raphic fire toward God and neighbors, became the strictest
keepers of God's commandments and became worthy of becoming the chosen vessels of the Holy Spirit. Many of them,
being motivated by the innermost divine inspiration, and
agreeing with the divine writings of the Old and New Testaments, wrote in their holy teachings, which were filled with
the wisdom of the Holy Spirit, about this divine prayer. And
they did this according to God's special providence so that
in later times this divine action would not be somehow forgotten. But many of the books written by them, through God's
sufferance because of our sins, were destroyed by the Saracens
who overtook the Greek Kingdom, while others, by God's
mercy, have been preserved to this day. No one possessing true
belief has ever dared to blaspheme this divine mental activity
and keeping of spiritual paradise, but everyone has always
treated it with great respect and extreme reverence, as something filled with great spiritual benefit.

"The devil, who is the source of malice and the opponent
of all virtues saw that through this mental performance of
prayer, the monastic host, choosing its good aspect, sits at

Jesus' feet in tenacious love, abiding by his divine commandments to perfection. He therefore started making every effort to discredit and blaspheme this saving action, and if at
all possible, to totally wipe it off the face of the earth. He
strived to attain this either by destroying books or by adding
soul-corrupting chaff to the heavenly wheat. Thanks to this,
people lacking reasoning ability, seeing those who arbitrarily
approach this activity and through self-exaltation reap chaff
instead of wheat and find perdition instead of salvation, blaspheme this holy action. Not satisfied with the aforesaid, the
devil found in the Italian lands the serpent of Calabria, the
heretic Barlaam, who in his pride resembles the devil in all
aspects. Entering him with all his power, he provoked him to
blaspheme both our Orthodox faith and this holy mental
prayer. Watch, then, O friends who dare blaspheme mental
prayer—are you, too, becoming co-participants with this heretic
and his sympathizers? Do you not tremble with your souls at
the thought of being anathematized by the Church as they
were, and of being alienated from God? What is your actual
lawful reason for blaspheming this most undefiled and thrice-
blessed thing? I cannot possibly understand this. Does the
calling of Jesus' name seem useless to you? It is impossible
to be saved by anyone else's name except by the name of our
Lord Jesus Christ. Perhaps it is the mind performing the
prayer which is defiled? But this too is impossible, for God
created man according to his image and likeness. Now God's
image and likeness are found in the human soul, which, being
God's creation, is pure and undefiled, so therefore the mind
also, being the principal sense of the spirit, is pure and undefiled. But it may be that blaspheming is due to the heart, upon
which, as on the altar, the mind ministers to God the secret
sacrifice of prayer? Again no. For the heart is God's creation
as well and like the whole human body, is very good. Thus,
if the calling of Jesus' name is a saving art, and the human
mind and heart are the work of God's hands, then why is it
wrong for a person to send forth mentally a prayer to the
most sweet Jesus from the depth of his heart and ask mercy
of him? Or perhaps, you are blaspheming and rejecting mental
prayer for the very reason that God, in your opinion, does

not hear the prayer performed secretly in the heart, but hears only the one uttered by the mouth? But this is slander against God, for God knows all hearts and knows in detail the most subtle thoughts contained in a heart, or those that are yet to appear—he knows everything, as the all-knowing God. He himself seeks such a secret prayer, sent forth from out of the depths of the heart, as a pure and undefiled sacrifice, and bids us: 'But when you pray, go into your room and shut the door and pray to your Father who is in secret; and your Father who sees in secret will reward you' (Matt 6:6).

"St. John Chrysostom, the mouth of Christ, the universal light, and ecumenical teacher, in his Nineteenth Homily on St. Matthew's Gospel, through the wisdom granted to him by the Holy Spirit, applies these words not to the prayer uttered by the mouth and tongue but to the most secret and voiceless prayer sent forth from the depths of the heart, which he instructs to perform not only bodily, and through the utterance of the mouth, but with the most earnest inclination, with every quietness and contrition of soul, with internal tears and spiritual pain, and with the closing of mental doors. And he cites evidence from the Divine Scriptures about this secret prayer—the God-seeing Moses, St. Hannah, and the righteous Abel—saying: 'But are you pained in mind and cannot help crying aloud?' But surely it is appropriate for one so exceedingly pained to pray and entreat even as I have said. Since Moses too was pained, and prayed in this way and was heard; for this reason God said to him, 'Why do you cry to me?' (Ex. 14:15). And Hannah too, her voice not being heard, accomplished all she wished, since her heart cried out (1 Sam. 1:13). But Abel did not pray only when silent, but even when dying, and his blood sent forth a cry clearer than a trumpet (Gen. 4:10), 'Groan, then, also, even as that holy one, I do not forbid it.' 'Rend,' as the prophet commanded, 'your hearts, not your garments' (Joel 2:13). Call upon God out of the depths, for it is said, 'Out of the depths I cry to thee, O Lord' (Ps. 130:1). From beneath, out of the heart, draw forth a voice, make your prayer a mystery. And elsewhere: 'For it is not to men that you are praying, but to God, who is omnipresent, hears even before the voice, and knows the secrets of the mind. If this is how you pray, you shall receive a great reward.' And again: 'For because he himself is invisible, he wishes your prayer to be likewise' (Hom. 19:4).

"So you see, my friends, that according to the testimony of the insurmountable pillar of Orthodoxy there exists another type of prayer besides the one uttered by the mouth, which is secret, invisible, voiceless, and sent forth to God out of the depth of the heart. As a pure sacrifice, as an aroma of spiritual fragrance, God accepts it, rejoices and is glad in it, seeing the mind, which especially should be dedicated to God, being joined with him by prayer! Fear and trembling overcome me at the sight of your foolish undertaking! But I will also ask you, are you blaspheming this most saving prayer for the reason that, perhaps, you happened to see or hear that one of the performers of this prayer damaged his mind, or took some sort of deceit seriously, or suffered some sort of spiritual harm, and you decided that the cause of all this was mental prayer? But no, no! Holy mental prayer, being activated by God's grace, purifies man from all passions, prompts him toward the keeping of God's commandments, and preserves him unharmed from all of the enemy's arrows and from deception.

"If anyone should dare to experience this prayer arbitrarily, not by virtue of the Fathers' teachings and without inquiry and the counsel of the skilled; being in addition haughty, passionate, and infirmed, living without obedience, and, to top it off, living a solitary and eremitic existence, even the trace of which he is not worthy of seeing for his arbitrariness—I declare that such a person easily falls into all of the snares and deceptions of the devil. What then? Can it be that this prayer is the cause of deception? Nothing of the sort! If you are defiling mental prayer because of this, then you should also defile a knife through which a small child might inflict a wound upon himself due to his foolishness, while playing with it. Then warriors, too, should be forbidden to bear the warrior's sword, lest some foolish warrior stab himself with the sword. But just as neither the knife nor the sword should be considered to be guilty of the harm caused by them, so also is holy and mental prayer, which is the spiritual sword, blameless in any evil. The guilt lies in arbitrariness and in the pride of the arbitrary, as a result of which they fall into demonic deception and undergo all kinds of spiritual harm.

"However, why am I taking so long to ask you about the reason for your blaspheming this holy prayer? I know, O friends, I know well the most fundamental cause of your blasphemy. It is, in the first place, your reading of the Holy Scriptures not according to Christ's commandment, without experiencing them; second, your mistrust of the teachings of our Fathers who teach about this divine prayer; third, your extreme ignorance, perhaps having never even seen the writings about it of our God-bearing Fathers, or at least not at all understanding the power of their words of divine wisdom— it is in this that the basic cause of your false teaching lies. If with the fear of God and total concentration, with an unquestionable faith, and with diligence and humility you read the patristic books, which contain all of the wisdom of the Gospel life, and are essential to monks for their spiritual benefit and correction and for the truly healthy and humble pattern of their thoughts, God would never have suffered you to fall into such a depth of evil blaspheming. Rather, he would have inflamed you with his grace through this activity toward his inexpressible love, so that together with the apostle you would have been ready to exclaim, 'Who shall separate us from the love of Christ' (Rom. 8:35). And not only would you not blaspheme it, but you would be prepared to lay down your soul for it, having perceived through the very action and experience arising from this mental concentration its inexpressible benefit to your souls. In order to deliver you and all sceptics from great spiritual harm, I cannot find a more appropriate remedy than to point out to you, insofar as the Lord will aid me in this, how our God-bearing Fathers, basing themselves on the immovable rock of the Holy Scriptures, teach about this all-holy prayer, performed mentally in the heart. And you yourselves, when you will see clearly and graphically the truth of the patristic teachings, which with the help of God's grace will have touched your souls, will be healed of your spiritual affliction, bringing to God your sincere repentance for your error and becoming worthy of his mercy and complete forgiveness of your transgression."

In the second chapter Starets Paisii explains the source of the Jesus prayer and the evidence for it from the Holy Scriptures presented by the Fathers. "Let it be known that according to the patristic writings there exist two types of mental prayer. One is for beginners and corresponds to action, while the other is for the perfect and corresponds to vision. One is the beginning, the other the end, for action is the ascent to vision. It should be known that, according to St. Gregory the Sinaite there exist eight primary visions, enumerating which he says, 'We enumerate the eight primary visions: the first is about God, without image and unoriginate, uncreated, the cause of all, the Triune Unity and the most-high essential Divinity; the second is the order of the mental powers; the third is the content of the existing; the fourth is the watchful condescension of the Word; the fifth is the universal resurrection; the sixth is the Awesome and Second Coming of Christ; the seventh is eternal suffering; the eighth is the Heavenly Kingdom without end.' I will now try, to the extent of my feeble mind, to explain in what sense action and vision should be understood. Let it be known (I say this to the simplest monks like myself) that the whole monastic effort, by which anyone, with God's help, labors unto love for God and for his neighbor, unto meekness, humility, patience, and all the other divine and patristic commandments, unto obedience of soul and body performed according to God, unto fasting, vigilance, tears, prostrations, and other forms of wearying the body, unto the very diligent performance of the rule of the church and the cell, unto the secret mental exercise of prayer, and unto weeping and contemplation of death—all such effort, so long as the mind is ruled by human sovereignty and choice, is called, as far as we know, action, while it can in no case be called vision.

"If someplace in the patristic writings the feat of mental prayer has been called vision, this is simply in common parlance, just as the mind, being the soul's eye, is called vision. Now, when helped by God in the above feat, a person will cleanse his soul and heart in particularly profound humility

from evil spiritual and bodily passions, God's grace, the
mother common to all, having taken the mind it had cleansed
by the hand like a child, leads it up the steps to the spiritual
visions referred to. God's grace reveals to the mind, to the
degree of its purification, inexpressible and incomprehensible
divine mysteries, and this is justifiably called a true spiritual
vision. This is the visionary or, according to St. Issac, pure
prayer, and from it come awe and the vision. But it is impossible for anyone to enter into these visions on his own through
arbitrary effort, if God does not visit him and does not lead
him into them by his grace. If anyone should dare to ascend
to such visions outside of the light of God's grace, then, according to St. Gregory the Sinaite, let it be known to such a
person that he is imagining dreams and being deceived by
the spirit of dreaminess.

"Having presented this discussion of active and visual
prayer, it is now time for us to show where divine mental
prayer has its cause. Let it be known that, according to the
unlying witnessing of our divinely-wise Father Nilus, the
Faster of Sinai, God himself gave to primordial man long ago
in Paradise the divine mental prayer befitting the perfect.
St. Nilus says, 'Having prayed, appropriately, start expecting
what is not appropriate, and stand manfully, keeping your fruit.
For this purpose you were appointed from the very beginning—
to till and keep and thus, having tilled, do not leave the
tilled without keeping it. If you do not do this you will not
derive any benefit from prayer.' Commenting upon these
words, the Russian light, venerable Nil, the desert Father
of Sora, who shined forth like the sun in Great Russia through
his mental performance of prayer, says, 'The saint takes these
words, "to till and keep it," from the Old Testament, for
the Scriptures say that God created Adam and settled him in
Paradise to till and keep Paradise' (Gen 2:15). By 'tilling,'
St. Nilus of Sinai means prayer, and by 'keeping,' he means
the necessary post-prayer avoidance of evil thoughts. Similarly
venerable Dorotheus says that primordial man, being settled
by God in Paradise, remained continuously in prayer. From
these witnessings we see that God, having created man in his
image and likeness, led him into the Paradise of sweetness in

order that he may till the gardens of immortality, i.e. divine, most-pure, most-high, and perfect thoughts, as St. Gregory the Theologian writes. This is nothing other than the fact that it was prescribed to the first man, as being of clean soul and heart, to remain continuously in visual grace-filled prayer, ministered by the mind alone, i.e. in the sweetest vision of God, and to guard it as a heavenly activity, as the apple of the eye, so that it would never depart from the soul and heart.

"But this prayer acquired incomparably greater glory when the most-holy Virgin, who is the holiest of all and more honorable than the Cherubim and more glorious than the Seraphim, beyond compare abiding in the Holy of Holies and having ascended through mental prayer to extreme heights of divine vision, was granted to be the spacious abode of God the Word, who is uncontainable by all creation. This is witnessed by St. Gregory Palamas, archbishop of Thessalonica in his *Sermon on the Entrance of the Most-Holy Theotokos into the Temple.* He says that the Most-holy Virgin, who remained in the Holy of Holies and learned from the Holy Scriptures about the human race perishing from its disobedience, was filled with great mercy and undertook a mental prayer to God for the speedy forgiveness and salvation of the human race. Here are his own words, worthy of angelic wisdom: 'When the God-child heard and saw all that was taking place, she was filled with great mercy toward the human race, and searching for a means of healing it and ministering to it which would be equal to such suffering, she found it necessary to address God immediately with her whole mind, assuming a prayer for us in order to compel the one who cannot be compelled and to lead him to us, so that he himself would destroy condemnation and having healed what was afflicted would establish a link with creation.' And further, 'Not envisioning out of all existence anything more appropriate to man than this prayer, and steadfastly striving to pray with all her effort, the Virgin acquires sacred silence as the greatest conversational necessity for those who pray. Any other virtue is a sort of ministering to spiritual afflictions and evil passions ingrained through faint-heartedness, while the vision of God is the fruit of a healthy soul, as a certain final perfection. Thus a person does not become deified through words or visible actions moderated by foresight, for all this is earthly and human, but through maintaining silence, thanks to which we reject and free ourselves from the earthly and ascend to God. Abiding on the heights of a silent existence, laboring patiently, day and night in prayer and worship, we somehow draw near to the unapproachable and blessed Essence. And in this way, patiently performing our prayer, which is penetrated by the light that is inexpressibly superior to the mind and senses, we see God in ourselves as in a mirror, having cleansed our hearts through sacred silence.' And elsewhere, 'This is why the Most Pure, having rejected a worldly existence and discourse, withdrew from people and chose a life that was private and unseen by all remaining unapproachable. At this point, having renounced all material bonds, all human contact as well as affinity for everything, and having surmounted her condescension to her own body she gathered her mind toward unity with him, and toward constancy, concentration, and unceasing divine prayer. By having set herself above all manner of strife and thoughts through this prayer which abided in her, she opened up a new and inexpressible path to heaven which is, if I may say so, silence of thought. Concentrating upon it, she surpasses all created things better than Moses, beholds God's glory, contemplates divine grace which in no measure is subject to sensory power. She also beholds the joyful and holy vision of uncorrupted souls and minds, and having become a participant in it, she is the radiant cloud of living water, the dawn of the day of the mind, and the fiery chariot of the Word.'

"We see from these words of St. Gregory Palamas that the most-holy Virgin, while abiding in the Holy of Holies, ascended through mental prayer to the immense height of seeing God and herself become an example of a life that is watchful of the inner man. She did this through the renunciation of the world for the sake of the world, the sacred silence of the mind, the silence of thoughts in unceasing divine prayer and mental concentration, and the ascent through action toward seeing God, so that, looking at her, those renouncing the world would undertake the indicated mental efforts, trying as much as they can to be her imitators through her prayers. And who can worthily glorify divine mental prayer, the performer of which was the Theotokos herself, instructed by the guidance of the Holy Spirit!

"However, it is time to show, in order that all sceptics could confirm and unquestionably verify the above, what evidence from the Holy Scriptures about this is cited by our God-bearing Fathers, who wrote according to the enlightenment of God's grace. Divine mental prayer has its unshakable foundation first of all in the following words of Lord Jesus: 'But when you pray, go into your room and shut the door and pray to your Father who is in secret; and your Father who sees in secret will reward you' (Matt. 6:6). As was stated previously, St. John Chrysostom explains these words as referring to the silent and secret prayer arising from the depth of the heart. St. Basil the Great, the flaming pillar, the flaming mouth of the Holy Spirit, and the eye of the Church, in commenting upon these words of the Holy Scriptures: 'I will bless the Lord at all times; his praise shall continually be in my mouth' (Ps. 34:1); instructs us wonderfully about a thoughtful mouth and thoughtful action, i.e. mental prayer. I quote him directly: 'his praise shall continually be in my mouth.' What the prophet says seems impossible—how can the praise of God be continually in man's mouth? When a person carries on a usual everyday conversation, he does not have God's praise in his mouth, and when sleeping he is silent, of course. So how can the praise of God be continually in man's mouth? Our answer to this is that there exists a thoughtful mouth of the innermost man, by means of which man becomes a participant in God's life-bearing Word, which is the bread coming down from heaven. The prophet speaks thus of this mouth, 'With open mouth I pant' (Ps. 119:131). God too, calls us to keep this mouth open in order to receive the true food: 'Open your mouth wide and I will fill it' (Ps. 81:10). A thought about God, once outlined and impressed upon the mind of the soul, can be called praise that is continually abiding in the soul. And according to the apostle's words, the diligent person can do everything for the glory of God. For every activity, word, and mental action has the force of glorification. The righteous person, whether he eats, drinks, or does anything else, he does it for the glory of God. Even when he sleeps his heart keeps watch.' From these words of St. Basil it is clear to see that besides the bodily mouth there is also the mental mouth and mental action and glorification, performed mentally in the innermost man.

"The great Macarius, who is synonymous with beatitude and is the Egyptian, or rather the universal sun, having shone brighter than the sun by the gifts of the Holy Spirit, says the following in his words about this prayer: 'The Christian should always keep the memory of God, for it is written, "For where your treasure is, there will your heart be also."' (Matt. 6:21). And the venerable and God-bearing ancient Father, St. Isaiah the Faster, cites as evidence of innermost instruction, i.e. of the Jesus Prayer, performed by the mind in the heart, the following words from the Divine Scriptures: "My heart became hot within me. As I mused the fire burned" (Ps. 39:3). The venerable Symeon, having shone forth in the royal city like the sun through mental prayer and the inexpressible gifts of the Most-holy Spirit, and having received for this from the entire Church the name of New Theologian, writes the following in his essay on the three types of prayer: 'Our Holy Fathers, heard the Lord's words as to how out of the heart come evil thoughts, murder, adultery, fornication, thievery, false witness, slander, and how these are what define a man (Matt. 15:19), and also that the inside of the cup and the plate should first be cleansed, that the outside also may be clean (Matt. 23:26). Therefore, having abandoned the thought of any other activity, they labored in this keeping of the heart, undoubtedly knowing that with the keeping of the heart they will easily succeed in any other activity, for without it no virtue can hold fast.' These words of the venerable one clearly indicate that the above words of the Lord were recognized by the divine Fathers as a testimony to and the foundation of the keeping of the heart, i.e. the mental summoning of Jesus. The same venerable one cites in evidence of divine mental prayer additional words from the Holy Scriptures: 'Rejoice, O young man, in your youth . . . walk in the ways of your heart and the sight of your eyes . . . Remove vexation from your mind' (Eccl. 11:9-10), and 'If the anger of the ruler rises against you, do not leave your place.' (Eccl. 10:4).

"And the apostle Peter says, 'Be sober, be watchful. Your adversary the devil prowls around like a roaring lion, seeking someone to devour' (1 Pet. 5:8). And the Apostle Paul, apparently in reference to the vigilance of the heart, writes to the Ephesians: 'For we are not contending against flesh and blood, but against the principalities, against the powers, against the world rulers of this present darkness' (Eph. 6:12). The venerable presbyter Hesychius, the theologian and teacher of the Jerusalem Church, who wrote a book in 200 chapters about the mental calling upon Jesus in the heart, i.e. about mental prayer, cites the following testimony about it from the Divine Scriptures: 'Blessed are the pure in heart, for they shall see God' (Matt. 5:8), and again, 'Take heed lest there be a base thought in your heart' (Deut. 15:9). And the apostle says, 'Pray constantly' (1 Thess. 5:17), and the Lord himself says, 'He who abides in me and I in him, he it is that bears much fruit, for apart from me you can do nothing' (Jn. 15:5). Our divine and God-bearing Father John Climacus cites the following testimony to this sacred prayer and true silence from the Holy Scriptures: 'The greatest of great and performer of perfect prayer said, "I would rather speak five words with my mind," and so on; and again, "I slept but my heart was awake" (Song 5:2); and also, "With my whole heart I cry" ' (Ps. 119:145). Our God-bearing Father Philotheos, the superior of the monastery of the Theotokos of the Burning Bush on Mount Sinai, who compiled a small book of invaluable gems of divine wisdom about vigilance of the heart, places the following words of the Holy Scriptures as an unshakable foundation for his teachings: 'Morning by morning I will destroy all the wicked in the land' (Ps. 101:8); and 'The kingdom of God is in the midst of you' (Luke 17:21); and again, 'Keep your heart with all vigilance' (Pr. 4:23); and still again, 'For I delight in the law of God, in my inmost self, but I see in my members another law at war with the law of my mind and making me captive' (Rom. 7:22-23). Our divine Father Diadochus, bishop of Photice, in his writings on the mental prayer of Jesus gives the following justification for it from the Holy Scriptures: 'No one can say "Jesus is Lord" except by the Holy Spirit' (1 Cor. 12:3), and from the Gospel parable about the merchant in search of fine pearls, this conclusion is made about prayer: 'This is an invaluable pearl, which a person can acquire at the price of all his belongings, and he can possess inexpressible joy over its acquisition.' Our venerable Father Nicephorus the Faster, in writing about the vigilance of the heart, likens this divine mental performance of prayer in the heart to a treasure concealed in a field and calls it a 'burning illumination.'

"Our divine and God-bearing Father, Gregory of Sinai, who attained the supreme vision of God through the performance of this prayer on Holy Mount Athos and other places, with the aid of divine wisdom wrote Trinitarian hymns which are sung weekly throughout the world, and also put together the Canon to the Life-giving Cross, cites the following confirmation about this divine prayer from the Divine Scriptures: 'You shall remember the Lord your God' (Deut. 8:18); and again, 'In the morning sow your seed, and at evening withhold not your hand (Eccl. 11:6); and again still: 'For if I pray in a tongue, my spirit prays but my mind is unfruitful' (1 Cor. 14:14); and, 'I will pray with the spirit and I will pray with my mind also' (1 Cor. 14:15); and, 'I would rather speak five words with my mind' (1 Cor. 14:19), and so forth. As a witness he cites John Climacus, who also associates these words with mental prayer. The most holy, most wise, and most erudite Mark, Metropolitan of Ephesus, who followed in the steps of the apostles and was the insuperable pillar of the Orthodox Faith, and who tore apart the spirit-contending heresies of the Latins as he would a spider web at the Florentine Council with the flaming sword of the spirit and the truth of Orthodox dogma, writes about the divine Jesus Prayer: 'It would be fitting, according to the commandment, to pray ceaselessly and send forth veneration to God through the spirit and truth. But the disposition toward earthly thoughts and the burden of bodily cares separate and hold back many from the kingdom of God which exists within us, and hinders our presence at the altar of the mind and our bringing to God of spiritual and verbal sacrifices according to the divine apostle, who said that we are the temples of the God who abides in us and that his divine Spirit also abides in us. There is nothing surprising if this happens to many of these who live according to the flesh, when we see certain monks, who having renounced the world, are mentally possessed by the actions of passions. Consequently, they are subjected to great anxiety which darkens the reasoning area of the soul and are therefore made incapable of attaining true prayer, in spite of all their desire to do so. Sweet is the pure and constant remembrance of Jesus abiding in the heart and the resulting inexpressible illumination.' Our venerable Father and Russian Saint Nil Sorskii, who wrote a book on the mental vigilance of the heart, uses the following words from the Holy Scriptures: 'For out of the heart come evil thoughts . . . These are what defile a man' (Matt. 15:19-20); and 'The Father must be worshipped in spirit and truth,' and so forth. Another light of Russia, the bishop of Christ Dimitrii, Metropolitan of Rostov, who wrote a work on the internal mental performance of prayer, cites the following passages from the Holy Scriptures: 'My heart says to thee, "Thy face, Lord, do I seek" ' (Ps. 27:8); and again 'As a hart longs for flowing streams, so longs my soul for thee, O God' (Ps. 42:1); and again, 'Pray at all times in the Spirit, with all prayer and supplication' (Eph. 6:18). Together with St. John Climacus, Gregory of Sinai, and the venerable Nil Sorskii, he associates all of these passages with mental prayer. So does the Church Statute, in presenting the Church's rules on reverences and prayer, cite the following passage from the Divine Scriptures about this divine prayer: 'God is spirit, and those who worship him must worship in spirit and truth' (Jn. 4:24). It also cites the testimony of the Holy Fathers from that area of their teachings which refers to mental prayer and follows this by stating, 'We conclude here our discussion of holy, sacred, and ever-memorable mental prayer' and then turns to the united prayer which is holy to all and is prescribed by the *ordo* of the Church. In this way, it is shown to us through God's grace that the God-bearing Fathers, being edified by the Holy Spirit have established the foundation of their teachings about the

mental ministering of the prayer which is performed secretly
according to the inner man upon the immovable rock of the
Divine Scriptures—the New and Old Testaments, from which,
as from an inexhaustible spring, numerous testimonies are
taken."

In the third chapter of his book on mental prayer Starets
Paisii says that this prayer is a spiritual art. "Let it be known
that the divine Fathers call this sacred mental performance of
prayer an art. Thus, St. John Climacus says in his twenty-third
sermon *On Silence*, 'If you have mastered this art, then you
know what I am speaking of: Sitting on the heights, observe
if you can, and you will see how, when, from where, how
many, and what kind of thieves are coming to steal the clus-
ters. Having become tired, this sentry will arise and pray,
and then will sit down again, continuing his original activity.'
St. Hesychius, the presbyter of Jerusalem says the following
about the same sacred prayer: 'Being of sober mind is a spiritual art which, with God's help, totally liberates a person from
passionate thoughts and words, and from evil actions.' St. Nicephorus the Faster considers the same subject: 'Come, and
I will reveal to you the art, or rather the science, of eternal
heavenly life, which leads its performer without labor and
sweat into the refuge of passionlessness.' The above Fathers
call this holy prayer art, I would think, because, just as a person cannot learn art by himself without an artist, he cannot
learn this mental performance of prayer without a skillful
mentor. Its mastery, according to St. Nicephorus, comes to
most and even to all through learning. Occasional persons require its mastery from God without learning, through the
painfulness of activity and the zeal of faith."

The fourth chapter of the book speaks of the kind of
preparation needed for anyone who may wish to undertake
this divine activity. Inasmuch as this divine prayer is above
any other monastic feat and represents the end of all labors,
the source of virtues, and the most subtle activity of the mind
hidden in the innermost heart, so does the invisible enemy of
our salvation lay upon it the snares of his various deceptions
and dreams, which are invisible, subtle, and barely conceivable
to the human mind. Therefore, one who wishes to learn this

divine activity must, according to St. Symeon the New Theologian, devote himself to complete obedience to a person who fears God, is a diligent keeper of his divine commandments, has experience in this mental feat, and is capable of indicating to his pupil the proper way to salvation. Through humility arising out of obedience such a person will be able to avoid all of the seductions and snares of the devil and to always exercise this mental activity peacefully, silently, without any harm, and with great progress for his soul. If, even having given himself over to obedience, he does not find in his spiritual father a mentor skilled in this divine prayer by his very actions and experience, he nonetheless should not fall into despair. Instead he should continue to abide in obedience that is truly in accordance with God's commandments with humility and fear of God, rather than in an arbitrary and self-willful existence which is usually followed by delusion. Placing all his hope on God, together with his spiritual father, he should obey the teachings of our holy Fathers who astutely instruct us in this divine activity, and should learn this prayer from them. In any case God's grace will hasten forth, and through the prayers of the Fathers, will without any doubt, guide the learning of this divine activity.

The fifth chapter contains the teaching on the quality and action of this divine prayer. St. John Climacus, in his twenty-eighth sermon *On Prayer*, says: "Qualitatively, prayer is the coexistence and unification of Man and God. Actively, it is the confirmation of peace, the reconciliation with God, the mother as well as the daughter of tears, the propitiation for sins, the bridge which passes over temptations, the shield from sorrows, the repelling of attacks, the activity of the angels, the food of the bodiless, the future gladness, eternal activity, the source of virtue, the cause of endowments, a secret accomplishment, food for the soul, illumination of the mind, the slasher of despair, the proof of hope, liberation from grief, the wealth of monastics, the treasure of those keeping silence, the mitigator of anger, the mirror of success, the indication of measure, the discovery of one's condition, the exponent of the future, and the seal of glory. For the one who prays, prayer is truly a place of judgment, the judgment itself, and the throne of the Lord's judgment in advance of the future throne." And St. Gregory of Sinai writes in his *Chapter 113:* "In beginners prayer is, as it were, a flame of gladness produced by the heart, while in the perfect it is activated fragrantly as a light," and elsewhere he says; "Prayer is the preaching of the apostles, the action of faith,—or better, direct faith—a feature of the trusting, love that is realized, the movement of the angels, the power of the bodiless, their activity and gladness, the gospel of God, the revelation of the heart, the hope of salvation, the sign of sanctification, the development of holiness, the knowledge of God, a manifestation of baptism, the betrothal of the Holy Spirit, the joyfulness of Jesus, the gladness of the soul, mercy of God, the sign of reconciliation, the seal of Christ, the ray of the mental sun, the morning star of hearts, the confirmation of Christianity, the manifestation of reconciliation to God, the grace of God, divine wisdom—or rather the beginning of self-wisdom, the manifestation of God, the activity of the monastics, the livelihood of those keeping silence,—or rather the source of silence— and the seal of the angelic life."

The blessed Macarius the Great says the following about prayer: "The most important thing in any good effort and the height of all activities is to persevere in prayer, by means of which we can always acquire through supplication the other virtues from God as well. Through prayer those who are made worthy are able to participate in God's holiness and spiritual action and to unite their minds, which are directed toward God, with him through inexpressible love. Whoever compels himself to abide patiently in prayer becomes enflamed toward God with divine zeal and a flaming desire out of spiritual love, and according to his measure, receives the gift of sanctifying spiritual perfection" (*Homily 40*, Ch. 2). St. Symeon, archbishop of Thessalonica, says the following about this same holy prayer: "This divine prayer of our Savior consists of the appeal: O Lord Jesus Christ, Son of God, have mercy on me. This prayer is supplication, confession of faith, the giver of the Holy Spirit and the bestower of divine gifts, the purification of the heart, the expulsion of demons, the indwelling of Jesus Christ, the source of spiritual ideas and divine thoughts, deliverance from sins, the ministering to souls and bodies, the giver of divine illumination and the source of God's mercy, the giver of revelations and divine mysteries to the meek, and it is salvation itself, for it carries within itself the saving name of our God—this being the name of Jesus Christ the Son of God which was betrothed to us" (Ch. 296). Likewise, the other God-bearing Fathers, writing about this holy prayer, bear witness to its action, to the ineffable benefit deriving from it, and to the progress through it in the exercise of the divine gifts of the Holy Spirit.

Seeing how this most sacred prayer brings its performer to such a heavenly treasury of various virtues, who will not become inflamed with divine zeal toward the constant performance of this prayer, so that through it sweetest Jesus would always be preserved in heart and in soul and to ceaselessly commemorate within oneself his most cherished name, being ineffably inspired to love him ceaselessly. The only person who will not feel a burning desire to approach this mental activity of mental prayer is the one who is overtaken by a predilection for worldly thoughts, who is bound by bodily cares which lead us away and alienate us from the kingdom of God abiding within us, who through his very action and experience has not tasted with his spiritual larynx the ineffable sweetness of this divine activity, and who has not understood what a treasured spiritual benefit is contained within this prayer. Those who wish to be united in love with sweetest Jesus, having scorned all the attractions and pleasures of this world, as well as bodily comfort, will not wish to possess in this life anything other than the constant exercise in the heavenly performance of this prayer.

In the final sixth chapter of his book starets Paisii writes about certain external methods of learning this prayer for beginners. Before presenting his instructions, we shall, in place of a preface apply to this situation a brief comment by one of our contemporary spiritual warriors who writes the following: "The aim of mental prayer is unification with God who is the Spirit, and with whom unification can therefore be only spiritual. As far as external methods used by certain spiritual warriors while practicing this prayer are concerned, these undoubtedly have secondary significance. The Fathers say that in the imperfect the human soul becomes integrated with the body. Therefore, the silence of the soul ought to be preceded by the silence of the body, i.e. its beatification, as John Climacus says, and for the integrity of the mind, which is necessary for prayer, certain external conditions of the body's environment and even of its position. But it would be erroneous to think that the feat of growth in spiritual prayer can depend on external conditions and methods. One thing is certain—that since the essence of prayer consists of praying in the heart with the mind, our mind should also be directed toward the heart. Everything else has secondary significance. Thus, in the Russian *Philokalia* all mention of external methods is omitted" (Bishop Feofan of Poltava). After this preliminary remark, let us turn to Starets Paisii's book. He writes: "In the ancient times the performance of mental prayer flourished in many places where the Holy Fathers were present, and there were many teachers of this spiritual benefit deriving from it, not finding it necessary to write of the actual method of this activity which is appropriate to beginners. When it was realized that those instructors of this activity who were genuine and removed from delusion were starting to decrease in number, then those who were motivated by God's Spirit, so that the true teaching on the beginning of this prayer would not become impoverished, described the beginning itself and the method by which beginners ought to learn this prayer, entering with the mind into the domain of the heart and performing mental prayer there without delusiveness.

"St. Symeon the New Theologian says the following about the beginning of this activity: 'True and unerring attention and prayer lie in the keeping of the heart by the mind during prayer, in addressing the Lord from within it, and in sending forth a prayer from its depths. Tasting here how good the Lord is, the mind no longer leaves the refuge of the heart and says together with the apostle: "it is good for us to be here," and, always overlooking those environs, expels the thoughts sown by the enemy.' Later, he speaks of the same in even clearer terms: 'Sitting in a silent cell in some solitary corner, attentively perform what I tell you: shut the door, turn your mind away from any fuss, and press your beard to your chest, adjusting your sensory eye in the same direction as your mind. Slow down your breath, in order not to breathe too freely. Make a mental attempt to find within the breast the place of the heart, where all of the spiritual powers naturally enjoy being present and where, first of all, you will find darkness and unremitting coarseness. Now if you continue to perform this action both day and night you will acquire—O wonder!—permanent gladness. For as soon as the mind finds the place of the heart, it sees that which it never saw—it sees air in the midst of the heart and itself wholly radiant and filled with reasoning. And from that time on, regardless of where the thought may arise from, before it becomes an action or an idol, the mind expels it by calling upon Jesus Christ and destroys it. At this point the mind, bearing a grudge against the demons, arouses natural anger against them and, expelling them, overthrows its mental adversaries. You will learn much else through the keeping of the mind, holding Jesus in your heart' (*On the Three Forms of Concentration and Prayer*).

"The venerable Nicephorus the Faster, teaching with even greater clarity about the entrance of the mind into the heart, says the following: 'First of all, let your life be silent, free from cares, and at peace with everyone. Then, having entered your cell, shut the door, sit down in one of the corners, and do as I tell you; you know that while breathing we inhale air, while we exhale it for the sake of nothing other than the heart, for the heart is the cause of life and of the body's warmth. The body attracts the air so that it may exude its warmth through breathing, and to receive fresh air for itself. Such activity is effected by the lungs, which being created porous by the Creator, constantly, like fur, draw air in and out. In this manner the heart fulfills that function for which it was made for the well-being of the organism. Thus, be seated, and gathering up your whole mind, lead it into that path through which the air goes to the heart and compel it to descend into the heart together with the inhaled air. Now when it enters there, what follows is neither unhappy nor joyless.' He writes further: 'Therefore brother, train the mind to leave from there unhurriedly, for at first it despairs much from internal seclusion and crowding. But when it becomes accustomed to this, it no longer wishes to remain in external wanderings, for the Kingdom of Heaven is within us. When we contemplate it there and seek it through pure prayer, everything external appears to us loathsome and hateful. Thus, if you enter with your mind immediately, as it is said, the place of the heart which I have shown you, give thanks to God, glorify him, and rejoice, always persevering in this activity, and it will teach you what you do not know. You also ought to know that when your mind is there it must not remain quiet and vain, but should have as its constant action and teaching the following prayer: Lord, Jesus Christ, Son of God, have mercy on me, and you should never cease this activity. It restrains the mind from self-exaltation, makes it unapproachable and elusive to the designs of the enemy, and elevates it to God's love and to daily divine desire. Now if having labored much, you are not able to enter the domain of the heart, do as I tell you, and with God's help you shall obtain what you seek. Do you know that the origin of each person's reasoning is found in his breast? Here, precisely, even when our mouths are silent, we speak, discuss, perform prayers, and do other things. Let this origin of reasoning say, after having removed any thoughts (you can do so if you wish) : Lord Jesus Christ, Son of God, have mercy on me. Compel yourself to exclaim this alone internally, instead of any other thought. If you maintain this order for a certain amount of time, the entrance to the heart will open up to you, as we have written to you, beyond any doubt, as we ourselves have discovered through experience. It will come to you with greatly desired and sweet concentration, and with the whole host of virtues; love, joy, peace, etc.'

"The divine Gregory of Sinai, also teaching how the calling of the Lord's name ought to be performed by the mind in the heart, says: 'sitting since the morning on the edge of your seat, take down your mind into your heart and keep it there. Bending down with tension, and experiencing discomfort in the breast, the shoulders and the neck, ceaselessly call forth with your mind or soul: Lord Jesus Christ have mercy on me.

When the frequency of repetition becomes too constricted and painful, perhaps even lacking sweetness (which takes place not because of the monotony of frequently eaten food, for it is said: 'Those who partake of me shall yet hunger' [Sirach 24:23]). Rather having directed your mind toward the other half of the prayer, say: Son of God, have mercy on me. And repeating this half many times, you should not change it often out of boredom or laziness, for plants which are often transplanted do not take root. Also, control the breathing of the lungs, so that it would not be too free. For the breathing of the air coming from the heart darkens the mind, prohibiting it from descending to the heart, and disperses thought. Keeping it away from the heart, it places it into the captivity of forgetfulness or prompts it to learn something other than what it should, leaving it to remain senseless in what it should not be. If you see the impurities of evil spirits, i.e. thoughts arising or being transformed in your mind, do not be horrified or surprised. Should positive understanding of certain things appear to you, pay no attention to them, but restrain your breath as much as possible, containing your mind in your heart and performing your appeal to Lord Jesus frequently and ceaselessly, you will soon burn and destroy them, striking them down with the divine name. For thus says Climacus: 'Strike the combatants with the name of Jesus, for there is no stronger weapon either on heaven or on earth.'

"Further on, the same saint, in teaching about silence and prayer, continues: 'You should remain sitting, in patience, for the sake of what is being said. Endure in prayer and do not get up quickly, being weakened due to painful effort, mental appeal, and frequent lifting up of the mind. Therefore, bowing your head and gathering your mind in your heart, call upon Lord Jesus for help. Sensing pain in the shoulders and frequent headaches, endure all this, seeking the Lord in your heart, for to you it has been given to know the kingdom of heaven, and to him who has will more be given' (Matt. 13:11-12). The same Father tells us how prayers ought to be performed: 'Thus said the Fathers: one—Lord Jesus Christ, Son of God, have mercy on me, the whole prayer. Another one stipulates only half of it—Jesus, Son of God, have mercy on me, and this is more convenient, due to the yet infantile state of the mind and to its weakness, for no one can purely and perfectly pronounce the name of Lord Jesus in secret by himself, but only through the Holy Spirit. Like an infant who cannot speak, he cannot yet perform this prayer articulately. He should not often change the names he calls upon because of weakness, but slowly, for the sake of restraint.' And again: 'Some teach the performance of prayer by the mouth, and others by the mind, but I find both to be necessary. For sometimes, out of despair, the mouth tires in pronouncing it, while sometimes the mind tires. However, it is necessary to appeal silently and uninhibitedly, so that the perception of the soul and concentration of the mind, which becomes inhibited by the voice, will not leave until the mind, becoming accustomed to its situation, succeeds in the activity and receives power from the Holy Spirit to pray mightily and variously. Then he will no longer have the need to speak with his mouth, and he will not be able to do so, being able to perform prayer to perfection only with the mind.' We see from the aforesaid that the above Fathers present a totally clear teaching on the methods of learning mental activity for beginners. The instructions in this activity of other spiritual warriors can also be understood from their teaching, although the latter did not express themselves with such clarity."

This concludes the book of Starets Paisii about the mental prayer of Jesus.

CHAPTER III

Wartime Calamities and Starets Paisii's Care for Refugees and the Move to Niamets

The peaceful life at Dragomirna was unexpectedly disrupted. In 1768, according to the starets' biographer, "there arose a terrible storm and morbid fear. Two empires, the Russian and the Turkish, set themselves against each other, spewing anger and breathing fire." Moldavia and Walachia became the theater of operations. The residents sought help in flight. Mountains, forests, and monasteries filled up with frightened refugees fleeing from the wrath of the Turks and the Tatars. The Dragomirna Monastery, which was located in an inaccessible spot in a huge forest, attracted multitudes of people seeking refuge. During the first weeks of Advent the monastery was so full of people that it was impossible to walk through it. The whole surrounding forest was full of refugees. It was a severe snowy winter. The starets, seeing the terrible want of the people, many of whom were barefoot and scantily clad, attempted to alleviate their condition by all possible means. He turned over half of the monastery to the needy, moving all the monks to the other half and placing them three, four, or five to each cell. He turned over the large and warm refectory to the plain folk, especially to the miserable exhausted women. The manager, baker, and cook were ordered to give food to all who came and required it. Some brought raw provisions and prepared their own food, while others received prepared meals and bread along with the monks. Bread was baked and meals were prepared continuously, in the desire to feed all of the needy. But soon the light of God's grace shone forth and the moon was darkened. The Russian Army crossed the border and entered Moldavia. The Turks fled, and the refugees began returning to their abandoned homes.

However, along with war there came other calamities— pestilence, poor harvests, and a three-year famine. The war lasted six years. Only in 1774 was a treaty concluded between Russia and Turkey, and the brethren of the monastery were able to resume their previous life. But a new misfortune befell them. No sooner did the Russian troops leave Moldavia than the Austrian Empress Maria-Theresa demanded from the Turkish sultan the part of Moldavian territory which was due her according to agreement for the help she had given. Contrary to the Moldavians' wishes the Austrians also included the Dragomirna Monastery into this section.

The starets was frightened by the forthcoming passage of the monastery into a Roman Catholic state. He foresaw that there would inevitably follow persecutions of the monastery on the part of the new authorities, which could lead to the destruction of the established community. All the brethren recognized the threatening danger together with the starets. At this time the starets received a letter from the superior of the Sekul Monastery in Moldavia inviting him to move to his monastery. Rejoicing at this invitation, the starets immediately wrote to the Moldavian governor and to the metropolitan, requesting permission to move to the Sekul Monastery with his brethren. After receiving permission, the starets began preparing for the journey. Out of fear of trouble and delays on the part of the Austrians he conducted all his preparations in the greatest secrecy. First, he secretly took the church items to Sekul, and then he bade the monks to prepare for the journey. All the monks, of whom there were 350 at the time, expressed readiness to go with their starets. But the starets did not take them all along immediately. He left 150 persons at Dragomirna, appointing two confessors for them, one Moldavian and another Russian, and making the former the head of the monastery and the latter, his assistant, he embarked upon his journey with the rest. In order to conceal his intentions from the Austrians, he pretended to send the monks for obedience to some monastery lands lying along the way to Sekul. He then went into the church, and after having prayed there with bitter tears, bestowed peace and blessings upon the remaining weeping monks and left the monastery, going toward the place where the monks who had left earlier were awaiting him. The starets joined them near the monastery windmill, and after a month's journey they successfully arrived at Sekul on October 14, 1775.

We find the following description of the Sekul monastery written by the famous traveling monk Parfenii:

> The monastery is located in the midst of the Carpathian Mountains, a two-hour walk from the Niamets Monastery. The road leading to it follows a ravine between such high mountains that the sun cannot be seen. The monastery is located in the most quiet and silent spot, in a most impassable desert, surrounded by mountains reaching up to the clouds and by dark, impassable forests, so that in the winter there is hardly any sunshine. Neither is there ever any wind, but there is always great silence, except for a small river flowing by the monastery, in which the water murmurs drop by drop. Truly the whole world of vanities with its temptations becomes concealed here from eyes and ears.

Incidentally, we know concerning the past of the Sekul Monastery that in the middle of the fifteenth century Starets Zosima's hermitage was located where the monastery now stands. Having come here with his disciples, as is supposed, from the Niamets Monastery, Zosima cleared out part of the forest, built a wooden church in honor of St. John the Baptist and several cells around it, and began their feats of prayer here. Neighboring residents soon found out about the hermits. Benefactors appeared. In 1595 a boyar named Nestor Ureke, *vornik* of Lower Moldavia, with his wife Mitrofania built a stone church at the monastery, where they were later buried. There are eternal vigil lights burning over their graves. A silk Holy Shroud is kept in the church, with gold and silver embroidery—the work of Princess Mitrofania.

Upon arriving at the monastery the starets soon wrote a letter to the monks who remained at Dragomirna. He exhorted them to perform God's commandments and to keep the teachings of the Holy Fathers. Although they had separated from each other according to place of residence, their assembly remained one. He had long wished to write to them, but was delayed as a result of bodily weakness and numerous duties and cares. He exhorts them to be sober and to initiate their improvement constantly by cutting off idle talk which deadens the soul; by not going from cell to cell without the spiritual confessor's blessing; by confessing all thoughts to him, through which all of the enemy's designs fall apart; and by reading the writings of the Fathers, from which the human mind becomes enlightened and zeal toward the fulfillment of the Gospel commandments increases, without the fulfillment of which one cannot be saved by faith alone. Let everyone participate in the labors of the common life according to his strength. Let them not assemble at the monastery gates for the purpose of idle talk. Where there is diligence, there God abides, a radiance shines forth, peace appears, Satan cannot find a place for himself, and passions depart. Where there is no diligence, the opposite takes place. Instead of good there is evil, instead of light—darkness, and instead of Christ—the devil. The starets pleads with the confessors to keep vigil over the hearts of the brethren.

The Sekul Monastery made a very gratifying impression upon Starets Paisii and the brethren by its secluded and quiet location. But at the same time they realized that this monastery was too crowded for their large brotherhood. There was a total of fourteen cells in the monastery. There were three, four, and five persons to a cell, and there still was not enough room. With the coming of spring new monks began arriving from Dragomirna, and it grew even more crowded. The building of new cells began. Everyone was overwhelmed with work. Some built cells inside the monastery, while others attached them to the walls in the manner of lark's nests, as was once done on Mt. Athos, and others built themselves quarters outside the monastery in the forest. Three years were spent in such labors and cares. During this period one hundred cells were built, and finally all of the monks who had moved from Dragomirna found a refuge for themselves.

Wishing to re-establish his communal statute at the new location, Starets Paisii again addressed the Moldavian metropolitan in 1778, requesting permission to use the previously approved statute in Sekul. He asked that after his death the new superior would be elected by the assembly of brethren from among the same brethren. A new superior ought to be elected from among those who had spent a long period of time under the most complete obedience without any vice. Through this obedience and annihilation of self-will they should have acquired profound humility, through which they are granted the gift of sound reasoning and acquire Christ's love equally for all the brethren, as well as the most profound peace. Enduring temptations and abuse over a long period of time and always reproaching themselves, they are liberated forever from irritability and anger and acquire meekness and simplicity. The candidate should be able to supervise the brethren and to minister to their souls.

For if no one can learn the art of healing on his own without the guidance of an experienced physician, there is even less possibility to learn the art of instructing souls without the proper training. Then the starets again recalls the history of his community and sets forth the basic principles upon which it rests. These are the following:

(1) *Poverty.* Total self-imposed poverty according to the monastic model, i.e. that none of the brethren have their own particular possessions until their death—neither money nor any other object, neither movable nor immovable possessions, to the most insignificant objects. Let everything necessary for life be considered common to all.

(2) *Obedience.* Each of the brethren in our assembly submits with his soul and body voluntarily to the virtuous yoke of obedience, which was established by the Holy Scriptures and the Holy Fathers, in order not to be self-willed and arbitrary and not to have, in anything, one's own will and reasoning. Instead, they should be subordinate and submissive to everything that is according to God and beneficial to the soul till their very death, and should not perform any action, even

if it be good in their opinion, without the knowledge and blessing of the starets.

(3) *Confession*. All the brethren should have confession as often as possible, and beginners should certainly do so on a daily basis. Each of them should reveal to his confessor all the secrets of his heart without concealing anything, for without private confession there is no possibility of obtaining the correction of one's soul and instructions for God's way.

(4) *Remaining with the brethren until death*. This is necessary so that all the brethren would, according to their promise made to God and to the eternal and secure bond of divine love, remain until their death with the assembly of brethren gathered in Christ's name. As he endures all the constraints of his life for the sake of the kingdom of God and valiantly suffers also all temptations and abuse, through which, as gold in flames, the monk's humility becomes purified, he reproaches himself in his heart and considers himself blameworthy in everything. And as a purchased slave, according to his strength, both of body and soul, with all diligence, much humility, and fear of God, he should be prepared for any type of service assigned to him, as is serving Christ's brethren and Christ himself.

(4) The reading of the Holy Scriptures and the teachings of the Fathers.

(5) Observance of the holy fasts and the rule of the Church, as well as of the cells.

(6) Ministering to the sick, the feeble, and the old within the assembly of the brethren and to those for whom there is no room in the infirmary.

(7) The fulfillment of monastery duties and assignments while observing God's commandments, so that love toward one's neighbor would not be destroyed, and the satisfaction of all housekeeping needs through one's own labor in one's own workshop.

The starets bequeathed these basic elements of his community, as well as his commandments, to his brotherhood in writing, which is witnessed to by his successor and disciple, the Starets Sofronii.

Little by little the monastery life at Sekul took its orderly and peaceful course. The same order of life was established at Sekul as had been at Dragomirna. During winter the starets would gather everyone in the refectory, read aloud patristic books, and teach the observance of God's commandments, obedience, humility, and fear of God. Seeing the brethren listening to him readily and making progress in their spiritual lives, the starets would rejoice and give thanks to God, who had given them this quiet and secluded place. The crowded conditions at the monastery and the poverty of life did not trouble him, for since his earliest days he had sought these things for the sake of Christ. What was more burdensome was that the church turned out to be small and crowded for the number of brethren, while the number of those wishing to live with the starets kept increasing, and the starets could not find it in his power to refuse to receive them.

The literary activity of the starets did not cease at Sekul either. His translation activity in particular began developing here. The establishment of a school for teaching Greek to novices was proposed, with the goal of attracting them to the work of translating and correcting patristic books, while for the time being the starets was sending the ablest students to Bucharest to study Greek there.

However, the starets' situation was unexpectedly changed. The starets himself speaks of this circumstance in a letter sent through the spiritual mentor Iakinf to his disciples Amvrosii, Afanasii, and Feofan, who were living in Russia at the Florishchen Hermitage in the Vladimir Province. The following took place. In the spring of 1779 the Moldo-Walachian governor Konstantin Muruzi sent to Sekul a certain quantity of supplies and wrote a letter himself to the starets asking to be informed of all the monastery's needs, promising his help. The starets responded with a letter of thanks and asked him to be allowed 500 levas to convert four large cells into workshops for tailoring, shoemaking, weaving, and for studying Greek with the young monks. The prince, interested in the starets' monastery, informed his closest boyars of this request: "Of course," they answered, "it is not difficult to fulfill the starets' request, but it would not do much good, since he lives in a monastery that is much too inadequate for such a significant brotherhood. The Sekul Monastery is crowded, the church there is small, and the road to it is rocky and difficult, going along the bottom of a deep ravine which fills up with water during rains, which makes the delivery of necessary items very difficult." Then the prince said: "I would like to make the starets more comfortable. Is there no monastery to be found in this country where the starets and his brotherhood could be better situated?" The boyars answered, "In our whole country there is no larger and more accessible monastery than Niamets, which is located a very short distance from Sekul." The prince was overjoyed and decided to write a letter immediately to Metropolitan Gavriil, asking his permission to move Starets Paisii to Niamets, where there was a large monastery. The metropolitan agreed, and the prince immediately sent a letter to Paisii, offering him to move together with the brethren to the Niamets Monastery. The starets received this offer in June 1779 and was again saddened.

The move to Niamets appeared to him, as well as to his closest assistants, extremely undesirable for many reasons. In the first place, he would have to leave a quiet and secluded monastery and go to a wealthy, large, and noisy monastery that was frequented by numerous worshippers. In the second place, the starets realized that by his move to Niamets he would inconvenience and upset the brethren there. In the third place, acknowledging his old age and fraility, the starets was wary of new cares and concerns which were inevitably connected with the move to the populated monastery and with the unification under a single direction of three diverse groups of monks, from Niamets, Sekul, and his own previous one. With the large number of brethren he foresaw the difficulty of his usual winter gathering of the brethren for the reading and discussion of patristic books. Finally, he was also wary that the numerous secular visitors at the monastery would bring the affairs of the world both into the monks' cells and into their very souls, and would hinder him in holding frank discussions with the brethren on various issues and inadequacies of monastery life. All this disturbed the starets deeply. He began grieving and lost his spiritual peace.

Finally, he decided to send a letter to the prince declining to move to Niamets. He pleaded with the prince not to insist upon the move to the Niamets Monastery and not to take away their peaceful and silent existence at Sekul. He described the spiritual harm which awaited the brethren at the new place, the dissolution of the established way of life at Sekul, and the destruction and perturbation of the Niamets brotherhood, capable of bringing about resentment and irreconcilable enmity, which would be fatal to both parties. He sent to the prince with this letter the senior Moldavian-speaking confessor, the reverential Irinarkh, who also knew Greek, gave him another confessor to keep him company, and began anxiously awaiting the response to his letter. Meanwhile, in July there came to see him from Niamets the superiors of the monastery, who had already heard of the forthcoming move of the starets and his brethren to their place. With tears they started begging the starets not to hurt them or upset their way of life, in which they had lived from their youth, in their old age, so that they would not have to bemoan their troubles before him till the end of their days. These complaints brought about a painful reaction in the starets' heart. He broke into tears, and, showing the prince's letter to the Niamets superiors, said: "You see, holy fathers, herein lies the source of the perturbation and grief, both yours and mine. But let Christ convince you that it never even occurred to me to commit any coercion over you and bring sorrow to your souls. You know that neither did we obtain Sekul through coercion, but because the superior who was there at the time, seeing our unhappy situation at Dragomirna, called us there himself out of his love for us. Do you really think that I would dare to commit an evil deed against you? With what eyes would I be looking at your faces, having hurt you in this way? How would I be able to approach God's Altar and partake of the Holy Sacrament, knowing that there are those who weep and cry out to God against me for my coercion? Let this not come to pass! I have already written to the prince and will again ask him to let both you and me remain undisturbed in our monasteries. For here, through God's grace, we have a profound peace." Placated and calmed by the starets' words, the Niamets superiors returned to their monastery.

In the meantime the starets' envoys came to the prince and handed him Starets Paisii's letter. When the letter had been read the monks explained all their circumstances in greater detail to the prince and begged him to leave the starets and his brethren at Sekul and not to disturb and upset their spiritual life. However, the prince did not heed them. He ordered a new letter to the starets to be prepared and made in it the following personal addition: "We are leaving this monastery at your disposal not only for the confirmation of your brotherhood, but also so that the order of your brotherhood would serve as an example to the other monasteries. Therefore, be obedient and go to Niamets, perturbed by nothing."

On Friday, August 9 the envoys returned with the prince's letter to their monastery. When the starets opened the letter and saw in it the words, "be obedient and go to Niamets," he broke into tears and his soul was overtaken by boundless sadness to such a degree that he could neither eat, drink, nor sleep, and his body was totally exhausted. All of the brethren were fearful, grievous, and anxious, lest the starets might die from boundless sorrow. In another of his letters Starets Paisii describes with what anxiety he awaited the return of the confessor Irinarkh from the prince, praying to God day and night for the fulfillment of his desire to remain at the same location. But Irinarkh arrived, and to the starets' question: "What has God sent us?" answered, giving the letter to the starets: "You will find out when you read it," and left the cell. At night, when it was dark and quiet, the starets started reading the prince's response, and after having read it, fell into total despair. He was being told not only to move to Niamets, but to move for the purpose of being an example to other monasteries. "Who am I," thought the starets, "to accept such a view of my unworthiness? I am weak and infirmed, almost dead both in soul and body. I cannot direct my own soul along the way of God's commandments, for I have accepted responsibility for the souls of the brethren gathered around me, and now an even heavier burden is being imposed upon me. Oh, my soul is in distress." The starets wept through the whole night. In the morning the older confessors and monks came to him and started tearfully begging him to cease his boundless sorrow and fortify himself with food. They said: "What benefit shall we have if you die before your time, and we shall remain alone without you? What will we do then?" The starets, seeing how much his spiritual children were grieving and weeping, remained silent for a while, and turning his spiritual gaze toward God, sighed heavily, wept bitterly, and said: "We are being crowded in, brethren, from all sides." Then, after getting up from the bed, he made the sign of the cross, bowed to the icon of the Mother of God, and said: "The Scriptures say: 'Every word may be confirmed by the evidence of two or three witnesses' (Matt. 18:16). If this is what you, brothers, say, then let God's will be done! Let us then go unwillingly." After this he fortified himself a little with food, but could not sleep. He then called three confessors and several monks and bade them to go with the prince's letter to the Niamets Monastery, gather together the whole leadership and all the brethren, read the prince's letter, and prepare cells for him and other brethren, whom he decided to take along to Niamets for the first time. The messengers did as ordered and returned to Sekul.

The starets, meanwhile, with the help of the senior brethren, decided which of the brethren were to move to Niamets and which forms of obedience would be assigned to them, and who would remain at Sekul. He left the direction of the Sekul Monastery to Ilarion, one of the confessors. After this he ordered that the bell be rung to gather the brethren in the church, came there himself, prayed with tears to God, and after announcing the prince's will to the brethren, gave his blessing to those remaining there, and having comforted them by saying that each one of them can always come to see him in any sorrow and spiritual or bodily need, left the church and embarked upon his journey. Since he was too weak to walk, a one-horse carriage was prepared for him, while the brethren, surrounding his carriage like bees, walked alongside, listening to his last instructions. The ill and the aged, having come out to him from the infirmary, wept for not being able to accom-

pany him, while the others spent over an hour in seeing him
off and returned to the monastery only upon his insistence,
when he reminded them of the forthcoming vigil. Some accompanied him all the way to Niamets, where they arrived on
the eve of the feast of the Dormition of the Holy Virgin, on
a Wednesday.

When the starets and the brethren approached the Niamets
Monastery all the bells started ringing and all of the Niamets
brethren came out of the monastery gates to meet the starets.
At their head there were three priests in felonia, one of them
carrying the Holy Gospel and the others carrying holy crosses.
Two deacons in robes held censers. The starets venerated the
Gospel and the crosses and entered the monastery, preceded
by the priests and deacons and accompanied by the brethren
of both monasteries singing the Canon to the Theotokos. Upon
entering the church, the starets venerated the icons and prayed
with particular zeal before the wonderworking icon of the
Mother of God, placing himself and his brethren under her
intercession, custody, protection, and care, and setting on her
all his hope for God. Incidentally, in his letter to the prince,
the starets reveals an early incident in his life—namely, that
before he had appeared at Mount Athos, in his youth, the
starets came to Niamets to venerate the wonderworking icon
of the Mother of God and had the honor of holding this holy
icon in his sinful hands three times. From that time on he felt
a great love for this holy spot, to which later, through God's
inscrutable ways, he was to move with his assembly.

After the starets had venerated the icons, two leaders of
the Niamets brotherhood, Ioasaf and Varlaam, hegumen and
prohegumen, gave the hegumen's place to the starets. When
the church's troparion and kondakion had been sung and the
litany and Dismissal Prayer had been read, the starets tearfully
told those who had gathered that he came to them not of
his own accord but by the decision and order of the prince and
the metropolitan, and asked everyone to maintain mutual
peace and mutual love. From the church the starets proceeded
to the cell which had been prepared for him and rested a little.
For the brethren who had arrived with him, fifteen cells had
been set aside, in which they settled under very crowded con-

ditions with several people to a cell. Only the confessors, due to the nature of their duties, were allotted individual cells. In spite of his great weariness, the starets was not able to fall asleep for a long time because of his great sorrow, although he had already remained sleepless for five days. At the beginning of the all-night Vigil he came to the church with great difficulty and heard the divine service while sitting, praying to the Most-pure Theotokos that she would comfort his soul, expel the darkness and sorrow which had enveloped it, and send him gratifying sleep. And when vespers had already ended, matins had begun, and the Gospel had been read, the desired sleep started coming to the starets. The starets went to his cell and climbed into bed, but fell asleep only at the break of dawn and slept sweetly for two hours. Upon awakening he felt relief in his head, a certain strength in his whole body, and the absence of any sorrow in his heart. When the Liturgy and the Moleben to the Mother of God had finished, everyone went to the meal with the festal icon, singing the troparion of the feast, and after the meal, upon returning to the church, they went to their cells. The starets invited the former heads of the monastery to his cell and spoke with them privately in a brotherly manner, promising to leave them at peace and not to oppress them in any way. And having reconciled themselves to all that had taken place, they took the skhema after a little while, and having lived a few years more, departed to the Lord. Only a few of the Niamets brethren left the monastery, while the rest joined the brotherhood, one assembly was formed out of two, and total mutual love and unanimity were established. The starets wrote to the prince describing his reception at Niamets and the unification of the two brotherhoods, and asked for help in setting up new cells. The prince thanked the starets for his obedience and promised to give them help both in the setting up of cells and in all their other needs.

Thus occurred the move of Starets Paisii with his brethren from Sekul to the Niamets Monastery. As previously, the Sekul Monastery remained under his direction, and the same order of life was established at both monasteries. The Sekul brethren often came to visit the starets, and once a year the starets would spend several days at Sekul. Here is how he describes these journeys in a letter to the same monks Amvrosii, Afanasii, and Feofan: "At around the Leave-taking of Dormition, when everything is ready for my departure, the brethren are called to gather at the church by the bell, and they enter singing 'It is Truly Meet.' After having venerated the icons and hearing the Litany and Dismissal Prayer, I am given a special place to sit because of my infirmity and start instructing the brethren both in Slavonic and Moldavian, asking them to pray for my successful journey, to labor in the fulfilment of God's commandments, and to preserve among themselves Christ's peace and every monastic propriety and reverence. After this I leave the church accompanied by the brethren, and having bestowed my blessing upon them, leave for Sekul. As I approach the monastery the confessor Dosifei, along with the ill and aged brethren, comes out to meet me, and steps aside having accepted my blessing. As I proceed further, the confessor Ilarion with all the brethren come out to meet me outside the monastery gates. Having given them my blessing, I enter the monastery accompanied by all the brethren. After performing everything according to the prescribed order, I go to my cell, where I live till the Feast of the Beheading of St. John the Baptist, the feast day of the Church. After the feast day, about two days before my departure from there, the brethren gather in the refectory after Compline. I give them my last instructions, one day in Slavonic, and the other in Moldavian. On the day of my departure from Sekul the farewells follow the usual course. Upon my arrival at Niamets I am greeted in the usual manner. As I leave the church for my cell, two monks who have looked after my cell during my absence greet me and accept my blessings. I enter my cell, thanking God for my safe return." At the end of the letter the starets adds: "The confessor Iakinf will inform you of our other matters—the construction of new cells around the monastery, the transfer of all of the Dragomirna brethren and a sizeable number from Sekul to this monastery, etc." During his stay at Sekul, the starets would receive brethren, who could freely come to him at any time and tell him of both their spiritual and bodily needs, while the starets would say to them: "If any one of you has a need, and grieves and complains about it, but does not come to me and inform me of it, then I am not answerable before God for such grief." To those in the infirmary who could not come to the starets themselves, he would send his blessings and all necessities through Father Dosifei, the head of the infirmary, who treated the patients with such love and care, that one could often observe him sitting all night at their bedsides and comforting them by giving them hope for their recovery and saying other heartening words.

It is at Niamets that the most difficult, but also the most fruitful, period of Starets Paisii's life and activity begins. The number of brethren who united around him in the common spirit of non-acquisitiveness, obedience, and love for God, their starets, and each other, grew here to 700 and more. Word of their exalted way of life and of their wise starets spread far throughout the whole Orthodox East. The starets had an extensive correspondence and many dealings with numerous spiritual figures not only in Moldavia, but also on Mount Athos, in Constantinople, in Russia, and in other places. Each traveling monk, each pilgrim, considered it his duty to visit the glorious Niamets Lavra, see its famous starets, and observe its strict communal rule and the splendor of the monastery services, in order to tell of all in their homelands and monasteries. During this period the starets' literary activity reached its greatest flowering. No longer was he working on the correction and translation of patristic books only by himself and among the circle of just a few friends, he also established a whole school for correctors and translators, and established, on a large scale, the copying of books being corrected and translated. Thus, he not only filled up the monastery library with his numerous manuscripts, but distributed them in a great number of copies far beyond the confines of his monastery, and especially among the monasteries and cells of the vast Russian land. He managed to raise within Russian monasticism the level of interest toward literary activities, the reading and copying of patristic books, and spiritual discussions, while making his Niamets Lavra the center and guiding light of Orthodox monasticism and a school of ascetical living and spiritual enlightenment for the Orthodox East. The Niamets Monastery served as a training ground for many Moldo-Walachian and Russian monks who later became disseminators of the Orthodox starets tradition and monastic communities according to the statutes of Paisii's Brotherhood in many monasteries.

As we commence our description of this period in Starets Paisii's life, let us first say a few words about the Niamets Monastery. According to His Eminence, the Bishop Arsenii, the Niamets Monastery has the same importance in Moldavia as does the Holy Trinity-St. Sergius Lavra of the Kievo-Pechersk Lavra in Russia. For many centuries it was the center of Ortho-dox enlightenment in Moldavia, having trained within its walls many Moldavian holy bishops and metropolitans who selflessly defended their native Orthodox Faith. It was a great school of moral life for the Orthodox people, offering in its monks examples of spiritual feats and devotion to faith. In the years of severe national ordeals, in the years of civil war between the princedoms of Moldavia and Walachia during the frequent wars with Turks, Poles, and Hungarians, and during hunger, fire, and other national calamities, Or-thodox Moldavia would gravitate toward it and find here material and spiritual support.

The monastery is situated in an exceedingly scenic area. At the point where the small mountain river Niamtsul bursts out into the expanse from the Carpathian gorges running between tall hills covered with an ageless coniferous forest, shine the walls and buildings of this monastery. With it are connected the best pages of Moldavian-Slavic culture and literature of the princedoms along the Danube. The monastery was established in the latter part of the fourteenth century. At that time three monks, Sofronii, Semen, and Siluan, came with their pupils to Moldavia, where Ioasaf was metropolitan. They came from Tisman and were pupils of St. Nikodim the Sanctified. The Moldavian governor, in most likelihood Petr Mushat the Warrior, built for them a small church in honor of the Ascension. The first document indicating the monastery's existence dates from 1407 when the monastery gained posses-sion of some villages, and together with the Bystritsa Monas-tery was ruled by a certain hegumen Domitian. The monastery kept expanding and prospering thanks to the generous contributions of the Moldavian governors, hierarchs, and other individuals. The history of the first years of the monastery's existence is also connected with the name of the famous preacher, the Metropolitan Gregory Tsamblak, who upon his arrival in Moldavia, supervised this monastery until approximately 1420. The monastery acquired its name, as did many areas around it, most probably from the citadel built not far from there by German crusader knights in the twelfth and thirteenth centuries. The ruins of the fortress still stand on a high cliff not far from Niamets.

The present Church of the Ascension was built in 1497 by the governor Stefan the Great, a fact to which the sign over the entrance to the church bears witness. In the early eighteenth century the superior at Niamets was the Hieromonk Pakhomii. Upon hearing of the famous Russian ascetic, St. Dimitrii of Rostov, he resigned as superior in 1704 and went to Russia to see St. Dimitrii and to venerate the holy men of Pechersk. He had the honor of speaking with St. Dimitrii a number of times, received from him a book written by his own hand, and returned to Niamets. After this he withdrew with a few monks to a barren spot, which is now the spot of the Skete of the Protection (a one hour's walk from the Niamets Monastery) and devoted himself to the feat of prayer. In early 1707 he was summoned from his solitude and was consecrated bishop of Romania. After ruling the diocese for seven years he again withdrew to the Protection Skete, and three years later he left to the Kievo-Pechersk Lavra, where he died in 1724. Shortly before his death he sent his will to the Protection Skete (which he had founded), incidentally including in it the statute of the skete. Thus, in the beginning of the eighteenth century there already existed vital contact between the Niamets Monastery and the Russian Orthodox Church, nor was this contact broken subsequently.

One of the churches houses a Holy Shroud of exquisite work, sewn in gold and pearl on crimson velvet. An embroidered inscription runs around this shroud saying that this shroud was donated to the church of the Niamets Monastery by Sister Mariia in 1741. According to tradition Sister Mariia

was the Grand Duchess Mariia Petrovna, daughter of Emperor
Peter the Great, who became a nun in one of the convents in
Moldavia. In the sacristy of the monastery there is a large
Russian Gospel, which two deacons would carry out for the
entrances. This Gospel was sent to the monastery from
St. Petersburg as a gift in 1764. In 1849 Emperor Nicholas I
gave the monastery ten complete sets of priestly vestments
out of fine parchment and money to build an infirmary. Em-
peror Nicholas II donated to the monasteries a full set of
priestly and diaconal vestments. The main holy object of the
Niamets Monastery is the ancient wonderworking icon of the
Mother of God. It is unknown when this icon was painted.
It was given by the Greek Emperor John Paleologus to the
Moldavian governor John the Kind, who in turn gave it to
the Niamets Monastery at the beginning of the fifteenth
century.

Upon settling at Niamets Starets Paisii started establishing
his usual order of monastic life here as well. First of all he
turned his attention to the order of services and prescribed
that it be performed as it had been in his brotherhood. Reading
and chanting were performed in two languages, Moldavian
and Slavonic. During matins, between the kathismata, two
exhortations were read, one in Slavonic and the other in Russian or Moldavian. During the Week of Praises the Akathist
to the Mother of God was read in Slavonic, Moldavian, and
Greek. Close contact with the Russian Church was maintained
in everything. The venerable Antonii and Feodosii of Pechersk
were commemorated in the dismissal prayers. Every September 21 a service was held to the Holy Bishop Dimitrii of Rostov, May 3 was the commemoration of the Venerable Feodosii
of Pechersk, July 10—of the Venerable Antonii, July 11—of
the Holy Princess Olga, and July 15—of Holy Prince Vladimir.

With the prince's help the starets added an infirmary and
hostels to the monastery and increased the number of cells
significantly. Care for the sick, the aged, and travelers concerned the starets in particular, for they would all come to
him and plead tearfully that he give them shelter at the monastery for the sake of Christ. The starets would place those who
needed it in the infirmary and would order Brother Onorii,

who was assigned the same task here as he had performed at Dragomirna, to give them all possible care and rest, and to show unceasing concern for them. He demanded that all infirmary workers serve the patients as they would the Lord, change the linen and wash the patients' hair weekly, clean their clothing, beds, and sheets from insects, and air out their clothing and hang it out in the sun as often as possible in the summer. The starets also demanded that impeccable cleanliness be observed within the infirmary and incense or some other sweet-smelling substance be burned in it daily. He would also order that more nourishing meals and the best bread and wine be given to the patients. And everyone was satisfied and tearfully thanked the starets for his concern. Traveling monks who dropped into the monastery could rest there as long as they wished—a week, two weeks, or a month, and nobody ever said a word of reproach to them. Some would ask the starets to allow them to spend the winter at the monastery, and he would grant them permission to do so. When summer would approach and they would proceed with their journey he would supply them abundantly with all the necessities for the road and would dismiss them in peace. The starets would also receive laymen suffering from various illnesses or being tormented by various spirits and having no place to lay their heads, and would feed them in a special infirmary from the common table. They would live there as long as they wished, with some remaining to their very deaths.

Ascension, the principal name day of the church, was celebrated with particular solemnity at Niamets. Even in earlier days Niamets had been a gathering place for great multitudes of both men and women of various callings, of both noble and simple origins, and who were both rich and poor. They came not only from Moldavia and Walachia, but from other lands as well, wishing to venerate the miraculous icon of the Most Holy Theotokos, and under the starets the number of worshippers grew even more. Paisii would try to accomodate all of them as well as he could. During the four days he would not have a moment to himself, with his cell doors open from morning till night. Anyone wishing to see him, be he rich or poor, could enter freely. He would receive everyone lovingly, thank them for taking upon themselves the task of the journey, and after blessing them, would send them off to the guest house or to other cells prepared for them. Before the feast the starets would appoint some of the more reverent and God-fearing brethren to look after the weaker ones, going through the monastery day and night, in order to avoid any temptation. In carrying out his wishes, the brethren would protect each other. At the conclusion of the feast everyone would thank Christ God and His Pure Mother, who had vouchsafed them to celebrate this holy feast of the Lord peacefully, successfully and joyfully.

The move from one monastery to another, and the merging of the starets' original pupils whom he had collected back at Mount Athos and Dragomirna with the communities at other monasteries could not take place without adverse effects on the monastery's internal life. According to the starets himself, the internal life of the community at Niamets was already not attaining the level at which it stood at Dragomirna. But the starets, as before, kept a close and solicitous watch over the life of the community. In church he would inspect them himself so that they would stand in a dignified manner with fear and trembling and would perform all of the prescribed prostrations. One day the starets noticed a novice walking around the monastery waving his arms and looking to and fro. The starets summoned his confessor and said; "Is this how you exhort your pupils? They are committing excesses and tempt the brethren." As punishment he imposed upon both of them the following rule: three days of prostrations in the refectory, so that others would learn not to commit excesses. In spite of all of the starets' efforts however, he was barely able to overcome those adverse influences which had a deteriorating effect upon the community. The starets' biographer asserts that by the end of his life "the level of our spiritual life declined irretrievably from its original unanimous, peaceful, and loving level originally found at Sekul and Dragomirna, the reasons for this being gossip, excess, concern with oneself, the abandonment of the reading of the holy writ and the Fathers, and discontinued self-scrutiny." The starets, who had foreseen all this, would often weep and forewarn the brethren. He would entreat everyone not to abandon the attentive reading of the Fathers, to hold fast to the narrow path of the Gospel, and to avoid a carefree pseudo-monastic peace-loving way of life. Pointing out other reasons for the slackening of community life, the starets' biographer says: "A tree orchard dies if there is too much transplanting, and likewise the spiritual orchard of our assembly has suffered from the moves and changes of our monasteries." At Dragomirna and Sekul the starets had conducted community lessons each evening, but these were stopped at Niamets, making the use of more books necessary. And the starets spent more time here on translations and corrections. Furthermore, visits by distinguished persons of both genders did much harm to the brethren. One peripatetic monk asked Paisii: "Father, how does your life here compare to life at Dragomirna?" The starets replied, "It gets worse with each year, and it is impossible to hold it at one level in spite of my efforts. This is due to the indiscriminate admittance of women and the abandonment of the assembly's teaching."

Of course, the decline in the level of spiritual life in Paisii's community was apparent only to the starets and his closest helpers, who evaluated the community's condition from the viewpoint of ideal monasticism. For an outside observer, even a monk and an ascetic, the life of the community appeared in a totally different light, as can be seen from the story of the Solovetsk hermit Feofan, who visited the Niamets Monastery when it was under Paisii. This Feofan came from a family of Ukrainian landowners. Orphaned at the age of twelve, he started managing his own land at sixteen. One day, as he was working in the fields, the divine light illuminated his soul, and his heart was filled with a feeling of particular tenderness. He unhitched his oxen, left his plough and land, and seized by love for Christ, set off for the holy places. He was admitted to the Pechersk Lavra in Kiev as a novice, where he spent seventeen years in various labors and was finally assigned to serve the ascetic Dosifei, who had been living as a recluse for over twenty years. He neither went out of his cell nor allowed anyone to enter. Those wishing to be blessed and instructed by him could converse with him through his cell window. His special gift of speech was combined with discernment—he could lay open hidden sins and encourage repentance, as well as warn against future calamities and temptations. It was this ascetic who taught the monastic life to Feofan, who soon developed a strong desire to visit the holy places marked by the events of Jesus Christ's earthly life. Feofan asked his starets to give him his blessing for this journey, but the starets replied, "You are going neither to Jerusalem nor to the Holy Mount. You will eventually be going elsewhere, but for now go to Moldavia, as this will benefit you." And the starets commanded Feofan to go to Podol (the lower part of Kiev), where he would find two Moldavian monks and bring them to the starets. Feofan went to Podol and did indeed find two Moldavian monks there. One of them was Sofronii, Paisii's friend and pupil who followed him as superior of the Niamets Monastery. Having completed a task given him by Paisii, Sofronii was already preparing for the return voyage when Feofan appeared to him and invited him to see the recluse. Dosifei asked Sofronii and his companion to take Feofan along with them to Moldavia. The Moldavian monks readily agreed to this, and Feofan came along with them, doing various favors for them during the journey. This did not turn out to be an easy journey for Feofan, due to harrassment by Turks and various privations they had to endure along the way, and as a result he even regretted that he had left Kiev. But it was not in vain that the wise starets sent him to Moldavia. When the travelers were approaching the Niamets Monastery Paisii himself met them and greeted them with the following words: "My child Feofan, your voyage to us wretched ones has not been in vain. God will count all your steps and will prepare his reward for you." Having become a recipient of the starets' kindness, Feofan first stayed at Niamets, later going to other Moldavian monasteries to look over their sites and to study monastic statutes and the conventions and customs of monastic life. Here is what he tells about the life of the Niamets monks. Their lack of acquisitiveness was complete—the cells contained nothing except for icons, books, and handcraft tools. The monks were particularly humble, and avoided pride and vanity. They did not know hatred and mutual offense, and if anyone happened to offend another because of carelessness or anger, he hurried to be reconciled with him. Whoever refused to forgive a brother who had sinned was expelled from the monastery. The monks' gait was humble, and upon encountering each other they exchanged bows. In church each stood in his assigned spot. Vain speech was forbidden not only in church, but everywhere else, both within the monastery and outside. There were 700 monks living with Father Paisii at the time, and when a hundred or a hundred fifty would gather for obedience, one of them would read out of a book or relate some edifying story. And if anyone started an unnecessary conversation, he was stopped immediately. Inside the cells some wrote books, others bound them, others spun thread, and still others sewed *klobuks* and *kamilavkas*, knitted beads, moved thread for cassocks and vestments for the monks, made spoons and crosses, and did various other handcrafts. Everyone was under the tutelage of spiritual fathers and instructors, and whoever would come to them would confess his sins and especially thoughts—the beginning of all evil deeds. And this was done twice a day—in the mornings they would announce what they had committed at night, while in the evenings they would tell about what they had done, said, or thought during the day, and all this was revealed in humility, without shame or guile. Without the spiritual father's blessing no one dared even to eat any piece of fruit, of which there are many in that land.

Feofan enjoyed life at Niamets to such a degree that he asked Paisii to leave him at his monastery for good, but the starets said: "Go to Russia and serve your starets a little longer, as he will soon depart to the Lord. Upon his blessing go save yourself wherever he directs you." Feofan parted with Niamets sadly. Paisii's parting words to him were: "My child, may God and the Most Pure One preserve you on any route. It is my belief that God will not let you be tempted beyond measure and will grant to you the lot of his chosen ones through the prayers of our Venerable Fathers Antonii and Feodosii, the Wonderworkers of Pechersk. May our meekness be God's blessing unto you. Give thanks to your pious starets and do not forget our poverty." Equipped with all the necessities for his journey, Feofan left Niamets and re-

turned safely to Kiev. Feofan also related the following interesting story. On his return trip from Moldavia, whenever he
would be detained by Turks asking him who he was and
where he was coming from, all he had to do was to show a
written pass from Paisii and the Turks would shout, waving
their arms: "Oh, Paisii, gaida, gaida, gaida,"—i.e. go ahead.
Seeing this, Feofan was amazed that the blessed starets was
known to the Turks and venerated by them to such an extent.

The same Feofan tells us of the purity of Orthodoxy in
Paisii's community, as well as of the heterogeneity of its population. When he was already living at the Solovetsk Monastery, Feofan was examining one of his pupils and asked him;
"Tell me, how do you put your fingers together to cross yourself?" The man showed him the three-fingered combination
and said, "In the same way, Father, as the Orthodox Church
teaches." Feofan then said: "When I was in the desert, I did
not forbid ignorant people to cross themselves with two fingers,
as long as they would go to church, but you should beware
of followers of the schism. When I lived in Kiev I saw no one
in all of the Ukraine who would cross himself with two fingers. I have also been in Moldavia, at the Niamets Monastery, which had over 700 monks from various lands—Moldavians, Serbs, Bulgarians, Hungarians, Hutsuls, Greeks, Arme-
nians, Jews, Turks, Great Russians, and Ukrainians, and all
of them crossed themselves with three fingers, and there was
not even a hint of crossing with two."

Likewise interesting is the story, related by Papadopulo-
Kerameus, of a noble Greek named Constantine Karaj, who
visited Paisii on Ascension. This Greek had earlier delivered
to Paisii a hermit's manuscript from his father, containing
instructions for monastics, and Father Paisii sent his father
in gratitude a copy of the manuscript written by himself in an
exquisitely beautiful and clear handwriting. The Greek wished
to see the starets himself and to venerate the icon of the Theotokos. He describes his journey with his wife from Pashkani
to the Niamets Monastery, delights in the scenery, and tells
of the welcome accorded him at Niamets. They were greeted
with ringing bells, which is an honor granted only to hospo-
dars and the most noble boyars. The starets himself, along

with fifty brethren in kamilavkas and cassocks met him at the holy gates. "We," he says, "hurried to leave the carriage, and approaching the starets, kissed his hand. Then we went into the church and venerated the icons to the singing of prayers, and then went to the starets' cell. For the first time in my life I saw with my own eyes an incarnate and unhypocritical holiness. I was struck by his face, which was radiant and pale, without a drop of blood, by his large white beard, shining like silver, and by the unusual cleanliness of his clothing and all his furnishings. His speech was gentle and completely sincere, and he had the semblance of a person who had totally renounced his body." After giving a brief biography of the starets and a description of his monastery statute, the Greek describes his visit to the various sections of the monastery. In one of the rooms he saw a great many shirts and other clothing, cassoks, and kamilavkas, all folded in attractive rows. Once a week the monks would come in to receive their clean clothes while special observers would make sure that dirty clothes would be left behind. He also saw the refectory, where all the brethren would gather together with the celebrant for that day. Fish and oil were served at the meals, and wine was drunk according to the statute. The presiding monk would first say: "To the glory of God," "To the health of the voivode," and finally, "To the health of all Christians." During the meal one of the monks would read from the lives of the saints at the ambo. There were no unnecessary conversations, but rather total silence, great cleanliness, and strict abstention. Four confessors would visit the cells daily and consider each individual case. Then the Greek goes on to tell how, after a rather prolonged stay in the starets' cell, the guests were taken to their assigned room, where they were likewise amazed at the unusual cleanliness and orderliness. Throughout their whole visit during the feast, they and other honored guests were served exquisite food—meat, fowl, chicken, fish, white bread, wine, and sweets. And all who had gathered in the courtyard of the monastery, about three thousand strong, likewise received as much bread, fish, and wine as they needed, with no payment required. After spending two days at the monastery, the travelers returned to Pashkani.

The starets' literary activities took an especially prominent place both in the life of the starets himself and in the community's life. Back in his childhood days he enjoyed reading and copying the Fathers. But at that time he would simply copy them, without questioning the correctness of the written material. At Athos his literary activity consisted of the examination and correction of Slavonic translations according to the oldest Slavonic copies. When this method of correction did not yield satisfactory results, the starets began studying Greek and collecting Greek originals of the Fathers, and already at Dragomirna he proceeded to correct Slavonic books against the Greek originals. Finding this to be unsatisfactory as well, the starets, to the extent that he had mastered Greek and had acquired the necessary reference books, finally undertook his own translation of the Fathers from Greek into Slavonic. At Niamets all of the starets' various activities began operating in a much more comprehensive and organized framework. With the help of specially trained monks, and under the starets' constant supervision, books were copied here, Slavonic books were corrected against the Greek originals, and new translations were made from Greek. The starets himself, in spite of his years and poor health, gave his assistants an example through his inexhaustible activity. Occupied all day with spiritual and housekeeping matters of the monastery, he would spend his nights translating and correcting books. According to his biographer, the starets worked beyond natural human capabilities. If the grace of God had not strengthened him, it would have been impossible for human nature to perform such work. One has only to visualize that the starets' whole right side, all the way to his foot, was so badly covered with sores that he could not even lie on that side. Sitting on his bed all bent over, he would barricade himself with books. Here were various dictionaries, a Greek and Slavonic Bible, Greek and Slavonic grammar books, and the book being translated. There also stood some lighted candles. And the starets, hunched over like a small child ,would write all night, forgetting both his weakness and his sores, and the necessity for rest and sleep. He would become so engrossed in his work, that he would neither hear the monastery bell, nor notice anything taking place around him, nor be able to answer questions directed toward him. In fact, the monk serving him at the time would not allow anyone to see him. When there would be a matter that could not be postponed, the attending monk would have to repeat his words many times to the starets before receiving a response from him. Forced to answer, the starets, with his pain and sighing, would hardly be in any condition to turn his attention from the book, as he would admit himself: "For me," he would say, "there is no harder work than having to answer any question while translating. By the time I turn my mind away from the book, I become covered with perspiration."

Incidentally, we should note that the starets possessed an unusual gift for writing which one rarely encountered in anyone. In his youth, for instance, he transcribed the book of St. Abba Dorofei. As big as it is, he was able to fit it on twenty-four sheets of paper, with each containing seventy lines of writing in the size prescribed for those books. Each letter was as thin as a hair and did not smear, but came out distinct and clean, and the necessary margins were left on the sides, on top, and at the botton. When an amazed pupil asked the starets if he had written that book with a pigeon quill, he replied; "No, with a goose quill."

In 1787 Paisii completed his major literary work — the translation of the ascetic writings of St. Isaac the Syrian from Greek. In his preface to this translation the starets gives a detailed description both of the external circumstances of this work, as well as of the difficulties he encountered while translating and the methods he used to overcome these difficulties. He writes:

In 1786 the Greek manuscript of St. Isaac's book was brought to me from Holy Mount Athos, and those who brought it entreated me to commence translating. The brethren of the monastery were encouraging me to do the same. Conscious of my old age and extreme frailty, as well as the tremendous magnitude of the book, the difficulty of the work, and the uncertainty of my final hour, I kept postponing the fulfillment of this request. But, on the other hand, I realized how God's

providence was granting me to see the Greek manuscript
of St. Isaac's book, which was brought to me for the spe-
cific purpose of translation, and took into account my
successful mastering of Greek and the fact that I had
the necessary references for translating. Sensing a desire
emerging in my heart to undertake the translation of
St. Isaac, and paying heed to the brethren's entreaties,
I started the new translation of St. Isaac's book during
Advent of that year. I based this translation on a printed
Greek book which I had received back at Dragomirna
from Nicephorus Theotoki in Constantinople, and used
the manuscript as a reference. And it was a great help
to me, indeed, without which, in spite of my best efforts,
having only the printed edition, my translation would
have been insufficient, since frequently certain words
found in the Slavonic book are also found in the Greek
manuscript copy, but are absent in the Greek printed
copy. This means that the early Slavonic translators
were using a similar Greek manuscript copy of the
book. Thus, as I translated from the Greek printed
copy, I simultaneously followed the Greek manuscript,
the early Slavonic copy, and the revised Dragomirna
copy word for word, carefully analyzing nouns and
verbs and taking into account, as much as possible, the
characteristics of both Greek and Slavonic. I performed
all this work with great spiritual joy, disregarding my
frailty and illnesses, and in this manner I finished my
translation in 1787.

Describing the translating difficulties he encountered and
the methods by which he overcame them, the starets writes:

Having worked long over the correction and translation of the Fathers, I have noticed that all of the
books in Greek convey the grammatical sense much
more clearly than the Slavonic translations. This is due
to the fact that Greek contains prefixes and suffixes
helping to clarify the grammatical sense of a given
word. Although Slavonic surpasses many languages in

its great beauty and richness of vocabulary, and is the closest of all languages to Greek in its formation of nouns and verbs and in its content and characteristics, it loses much, however, from the absence of these explanatory particles. For although the pronouns *izhe, on, sei*, and *toi* are used in Slavonic instead of the Greek particles, these still cannot be applied with as much accuracy as they are in Greek to all words and cases, except for the vocative, and cannot give the Slavonic translation as clear a sense as we find in the Greek books. Besides, all of the masculine and feminine Greek nouns, be they used with or without particles, are pronounced differently in the nominative and accusative cases, resulting in a clear interpretation of the message, while in Slavonic inanimate masculine nouns ending in a hard or soft sign, and feminine inanimate nouns ending in a soft sign, have the same ending in the nominative and accusative, making the sense of the message more ambiguous. Furthermore, although in Greek and Slavonic all neuter nouns in the nominative, accusative, and vocative cases, both singular and plural, are pronounced the same, many Greek feminine nouns end up being neuter when translated into Slavonic, and as a result acquire the same endings in the nominative and accusative cases, greatly increasing the difficulty of interpreting the message.

Noticing all of this, and wishing that my book and my translations in general would have a clarity more closely approximating the clarity of the Greek books, I noticed also that the books of that most wise and profound language preserve assiduously and with all circumspection the proper spelling of all the words. Thus, although this language has many words which are pronounced the same in both the singular and the plural, it does not content itself with only one pronunciation, but denotes each word with its appropriate spelling. Noticing this, I made it a rule in my translations to preserve the proper spelling most thoroughly in all singular and plural nouns, without bypassing a single one, save out of error or forgetfulness. And I assure my readers, that in my translation, words used in the singular should be understood in the singular without any hesitation, while those used in the plural should be understood in the plural. Because of this my translation achieves greater clarity of the Slavonic message.

In explanation, the starets writes the following:

As mentioned before, Slavonic inanimate masculine nouns ending in the hard or soft sign, and feminine ones ending in the soft sign, have the same ending in the nominative and accusative cases, and if they are not used in conjunction with a verb of the active voice or other modifiers, it is impossible to determine their intended case. Let us consider, for example, *dobrodetel'* —*dobrodetel'*. It is unclear which of these two words is in the nominative case and which is in the accusative. In Greek, thanks to the different endings, there is no such ambiguity.

In order to eliminate this ambiguity in the Slavonic text Paisii places a dot above a word being used in the accusative case: *dobrodetel'* — *dobrodetel'*, or *dobrodetel'* — *dobrodetel'*. The necessity of such a designation becomes particularly clear when certain phrases are examined:

'Dobrodetel' rozhdaet strakh Bozhii,' 'Strakh Bozhii otgoniaet lenost.' These phrases acquire totally different meanings, depending on which word is the subject and which is the direct object. If in the first phrase a dot is placed over the word 'dobrodetel'' [virtue], the meaning of the phrase will be that virtue is generated by the fear of God, and if a dot is placed above 'strakh' [fear], the meaning will be that the fear of God is generated by virtue. The same also occurs in the second phrase, depending on where the dot is placed. If the dot is placed over 'strakh,' the meaning is that the fear of God is driven away by sloth, while if it is over the word 'lenost,' it means that sloth is driven away by the fear of God. Here is another example of employing explanatory dots in another manner: 'If you will keep my commandments I will send you a Counselor, even the Spirit of truth, whom the world cannot receive, and he will teach you all truth.' In Greek 'Counselor' is masculine and 'Spirit' feminine, while in Slavonic both words are masculine. The dots indicate to which words 'whom' and 'he' refer, and without them the Slavonic text would have been ambiguous.

The starets goes on to write:

> In translating this book, as well as in all my other translations, I always employ the so-called literal method of translation, which was used to translate the Holy Scriptures and all Church books into Slavonic. In translating by this method, I maintained the features of both languages as carefully as I could, employing for clarity wherever necessary in the Slavonic, the verbs 'est'.... and 'byvaiu' [forms of 'to be'], and instead of particles the pronouns 'on' ['he], 'toi' ['that'], and 'sei' ['this']. All of this, employed in the appropriate places, gives the translation the necessary clarity. It is also important to know that I render quotations from the Holy Scriptures as they appear in the Greek original, not allowing myself to change them and render them as they appear in the Holy Scriptures, fearing the arrogance of arbitrariness. So that my translation may be precise in every way, I render them as I find them in the Greek book.

It is evident from Paisii's above description with what care he worked on his translations of the Fathers. And it is not surprising that, according to knowledgeable persons, Paisii's translations are valuable not only for purposes of religious edification, but also for research purposes.

Paisii's translations surpass all previous translations of

the Fathers in that in his work he did not limit himself to
only one copy of a book in a particular language, but tried
to obtain copies or printed texts of the book being translated
in various languages and from various periods. He would
then compare them with each other, checking them in order
to determine the most correct rendition, and would include
variant readings in the margins, allowing the reader himself
to be convinced first-hand of the correctness of the rendition
offered by the starets. Such a method of translating the Fathers
into Slavonic had not existed before Paisii's time. The earlier
translations, which had not always been based on Greek
originals but often on Bulgarian, Serbian, Latin, or Polish
translations, frequently featured ambiguity of meaning, forcing Paisii to adopt a more thorough and careful approach to
this work.

N. Popov, one of the researchers of the manuscripts of
Paisii's school, describes Paisii's translation work in his book
Rukopisi Moskovskoi Sinodal'noi (Patriarshei) Biblioteki
(2nd ed., Simonov Collection), and, using the starets' revision of St. John Climacus' book as a basis, says the following:

> The starets translated from the printed Greek copy,
> but he also included additions to the printed text which
> are taken, judging from the comments in the margins,
> from the manuscript copy. Other footnotes suggest that
> the translator had at his disposal not only a Greek or
> Slavonic copy, but a whole series of different copies.
> There are many comments on the margins of the *Ladder*
> testifying to the great amount of work which went into
> the juxtaposition of the Slavonic text with Greek manu-
> scripts and the printed edition. Moreover, it becomes
> apparent that the translator exercised strict selectivity.
> For instance, at one point he adds the following foot-
> note: 'The printed copy contains the following words
> as well (citations follow), while these words are taken
> from the other book. Therefore, I did not include
> these words in the translation, since they are not found
> in other Greek and Slavonic texts.' There are footnotes
> clarifying one or another passage on the basis of cer-

tain passages . . . Before Paisii Velichkovskii we do not encounter such a critical approach to a text in any of our writers.

We have already seen that the starets himself considered it necessary to conduct his translation literally, i.e. by translating from Greek into Slavonic word for word, after having established through comparative analysis the correct version of a book, without changing in any way the Greek word order. Of course, such a method of translation, which does not conform to the requirements of Slavonic and Russian word distribution patterns, does not always make clear and obvious the message of a book's author, and makes it necessary to first rearrange the words in order to discover the meaning of one or another phrase, which undoubtedly makes it difficult to read and understand a book. But on the other hand, this eliminates the translator's arbitrariness in phrase formation, which might cause the meaning of the original to be altered. It must also be noted that the starets possessed great spiritual experience, profound insight, and subtlety of perception, which were illumined and cultivated by his feats of prayer and purity of life. He could therefore penetrate deeply into the meaning of the book he was translating and select the most precise and appropriate words to express the ideas in the original, making his translations, although semantically somewhat cumbersome, precise to the highest degree akin to the spirit of the author being translated, and especially valuable as a result. In precision, expressiveness, power, and profundity of exposition his translations surpass not only previous translations, but also later translations by more learned persons—a fact which even a superficial comparison can confirm.

At Niamets the starets organized the work of copying and translating on a very large scale. He surrounded himself with a sizeable group of assistants, giving them special training for the book trade. He would teach them Greek and then send them to the Bucharest Academy to master it. Some of his assistants would translate the Fathers under his immediate supervision, while others would transcribe them. The work took place either in the cells, or in a common room, or finally,

in the quarters of the starets himself. The demand for manuscripts was very great not only among the brethren of the
Niamets Monastery, but among other monasteries and private
individuals. There was much work for the transcribers. The
manuscripts still bear the names of some of the starets' col-
laborators in the book trade These include his closest assistants
Ilarion, Makarii, and Onorii. Further names mentioned in the
manuscripts include Schema-Monk Afanasii, Confessor Nafa-
nail, Monk Pavel, Scribe Mikhail, Monk Ioannikii, Monk
Sil'van, Scribe Iakinf, Monk Nazarii, Monk Mitrofan, Monk
Kiriak, Deacon Timofei, Monk Gervasii, Hiero-Schema-Monk
Nikolai, Monk Filimon, Filipp, Monk Feofan, Monk Antonii,
Scribe Emmanuil, Hieromonk Ignatii, Scribe Sofronii, Scribe
Spiridon, Scribe Nikodim, Priest Sofronii, Scribe Gerasim,
Monk Sadof, Scribe Ierofei, Ieronim, Scribe Savva, Scribe Ser-
gii, Priest Dosifei, Scribe Serapion, Hierodeacon Kornilii,
Scribe Platon, and others.

Due to the zealous work of this group of trained collaborators, there appeared a large amount of revised translations
of patristic books and very many copies of them. According
to Professor A. I. Iatsimirskii, out of a thousand manuscripts
kept in the Niamets Monastery library, and written at various
times in Moldavian, Greek, Latin, Italian, German, Hebrew,
Arabic, Turkish, Syrian, Bulgarian, Polish, French, and Slavonic, 276 can be placed in Starets Paisii's time, and over 40 were
written by the starets himself. For all that, the Niamets manuscripts amount to a mere portion of all the manuscripts which
were produced by the starets' collaborators and which were
distributed among the monasteries and monastic cells of the
Orthodox East, especially within Russia and among secular
individuals.

Professor A. I. Iatsimirskii enumerates the manuscripts
written with the starets' hand: which include: (1) St. Anthony
the Great—*Counsels on Human Nature*; (2) The Theology
of St. John of Damascus; (3) St. Basil the Great—*Monastic
Rules*, (4) *Homily on Fasting*, (5) *Against Eunomius*; (6)
excerpts taken by Starets Paisii on the procession of the Holy
Spirit, from the works of Gennadios Scholaris, Patriarch Dositheus of Jerusalem, Mark of Ephesus, Athanasius of Alex-

andria, John of Damascus, Patriarch Eulogius of Alexandria, Justinian's *Confessions*, and Patriarch Ephraim of Antioch: (7) excerpts taken by Starets Paisii from the works of John Chrysostom, John of Damascus, St. Philotheus, Patriarch Sophronius, Evagrius Ponticus, Patriarch Germanos of Constantinople, St. Isaiah the Hermit, St. Gregory Palamas, and Maximus the Confessor; (8) the treatises of Gregory of Sinai; (9) St. Gregory Palamas' Letter to Xenia—*On Those Who Keep Silence* and (10) *Letters of Direction*; (11) St. Diadochus, Bishop of Photice—*Chapters on Spiritual Perfection;* (12) St. Dionysius the Areopagite and others on mental prayer; (13) the teachings of Abba Dorotheus, (14) *The Life of St. Gregory of Sinai*, a work by Patriarch Callistos of Constantinople; (15) the exposition of apostolic and patristic canons according to the epitomes of the deacon Alexis and the canonist Aristenus; (16) the ascetical works of St. Isaac of Syria; (17) the teachings of Joseph Vrienius with an appendix containing the letters of Pope John to Archbishop Photius of Constantinople (18) Callistus the Cataphigiote—*On Divine Unity and the Life of Vision*; (19) The Canons for the Twelve Major Feasts in two columns, the left containing their old translation, and the right containing the new; (20) *The Ladder* of St. John of Sinai; (21) the teachings of St. Macarius of Egypt; (22) the moral and ascetical treatises of St. Mark the Faster; (23) St. Mark of Ephesus—*On the Procession of the Holy Spirit, Against the Latins*; (24) the teachings of St. Nicethas Stethatos; (25) the works of St. Peter of Damascus (26) the responses of the Orthodox to Catholic violence (on the Union)—this is the autograph of Starets Paisii's translation from the Greek work, printed in Chalcides in 1775; (27) *Paradise*, by Patriarch Callistus of Constantinople and Ignatius Xanthopoulos; (28) An anthology containing excerpts taken by Starets Paisii from Dionysius the Areopagite's works on baptism, from Maximus the Confessor, from the Apostolic Canons, from Matthew Blastares' *Syntagma*, from the Canons of the Ecumenical Councils, from John Chrysostom, and from Bishop Theophylactes of Bulgaria on baptism; (29) an anthology containing Dionysius the Areopagite's works on baptism, John Chrysostom's and Theodore the Studite's on the same subject, a letter by Dionysius the Areopagite, and Theodoret of Cyrus *On the Seventy Weeks*; (30) An anthology containing the condemnation of Barlaam's and Akyndinus' heresy, selections from Basil of Caesarea and Theodore Studite, edited by the master and logothete Symeon, and the Prayer of Tenderness; (31) an anthology containing the *Synodiakon for the Week of Orthodoxy, On the Seven Ecumenical Councils, On the Annunciation* by Patriarch Germanos, *On the Transfiguration, On The Burial of Christ, On the Dormition, On the Annunciation*, and *On the Nativity of the Theotokos* by John of Damascus and *A Praise to the Holy Theotokos* by Epiphanius of Cyprus; (32) an anthology containing the teaching on prayer of Hesychius, presbyter of Jerusalem, and on human nature by Anthony the Great; (33) *A Light to Those in Darkness*, for Latins converting to Orthodoxy; (34) the sermons of Symeon the New Theologian; (35) a clean copy of the same; (36) Symeon the New Theologian—*To the Apostates*; (37) *On the Priesthood* by Symeon of Thessalonica; (38) the sufferings of the martyr St. Anastasius the New, who suffered in the city of Gelvina; (39) the *Faktikon* of Nikon of the Black Mountain; (40) *Chapters on Sobriety* by St. Philotheus of Sinai; (41) *One Hundred Chapters* by St. Thalassius of Libya with St. Philemon the Hermit's appendix "On Silence"; (42) *Commentary on the Song of Songs* by Theodoret of Cyrus; (43) *Teachings* by Theodore of Edessa; (44) *Antirrhetics* by Theodore the Studite.*

Professor Iatsimirskii also lists the manuscripts written by the starets' pupils by his choice and appointment. But it is impossible for us to enumerate all of them. The writings of certain Church Fathers can be found in these manuscripts in a particularly large number of copies. Such, for instance, are the writings of Theodore of Edessa, Philotheus of Sinai, Symeon the New Theologian, Peter of Damascus, John Climacus, Hesychius of Jerusalem, Isaac of Syria, Abba Dorotheus, Gregory Palamas, Basil the Great, and others. Appar-

---

* When we were at Niamets we were able to see some of these manuscripts of the great starets, written with great clarity and elegance. Fr. S. C.

ently there was an especially great demand for these manuscripts.

Many of these manuscripts are anthologies containing passages from the Fathers on dogmatic, liturgical, moral-ascetical, and canonical questions. The starets himself enjoyed compiling such collections and encouraged his pupils to compile them. According to the starets, it is not enough to limit oneself to reading the Fathers, since during such reading the reader's attention and mind do not always keep sufficient track of the book's content. In order to bring about a better connection of the mind and attention with the content of the book being read, one has to follow the text of the book word by word, and this is best achieved by copying the book. The very slowness of this work allows a fuller and clearer penetration into the sense of the material being copied. In this process the book's content grows more akin to the reader's soul and makes a deeper impression on it. It is not always possible to copy all of a book, nor is this always necessary. Sometimes it is enough to copy out the more significant and interesting passages, so that they would always be at hand, allowing one to reread them or use them for literary work, a letter, or making them known to someone else. A clearer and more comprehensive treatment of a particular topic can be attained by taking excerpts from the various church Fathers, who wrote on the same topics. The result is a theological-ascetical encyclopedia, a dictionary explaining all concepts entering into the sphere of the religio-moral life and world view of the Christian.

This author had possession of several such anthologies of patristic sayings and discussions which came out of Starets Paisii's school. One such collection was written by Archimandrite Moisei, head of the Kozel'sk Optina Pustyn' during his eremitic life in the Roslavl' forests of the Smolensk District. Entitled *On Monastic Feats*, it was compiled between 1812 and 1822 and contains valuable excerpts from the Fathers on internal spiritual life, selected in consecutive systematic order. It did not appear in print and was kept at the Optina Hermitage library before the Revolution. Another anthology was written by Starets Paisii's pupil Schema-monk Afanasii (a former secretary of the Senate). This was the same Afanasii

who brought Paisii's translation of the *Philokalia* to Metropolitan Gavriil of St. Petersburg, and who later lived at the
Svensk Monastery in the Orel diocese, where he died in 1811.
Before his death he entrusted his anthology in 1810 to another
Schema-monk Afanasii, a former captain of a Hussar regiment, who later lived at the Ploshchansk Hermitage of the Orel
diocese, where he died in 1825. Afanasii's collection contains
excerpts from the Fathers on various questions of religio-
moral life, e. g. on fasting, prayer, pride, etc. Numerous excerpts from the Fathers are given on each question, thus giving
them comprehensive treatment. All the other collections have
similar features.

Starets Paisii's literary work at Niamets and other places
was not limited to translating and copying the Fathers. He
led an extensive correspondence with many people on various
questions of spiritual and ecclesiastical life. The next chapter
will introduce us to this correspondence.

Starets Paisii in His Correspondence With Various People on Various Questions of Christian Faith and Life

Starets Paisii's growing fame as a teacher of spiritual life induced many to turn to him with written queries. The starets would respond to these with letters which were sometimes so lengthy, that both their magnitude and style made them look like major essays. In these letters he expressed his ideas and gave advice on various issues of monastic life and church life in general. His letters on questions of monastic life come from all the periods of his life on Mt. Athos and in Moldavia. And some of them, the ones which speak of the starets' literary activity and present his ideas on monasticism, have already been quoted in various places in this book. We shall now quote from his other letters which have not yet appeared in print.

When the starets was at Dragomirna Hieromonk Sofronii, head of a skete called Pubai, came to him to ask for priests to organize a community. The starets wrote to him:

We do not know how to respond to your request for a priest to organize a community. We are ourselves still in the beginning stage, and we need instruction in many matters ourselves. We can only tell you how you could organize a community according to the Holy Scriptures and the rules established by the Fathers. First of all, it is necessary that the head be knowledgeable in the Holy Scriptures, just, capable of teaching his pupils, full of truly unhypocritical love for all, meek, humble, pa-

tient, and free from anger and all the other passions—
love of money, vainglory, gluttony, etc. . . . Pupils, on
their part, should be in their superior's hands as a tool
in the hands of a craftsman or as clay in a potter's hands.
They should do nothing without his blessing and have
no possessions but instead have everything, including
books, a place to sleep, and other things, only upon
his blessing, so that they would be like the dead before
their deaths, without their own will or reasoning. Such
should be the rule of faithful novices. And no matter
where your skete may be located, it should not be under
the authority of another monastery, but should be ruled
independently and in such a way that the brethren
would find salvation through their leader, just as the
latter finds salvation through the Lord. And this order
ought to be confirmed with the blessings of both parties—the state and the local bishop. There should be
no women allowed in your skete. Only in this way can
you, with great difficulty, realize the kind of life which
would bring salvation to you and be pleasing to God.
And if anyone of you wishes to move here, only the Lord
knows if he is able to have such zeal so as to suffer to
the end the need and poverty of our life in things,
food, in the cells, and in everything else. This is all
we can say to you out of our inability. And let our Lord
and God Jesus Christ be your Light and Mind for your
holy salvation and eternal life.

As is known the starets would send his pupils from Sekul
to Bucharest to have them learn Greek. He wrote to two such
pupils, Dorofei and Gerontio, along with a small sum of
money, a letter warning them about the fact that they are
being encouraged to eat meat with the bishops' approval. The
starets writes: "It seems to me that according to the correct
sense and determination of the Holy Orthodox Church even
an angel should not submit in this matter." He turns their attention toward the essay on the eating of meat by monks
of Starets Vasilii, who wrote it not without the grace of the
Divine Spirit.

After the Flood, because of human weakness, the Lord allowed the eating of meat, but the monastic way of life corresponds to life in Paradise, where meat was not eaten. And although at the beginning of monasticism there were deviations from this practice in places, especially in large cities, St. Savva the Sanctified established abstention from meat. And this became the general rule in all lands. Thus it cannot be claimed that abstention from meat is merely a local custom. And this cannot be left to the discretion of each person. Neither is it true that abstention from meat harms the health. And we should not avoid those who eat meat, but should rather please God more than people, and those who tempt you, seeing your steadfastness, will praise you themselves.

The starets reminds his pupils that both the brethren of the monastery and the hermits would be led into temptation and distress, had they learned that they had started eating meat.

In his letter to Russia to the nun Maria Petrovna Protas'eva, head of St. Aleksei Community in Arzamas, the starets explains the importance of obedience, as the basis of monastic life. M. P. Protas'eva, who came from a wealthy family, had a yearning for the monastic life from her youth. Her father, having long resisted the realization of her wish, finally gave in to her pleas and placed her in the Girls' Convent in Kostromna. She was the spiritual daughter of the famous Starets Feodor Ushakov, and with his blessing was chosen by the sisters to head the St. Aleksei Community in Arzamas. Upon the death of Starets Feodor, Maria Petrovna turned to Starets Paisii for guidance. The starets' letter to her begins with a reference to Christ the Savior's words:

'I came to cast fire upon the earth; and would that it were already kindled!' (Lk. 12:49). The holy apostles accepted this divine fire into their hearts, and fired with flaming love toward the Lord, left the world and everything in it and followed Christ. They gave themselves to him both in soul and in body, and renounced both

their will and reasoning, so that they could say with
great joy: 'Lo, we have left everything and followed
you' (Mt. 19:27). They kept this holy obedience to
the Lord in their hearts to the end of their lives, im-
printing it in our memories through their experience of
innumerable temptations, diverse deaths, and the pour-
ing out of their blood unto the last drop. That same divine fire of love and obedience was accepted by the holy
martyrs who joyously suffered various tortures, and the
cruelest deaths for Christ. This same divine flame was
accepted by all our venerable and God-bearing Fathers,
who had fled the world and all that is in the world,
and who dwelt in communities in total obedience and
severance of their wills, labored in deserts, mountains,
and caves, walked the straight and narrow path, participated in Christ's crucifixion, spent their lives in
hunger and thirst, in all kinds of cruel sufferings, and
in unceasing prayer and tears, and kept the Gospel
commandments purely and without defilement in everything. And this same fire of divine grace was accepted
by all the true holy servants of Christ, people of all
ranks and calling, who meticulously observed the soul-
saving Gospel commandments, without the fulfillment
of which salvation is impossible through faith alone.

He thereupon indicated that this same divine fire had inspired the one to whom he was writing his letter as well, and
that for the sake of Christ's love she endured much grief and
persecution. After reviewing certain circumstances of her life
and heeding her request to give her helpful instruction in her
difficult circumstances, the starets then speaks of the meaning
of obedience.

Since you have discovered the fruits of blessed
obedience and the fruits of accursed disobedience
through action and experience, I ought to say to you a
few words about holy obedience also. Divine obedience is so essential for truly pleasing God that it is impossible to serve God without it. This is why holy obedi-

ence was implanted by God in three locations — in heaven, in Paradise it was in its primordial inhabitants, and on earth it was in the holy disciples and apostles of the Lord. And in these three locations there appeared the fruits of both blessed obedience and accursed disobedience. In heaven, the heavenly powers, having observed obedience to God, were made worthy, through the illumination of the Holy Spirit, to abide in him eternally and immutably. As for the devil, although he belonged to the angelic host, he fell from obedience by his own decision and became proud, and was therefore cast out of heaven together with the other powers which had stepped away from God and listened to the wicked advice of the devil. Having lost the divine light, he voluntarily became darkness, an enemy of God and of the salvation of Orthodox Christians. In Paradise, as long as its primordial inhabitants were truly obedient to God, they enjoyed the vision of God and various gifts of the Holy Spirit. When, by their own will, they heeded the devil's advice, fell away from obedience, and, having desired to become equal to God, became proud, then they were condemned to death by God, were cast out of Paradise, and became responsible for the death of the whole human race. And if the Son of God, through his obedience, would not have put an end to Adam's disobedience, the human race could not have retained any hope at all for salvation from death and eternal perdition. Such were the fruits of obedience and disobedience in the primordial human beings. Finally, on earth, Christ the Son of God, having descended from heaven not to do his own will but that of the Father who sent him and to whom he was obedient even unto death on the cross, implanted his divine obedience in his holy disciples and apostles. Those of them who remained in this obedience even unto death brought all the universe through their preaching to the knowledge of God and now rule in heaven together with their Lord and Teacher, Christ. Judas, having fallen away from obedience and having obeyed the devil instead of the Lord, fell into despair, hanged himself, and perished forever both in body and in soul. Thus the fruits of obedience and disobedience appeared on earth also.

Upon this divine obedience, planted on earth by our Lord Jesus Christ himself, the whole monastic order is based, be it cenobitic monasticism, two or three monks living together, or monks living in the desert. All of them generally began their monastic lives with obedience and in this way avoided, with God's help, devilish deception. Whosoever began his monastic life arbitrarily would be plagued by devilish temptations, from which may the Lord deliver us by his grace.

At the letter's conclusion the starets enjoins M. P. Protas'eva to make her life an example to the sisters over whom she had been placed as head.

Guide them to the path of salvation, showing them the example of various good deeds with God's help, through the diligent performance of the Gospel commandments, love for God and neighbor, meekness and humility, the profound peace of Christ always and to everyone, maternal mercy, patience, and long-suffering, tearful prayer, consolation, and impetus for any good deed. Bear all their burdens and infirmities with God's love, while burning with God's love toward them as to sisters and disciples of Christ, guiding them assiduously to true obedience to God in everything, to the cutting off, or rather mortification, of their resistant wills, and to the abandonment of their minds and reasoning. Always consider yourself, in your secret heart and soul, to be dust and ashes before God, the most sinful of all people. Likewise, compel yourself to be an example to your sisters through the observance of the commandments of the holy Fathers, physical labor according to your strength, adherence to the rule of the church as much as you are able, great and lesser reverences, and also the rule of the cell established by the Fathers, which you should perform with the fear of God, prayers, psalmody, and readings. Diligently, with much attention and reflection, read in the Fathers about the prayer performed by the mind in the heart, which is the truest and most pleasing to God of the monastic feats. Should you, with God's help, acquire a correct understanding of this prayer through studying the Fathers, compel yourself to fulfill it, appealing to God for help, and your soul will be aided greatly by it. Compel yourself to judge no one, for the sole righteous Judge is Christ the Lord, who will give to everyone according to his deeds. Condemn only yourself, and you will not be condemned at his second and awesome coming. From your whole heart remit the sins of whoever sins before you, and your Father who is in heaven will remit your sins.

With these words the starets concludes his letter to M. P. Protas'eva.

In the summer of 1793 a petition signed by thirteen monks and all the brethren of the Polianovoronosk Monastery in Moldavia against one of its hieromonks named Feopempt, was given to its head, the hiero-schema monk Agafon. Feopempt was being accused of blasphemy against patristic books which taught the mental prayer of Jesus and of calling those who read these books heretics and free-thinkers, while these books, according to the petitioners, were received from Starets Paisii's monastery. The petitioners demanded that Feopempt prove, in an assembly of brethren, that they were heretics. All the monks gathered in the church and sent for Feopempt, but he did not come. Then they went to his cell and asked why he called them heretics. Feopempt answered that all the books they were reading were chimeras and that they were all deceived by them. He called the holy prayer of Jesus a heresy and said that this heresy came out of the Moshen Mountains and later reached Starets Paisii, this latter having taken place about thirty years prior to these events. After this the Niamets confessor Iakinf came to the Polianovoronsk Monastery and tried to reason with Feopempt, but was answered in the same way as the brethren. They then decided to write to the Niamets archimandrite, Starets Paisii, describing all the circumstances of the matter. The starets received the letter July 19, 1793. Thirty years before this, when he was still at Dragomirna, he had actually written an essay on the Jesus Prayer, but not in praise of the heresy which had then appeared among the monks in the Moshen Mountains, but in rebuttal to it. He was proving the holiness and correctness of the Jesus Prayer by referring to numerous testimonies of the Fathers. And now he was again writing in defense of mental prayer. He adds new proofs to his previous ones, taking them from the Fathers. Let us quote the concluding words of starets Paisii's letter:

> I plead and ask you from my whole heart to have undoubting faith in the Fathers and in the teachings contained in them, for they agree in all respects with the Divine Scriptures and with the minds of all the ecumenical teachers and the entire Holy Church, because one and the same Holy Spirit was working in them. The teaching found in the Fathers is truly instruction for monks wishing to be saved, and in keeping it you should flee and remove yourselves from the blasphemies of the blasphemer of the holy books of our God-bearing Fathers who has appeared among you. For neither he nor others like him can introduce a single witness to their sophistry and blasphemies, but base themselves merely upon the sands of their own perverted and God-opposing minds, inspired by the father of lies, the devil. You, however, are faithful and true sons of the Orthodox Church and are established upon the immovable rock of faith, for you have our venerable and God-bearing Fathers as a great number of witnesses (see the enclosed list) to the true observance of God's commandments and about this holy prayer. Follow their holy teachings, and compel your souls and bodies to do everything that is good and pleasing to God according to the strength of each, with the cooperation of God's grace. I ask and entreat you to have nothing to do with this blasphemer if he will not

decide to repent. If possible, send him away with love, so that your life would be quiet and peaceful and without trouble, to the glory of God and the salvation of your souls, which I earnestly desire for you.

When the brethren of the Polianomerul'sk Monastery chose the Hieroschema-monk Aleksei as their starets, (this was the same Aleksei who once came to Dragomirna to administer the schema to Starets Paisii) some of the brethren, knowing Aleksei's meek and humble nature, doubted if he could be a good leader and wrote about this to Starets Paisii. The starets responded with the following letter: "Do not worry about his gentleness and humility. In this lies the root and foundation of the Superior's position. The Fathers write that to his brethren the Superior should happen at the devil's prompting, in order to enable him to give an example to the brethren of patience and chaste living. Neither should you worry that apparently he is not familiar with housekeeping, for God is mighty and will take care of this through other brethren. What you need most for your salvation is the ability to provide well for the brethren's souls according to the divine commandments and the teachings of the Fathers. Do not worry about his bodily weakness when he is healthy in spirit and in spiritual reasoning. Therefore, O beloved and most honorable brothers in the Lord, I tearfully entreat you as I fall down to your feet, do not disdain my advice, but accept the most honorable Father Aleksei, a pastor and guide whom God has granted to you. Knowing the fraility of his health, do not demand from him physical labor beyond his strength, but take care of him in every way, so that his strength would not be exhausted before its time to the detriment of the brothers' benefit. It will be enough for him to sit in his cell, taking care of his health, reading edifying books, and being ready to give the brethren wholesome and edifying advice at the right time. Likewise do not ignore him in external housekeeping matters as being inexperienced, but in every undertaking, in each activity, always receive his blessing and advice with all humility, even if in one matter or another it may appear to any brother that it is unnecessary to ask the father, for he knows well enough himself what to do. This comes from the evil one. The procedure which comes from God and the Fathers is that in any matter, even one in which a brother is very experienced, he should first consult the Superior, and without imposing his own opinion upon him, wait for him to reflect upon the matter and make a decision. For the brother ought to still his intention completely, and as if knowing nothing, approach the father and ask him if one or another matter has his permission and blessing, and do whatever he may say. Then God, seeing the brother's humility and true obedience (for there is no obedience without humility), will convince the Superior's heart through his Holy Spirit to give a helpful response to the one making the request and through his invisible grace will help the novice in the matter he has commenced. And if the Superior, without being compelled to, says himself, 'Do as you wish,' then, with the fear of God and placing your trust in the father's prayers, commence however God may instruct you. Having fulfilled your obedience or having returned from a journey, come to the father again, and having told him in detail all that was done, fall to his feet asking forgiveness if you had done any wrong, for total absence of sin is found only in angels. Thus, become humble before each other, have God's love among yourselves, and may you have one soul and one heart through the grace of Christ."

A certain priest who was a childhood friend of the starets and his colleague at the Kiev Academy, and who was in continuous correspondence with him, wrote to him about his desire to become a monk. The starets answered the following: "In this matter, my beloved, there is a great inconvenience. For according to John Climacus, a married man is like one whose hands and feet are bound. He would have liked to become a monk, but he cannot. In addition, you are responsible for the flock of Christ's wise sheep, and to simply leave this flock, as you would have to, would not be without danger. Finally, the habits you have acquired during your long life in the world, such as the love for wife and children which has naturally implanted itself, and attraction to the world and to the worldly, are likewise not easy to overcome. Finding yourself in such circumstances, how could you free yourself from these hardly resolvable bonds? In the first place, my beloved, in this matter you should seek spiritual counsel from your God-given helper and resolve this matter with her acquiescence. Secondly, you should provide for your children lawfully and according to God. Thirdly, and this is the most important consideration, you should ask your bishop's blessings for this holy undertaking—will the Holy Spirit inspire him toward this, and also toward the selection of an experienced successor to you for your flock? If this is how you arrange this matter, it will be mighty and unshakable according to God, and will earn praises from God and men. And even if all the indicated obstacles were to be removed by the grace of God, you should take account of your spiritual treasures with great discretion, so as not to turn out to be similar to the builder of the Gospel, who, having miscalculated his means, started building a tower and could not complete it, and so that this cup, with the tears and bitter bread of monasticism, would not be to your condemnation on the Day of Judgment for your indiscretion. For according to Climacus, no one will enter the heavenly dwelling with a crown of victory if he will not perform the first, second, and third renunciations: the first is the renunciation of the world and everything in it, the second is of the will and reasoning, and the third is of the vainglory which accompanies obedience. The first of these is the least difficult, but only for those who love God. The second demands feats and bloody labors unto death. The third is attained through constant self-reproach. All three require God's invisible help, without which none of them are realizable. And so, if you hope, with the help of God's grace, having overcome all the difficulties indicated at the start, to really renounce the world and everything in it, to renounce likewise your will and reasoning and to give yourself to obedience performed according to God and his commandments even unto death, to give up all your possessions to the smallest object, to regard yourself as the least and the last of all, and to endure with magnanimity the mental struggle which is constantly being dealt upon the servants of God by the invisible enemy of our souls, as well as hunger, thirst, lack of everything, curses, dishonor, and all persecution and sorrow which characterize monastic life—if you are prepared to endure all this amiably until death for the sake of God's love, rejoice and be glad, praise God, and believe, without question, that God, through his wondrous fortunes, will bring your God-pleasing intention to completion, you will be accounted worthy, even at the eleventh hour of your life, to work for God in an angelic manner. However, have no doubt that you will receive in heaven from God's bountiful hand a reward equal to that of those who have worked for God as monks from their very youth to old age."

We will now turn to those of the starets' letters in which he speaks out on questions concerning the Church in general. In these letters we see the starets coming out in defense of the purity and truth of Orthodoxy with the same clarity, power, and fortitude with which he establishes the foundations and order of monastic life in previous letters. In certain instances his word may seem to us to be too severe, but this is because we have ourselves become too weak these days.

A priest by the name of Ioann, apparently a Uniate, had doubts as to the truthfulness of his confession and turned to the starets, asking him to resolve his perplexity. The starets writes to him that: "the Holy Spirit himself, proceeding from the only Father and resting on the Son through his grace has inspired him to turn with his question to a humble and sinful, but Orthodox son of the Eastern Church," and expresses his readiness to clear up his bewilderment in a few words. "The Uniates' primary and most significant error lies in the teaching which they have accepted from the Romans, that the Holy Spirit proceeds both from the Father and the Son. This is the primary and most significant of all heresies, for it contains a concept of God, who is one in the Holy Trinity, that is incorrect and against the Holy Scriptures. Whoever professes that the Holy Spirit proceeds from the Father and the Son conceives of two sources within God, one in the Father and the other in the Son. But we, the Orthodox, profess that God has one source in the Father, as our Lord Jesus Christ himself has taught us in the Holy Gospels, saying that the Holy Spirit proceeds from the only Son. He says: 'But when the counselor comes, whom I shall send to you from the Father, even the Spirit of truth, who proceeds from the Father, he will bear witness to me' (Jn. 15:26). And the apostle says: 'Every good endowment and every perfect gift is from above, coming down from the Father of lights' (Jas. 1:17). Do you see? He says, 'Father of lights,' meaning that the Father is the root and source of the Divine. Two lights, the Son and the Spirit, have their pre-existent being from a single light, the Father, the Son through begetting and the Holy Spirit through procession.

"The God-inspired prophet David says: 'By the word of the Lord the heavens were made, and all their host by the breath of his mouth' (Ps. 33:6). You see, the Lord is what he calls the Father, the word—the Son as pre-eternally begotten from him, and the breath of his mouth (and not theirs)—the Holy Spirit, who proceeds from the one Father. Other evidence from the Old and New Testament can be found to prove beyond a doubt that the Holy Spirit proceeds from the one Father and rests on the Son, as the Baptism of the Lord shows.

"And all the holy commentators on the Holy Scriptures and ecumenical teachers of the Church say in unison that the Holy Spirit proceeds from the Father, and have written nowhere 'and also from the Son.' Thus, if the Uniates agree with the Romans in such a grave heresy, what hope of salvation do they have, unless they reject this Spirit-denying heresy and do not reunite to the Holy Eastern Orthodox Church?"

The starets goes on to convince the priest to hasten to flee from the Unia, just as Lot fled from Sodom. "Do not spare," he writes, "either possessions or relatives, should they not wish to heed you, but proceed to save your own soul from destruction. For there is nothing more necessary for you than the soul, for which Christ died. As you flee, do not let your heart look back for the sake of your rapidly perishing estate, for better you should be impoverished than blaspheme the Holy Spirit, as do the Romans. Forsake and flee the Unia as soon as possible, lest you die while in it, and lest you be counted among the heretics rather than the Christians. And not only should you forsake it, but counsel others to leave, if you know in your conscience that they will heed you. Should they not heed you, at least go away yourself from the net of of the enemy and unite in heart and soul to the Holy Orthodox Church, and in this way, upholding the undefiled faith along with everyone and fulfilling Christ's commandments, you will be able to be saved."

In 1794 the starets received from Russia a series of questions from a group of persons, whom he himself called true servants of God, performers of Gospel commandments, and great zealots of righteousness. They were the junior deacon of the church at Vasil'evskoe village, Aleksandr Matveev, Ioann Petrov, Matvei Sakovlev, Andrei Ioannovich, the widow Evdokiia, Ivan Sergeevich from the village Palekka, Afanasii Nikitich, and others.* As can be seen from the questions, all these people are greatly worried about the matter of salvation, live among schismatics (perhaps some of them were schismatics), are troubled about many perplexing matters, and earnestly wish and hope to receive from the starets a word of instruction which would be beneficial not only to them, but also to people around them.

All of the starets' responses are directed primarily toward warning against schismatic errors. Because of their extensiveness we cannot quote them in full and will mention only those which might have more to do with the present.

The starets prefaces his responses with the following introduction: "I received your second letter with particular joy through our beloved brother, the monk Feofilakt, and I praised God for the zeal which you have for the undefiled preservation of the Orthodox faith and the apostolic traditions and rules contained in the holy Church. This zeal of yours is divine and wise. Being inspired by it, you exhibit such love for me and such a faith, that in spite of my lack of education, you turned to me with questions which go far beyond my ability and intelligence, and are subject more to conciliar consideration by the Church than to my ignorant explanation. At the same time you wrote your questions to me with such a statement, that you will accept my responses and decisions with complete trust. I praise you greatly for your confidence in me,

---

* From the letter of starets Sofronii, Starets Paisii's disciple and successor, to M. P. Protas'eva, it is clear that Afanasii Nikitich was an icon painter from the village of Palikha, and helped Niamets in book printing.

but judge for yourselves, how can I give responses and solutions to your questions, even if I wished it with all my heart, being first, as I said, a simple and ignorant man, and secondly, not having the necessary books to do it. And I do not know what I should do—should I leave your questions without a response, or should I answer somehow according to my weak intellect? Having been so puzzled for a while, I decided to give way to your love for me, your faith and your zeal. I was touched the most by the fact that you are asking and beseeching me for an answer by the Holy and Life-Creating Trinity. Taking all this into consideration, I was overcome by your love, and I pray to the Almighty Christ God that he may help me through his Grace to begin this undertaking and to fulfill it according to the true and faultless mind of the Holy Apostolic Church.

"And so, your first question amounts to the following: Can a true Christian have and read books forbidden by the Church which are being secretly reprinted in a sacrilegious manner by schismatics and being distributed by them among the people, or should this be not done? My answer is that the Divine Church forbids reading heretical books and holding discussions with heretics. In a book on the profession of the Orthodox faith, there is a question asking what is the fifth commandment of the Church. The answer is that those who are unlearned in the Holy Scriptures and other necessary fields should not read heretical books or listen to the harmful teachings of heretics, or even speak and have dealings with them, as the psalm-singer prophet says: 'Blessed is the man who walks not in the counsel of the wicked, nor stands in the way of sinners' (Ps. 1:1). Elsewhere the Holy Scripture says: 'As for a man who is factious, after admonishing him once or twice, have nothing more to do with him' (Titus 3:10). Watch carefully and note that the Divine Church does not command everyone not to read heretical books and not to hold discussions with heretics, but only those who are unlearned in the Holy Scriptures and the various fields of learning. It is very easy for the latter, as they read heretical books and get acquainted with their teachings, or carelessly enter into conversations with heretics, to succumb to their ungodly and perverted sophistry. In the eyes of ignorant people, heretical teaching often appears to be truthful, while actually being unquestionably false. Just as Satan, being darkness, becomes transformed into a radiant angel, so do heretical teachings, being darkness and totally alienated from the light of God's Truth, often appear to people who are unlearned in the Holy Scriptures and various fields to be somewhat similar to the truth. This is why the Church forbids those who are unlearned in the Holy Scriptures and the other fields to read heretical books and to have discussions with heretics, so that they will not, due to their unsophistication, be harmed by their teachings. Those who have studied the Holy Scriptures and the other fields are exempt from this commandment. Such are the Holy Fathers, the pastors, and the teachers of the Church. Not only were they instructed to perfection in the Holy Scriptures by the grace of God, but they also mastered the other fields of knowledge, surpassing in worldly wisdom not only their instructors, but also all the ancient philosophers. These God-bearing Fathers of ours saw how various heretics, proud of their wordly wisdom, would turn the Divine Scriptures into a weapon of their philosophy, interpreting them in an erroneous and perverted sense through philosophical proofs and bringing constant strife into the Church of Christ through their teachings. Thus the Fathers would read their false heretical teachings, and subordinating their philosophies to the Divine Scriptures in every respect, would perceive the heretics' errors clearer than the sun, and through the invincible double weapon, i.e. theology and philosophical proof, would rend asunder all their heretical stratagems as a spider web and would defend God's Church by the word of truth from all heretical attacks. For philosophy, too, if used correctly, as the Holy and Apostolic Church teaches us, corresponds to God's truth to such an extent that it cannot be surpassed by any heretical verbal stratagems. If used contrary to the true sense of the Holy Scriptures and the Holy Church, as is done by the heretics, it becomes opposed to God's truth, and since it upholds lies it gets vanquished by truthful evidence. Thus, one who starts reading schismatic books must lack neither theological knowledge nor worldly learning. For the one who does not have the appropriate knowledge, it is better to obey God and the Church commandment which says: 'Do not read heretical books and do not take part in discussions with heretics.'

"You go on to ask: 'If one has certain doubts about the traditions of the Catholic Church and does not obey its orders, e.g. crosses himself with two fingers, and likewise has doubts about any other church decisions and refuses to submit to them—do such people have hope for salvation, even if they had performed good deeds, or not? And can a priest admit such people to Confession and Holy Communion, or is this absolutely against the truth? Inform us, who are miserable and accursed, for the sake of God.'

"In answering your question I find it appropriate to tell you of an incident which I recall. In 1746, having come to a certain monastery where monks of Russian background were living, I found there four schismatic monks living in the wilderness not far from the monastery. A certain Hieromonk Osiia was trying to convince them to abandon the schism and all their customs which are in confllct with the Church, enter into communion with the Church, submit to it in every way, and receive in this manner certain hope for salvation. They expressed their readiness to accept all the traditions and customs of the Church, if only they would be allowed to cross themselves with two fingers. They absolutely refused to cross themselves with three fingers in the Orthodox manner. Hieromonk Osiia reassured them and said he would request such permission and blessings from the ecclesiastical authorities, if only they would be obedient to the Holy Church in all the other traditions and customs. Having completely put their trust in his promise, the schismatic monks left their dwelling in the wilderness, moved to the monastery, started building their cells, put on monastic garb according to the tradition of the Orthodox Church, and often asked Osiia to hurry and fulfill the promise he had given, but he kept putting it off. Finally, during the fast of the Holy Apostles, at their urgent plea, he went with them to Jassy, the capital of Moldavia, where Sylvester, Holy patriarch of Antioch, happened to be at the time, a holy man full of the wisdom of the Holy Spirit, along with Metropolitan Nicephorus of Moldavia, who was a Greek and a very wise man. Having introduced the schismatic monks to them, Hieromonk Osiia told them, in detail, how he kept trying to convince them to enter into communion with the Church and how they were prepared to accept and observe all the Church traditions and customs, and that they were asking for only one thing with tears of condescension—that by the blessing of the holy cross they would be allowed to cross themselves with two fingers. Then with the greatest spiritual peace they would accept communion with Church. In no case would they agree to cease crossing themselves with two fingers and to adopt the three-fingered formula. Having listened attentively to this story the holy patriarch and the eminent metropolitan said: 'If you wish to join the catholic Church with all your heart, then you should without any doubt and in all sincerity accept all apostolic traditions and customs of the Church, without any exception. Then the Church would also accept you into her communion as beloved children with great joy. But since you do not agree with all the apostolic traditions and customs of the Church, but maintain steadfastly and unwaveringly your self-conceived two fingered formula, do not wish to submit to God's Church in this matter, and ask and beseech the Church to accept you into communion with your two-fingered formula, how can the Church fulfill your wish? Is it possible that in one and the same catholic Church there would be two customs disagreeing with each other and opposed to one another, that the very same Christians would cross themselves in different ways? And what kind of agreement would there be among Christians then? Would not the schism between them be apparent? And the Divine Church will in no case admit you into her communion with such a two-fingered formula, for if it would do so, it would create a schism in the whole Greece and all Orthodox lands, similar to the one that had been created in Russia by ignorant people. But may the Church not become the cause of a schism! Therefore, be certain that the Divine Church cannot agree to your proposal in any case, and do not ask us any more about this, as it is something impossible, but go back and remain no longer in the monastery where you are living, for you, being disobedient to the Church, cannot have anything to do with the

Orthodox monks who live there.' Upon hearing such an answer from the holy patriarch and the most reverend metropolitan, the monks left and, returning to the monastery, were very unhappy with Hieromonk Osiia, who had deceived them with his promise, and having showered him with heavy reproaches, returned to their schismatics at their original dwelling place.

"Now judge for yourself, lovers of Christ, if the Church did not accept into its communion schismatic monks who were ready to accept all apostolic and ecclesiastical customs, for the sole reason that they would not give up crossing themselves with two fingers, then how can she accept those who, as you write in your question, have doubts concerning the traditions of the catholic Church, do not heed her orders, and do not wish to submit to Church rules in many other ways? You ask if they have hope of salvation, at least for their good deeds, and can a priest absolve them at Confession and give them Holy Communion? And you beseech me to give you an authoritative answer. My answer to you is that in my view, there can be two kinds of schisms, one when someone is in schism, and when one also leads others into schism, driving them from the Church with his ungodly teaching. One who is in such a schism, even if he performed all the good deeds, and even if he had poured out his blood as a martyr for Christ, which unquestionably surpasses all good deeds, he can in no case expiate this mortal sin, i.e. the schism. Now if a man cannot expiate his schism even through martyrdom, what hope can he have for salvation? And how can a priest absolve him at Confession without his sincere turning toward the Church and allow him to have Holy Communion? This is absolutely impossible and will be against the truth of the Holy Church of God.

"I will not give a verbatim rendering of your next question, but will mention only its essence. 'Has any Eastern council lifted the curse and anathema which the Eastern patriarchs had earlier imposed at a council upon those against the catholic Church, i.e. upon those crossing themselves with two fingers or refusing to submit in some other way? And can any bishops lift this curse without the council's knowledge and the consent and will of the Eastern patriarchs? And if none of the bishops can lift this anathema without the will of the Eastern patriarchs and if it is not lifted by the patriarchs, then would not certain Christians be dying in opposition and unrepentant, in this conciliar anathema? Woe to us! And will such people be pleased by such commemoration by the Church? Do not fail to give us a truthful explanation of this matter as well.'

"My answer is that a curse or anathema upon those opposing the catholic Church, i.e. upon those crossing themselves with two fingers or resisting and not submitting to the Church in some other matter, which has been imposed by a council of Eastern patriarchs, remains through the grace of Christ firm, unshakable, and irreversible till the end of the age. You also ask if any Eastern council has lifted the anathema which has been imposed. And I answer, could there be such a council, except for one in opposition to God and the Holy Church, which would assemble to repudiate the truth and confirm falsehood? There would never be such an evil council. And you ask if any bishops can lift such a curse without the council's knowledge and the consent and will of the Eastern patriarchs. And I say that this is totally impossible. Keep in mind that all the bishops receive the same grace of the Holy Spirit when they are consecrated and are obliged to guard, as the apple of the eye, the purity and immaculacy of the Orthodox faith, along with all the apostolic traditions and the rules of the holy apostles, ecumenical and local councils, and the God-bearing Fathers contained in the Holy, Catholic, and Apostolic Church. From the same Holy Spirit they received the authority to bind and loose according to the order established by the Holy Spirit through the holy apostles in the Holy Church. The bishops did not receive the authority to destroy the apostolic traditions and rules of the Church from the Holy Spirit. Therefore, neither the bishops nor the Eastern patriarchs can lift the above anathema placed on the opponents of the catholic Church, as having been imposed correctly and in accordance to the holy councils. And if anyone would attempt to do this, it would be against God and the Holy Church. You also ask that if none of the bishops can lift this anathema without the Eastern patriarchs, has it not been lifted by the latter? I answer that not only any bishop without the Eastern patriarchs, but the Eastern patriarchs themselves cannot lift this curse, as has sufficiently been said already, for such an anathema is eternally irrevocable. You ask: 'Will not some of the Christians, in their opposition and lack of repentance, be dying under this conciliar curse? Woe to us!' I answer that your question contains three puzzles. The first is 'some of the Christians,' the second is 'will they, in their opposition and lack of repentance, be dying under this conciliar curse?,' and the third is 'Woe to us!.' In the first instance I am puzzled as to what sort of Christians these are, when they oppose the catholic Church without repentance? Such people are unworthy even to be called Christians, but are called schismatics according to the fair judgment of the Church. True Christians obey the Holy Church in everything. The second question: 'will they in their opposition and lack of repentance, be dying under this conciliar curse,' also puzzles me. For how could these so-called Christians, being unrepentant in their constant insubordination to the Church, not die under this conciliar anathema? Are those about whom you are perplexed immortal, will they be dying? And how can they not die, being mortal, and in addition being under an anathema, which makes them doubly mortal, both spiritually and bodily, as countless schismatics are always dying without having repented under this same conciliar anathema? Similarly, these so-called Christians will also, if they do not turn to Christ's Church wholeheartedly with true repentance, undoubtedly die under the above-mentioned conciliar anathema. My third puzzlement refers to your words, 'Woe to us!' These words introduce the thought into my soul—are you not those certain Christians, who have been opposing the Church without repentance, and who stand in fear and trembling before the anathema imposed by the catholic Church upon such enemies, and this is why you are asking in such detail if any Eastern council has lifted it? Afraid of dying under an anathema and not being able to endure constant pangs of conscience, you thus cry out, 'Woe to us!.' If you are true Orthodox Christians, in all things obedient to the Church, which has given birth to you through Holy Baptism, if you cross yourselves with the three fingers of the right hand according to the tradition of the holy apostles, and if you are asking me not about yourselves but about others, then neither does the above-mentioned anathema extend to you, and therefore by no means should you say about yourselves so plaintively, 'Woe to us!' It was these words of yours which suggested to me the above opinion of you, and may it perish from my soul! I am asking you to give me a full confirmation of what you have in mind in the circumstance which you mention, for we have nothing to do with those who oppose the Holy Church and cross themselves with two fingers. You also ask if it would be proper for the Church to commemorate them. My answer is that if you are speaking of those who oppose the catholic Church and die in their opposition and lack of repentance, then believe me, it would not only be improper for the Church to commemorate them, but it would also be against God and the Holy Church, and a priest who would dare to commemorate such people commits a mortal sin. Commemoration of the dead is the main part of the bloodless sacrifice brought in behalf of Orthodox Christians, both living and dead. If anyone, even an Orthodox Christian, sins openly without repenting, the Holy Church forbids the presentation of the bloodless sacrifice on his behalf till he completely abandons his sin and sincerely repents. If the Church does not allow the presentation of a bloodless sacrifice on behalf of an obvious and unrepentant sinner who is Orthodox, can it allow such a presentation on behalf of one who dies without any repentance for opposing the Holy Church? Absolutely not. St. Symeon of Thessalonica testifies about the obvious sinner, that he ought not to partake of Holy Communion and that it is impossible to present the bloodless sacrifice on his behalf, in the following words: 'There is no place for the unfaithful or for those who think differently. Thus no priest should ever present the sacrifice or make commemoration on behalf of an obvious and unrepentant sinner, for this sacrifice is unto his condemnation, as is the reception of Holy Communion unworthily and without repentance, as the divine Paul says about this' (Cod. 11:29). The same Symeon says, concerning those on whose behalf particles are to be offered: 'Priests should not accept, indiscriminately, offerings of the faithful who are obvious sinners, but should demand repentance first. For Communion takes place through the offered particle, and it is not proper for an unworthy person to partake of this sacrifice.' And he also says, concerning the priest's obligation to observe carefully on whose behalf he is offering a particle: 'While an offering on behalf of those making it worthily can be quite beneficial, one made on behalf of unworthy persons can be equally disastrous and harmful, to the extent that this is possible for people. For a particle brought in someone's behalf, being placed near the divine bread which had just been sanctified and become the Body of Christ, partakes of this holy thing right away. When placed into the cup it unites with the Blood also, and in this way communicates grace to the soul in whose behalf it is being offered. For there is mental communion, and if a man is approaching reverence, or is from among sinners but has repented, he accepts with his soul the Communion of the Holy Spirit invisibly, as we have said. As we have become convinced, his body is benefitted in many instances. This is why the priest should observe closely, so as not to receive an offering from anyone who wishes to present one, and should not make any on behalf of those who sin without any shame, so as not to be condemned along with them.' Such are the words of St. Symeon, or rather of the entire Holy Catholic Church, for he is speaking in agreement with the catholic thinking. It therefore follows that those dying without repentance and in opposition to the Holy Church should never be commemorated by the Church. Whoever dares to commemorate such people shall give an awesome answer for it before Christ God on the day of His Awesome Judgment.

"You next ask if one who has died in a Church schism can be buried in the Church according to the Christian rite and be commemorated, or if this is totally unacceptable due to unbelief. I answer that in your previous questions you call those opposing the Holy Church and not heeding her commands not schismatics, but 'some of the Christians.' But in your present question you are openly asking about one who dies in schism, as if such a person were incomparably worse than the above-mentioned. We, however, do not separate in any way the above-mentioned from schismatics. Now if this person who died in schism is worse than the above-mentioned, is he not from among those who are called the *khlysty* or self-immolators, and whom we call not simply schismatics, but complete atheists. But no matter what the schismatic persuasion of the deceased about whom you are asking might be, I will cite the response of Macarius, the Holy Patriarch of Antioch to Nikon, the Holy Patriarch of all Russia (from the final section of the book *The Tablet*) in order to resolve this question: 'We accepted, from the time faith began, the tradition from the holy apostles, Fathers, and the Seven Ecumenical Councils, to make the sign of the most honorable cross with the three first fingers of the right hand, and whosoever of the Orthodox Christians does not cross himself in this manner is a heretic and we deem him to be excommunicated from the Father, Son, and Holy Spirit and subject to the anathema.' And is not the person who has died in schism, about whom you are asking, the same as one who does not cross himself with three fingers? If the one who has died in schism is the same as this one, can he be buried and commemorated according to the Christian rite?

"Your next question concerns the following. Certain priests, pandering to human license, perform confessions and marriages according to the old *Trebnik* and oblige the schism in opposition to Church Tradition. Would this result in any illegality or obstacle to the action and performance of the sacraments? For both clergy and laity are deceived by this due to their misjudgment and conceit, and this causes us great sorrow, temptation, and doubt.

"My answer is that priests who oblige the schism are greater mortal sinners before God than those pleasers of men 'whose bones God scattered.' For in pandering to human license and obliging the schism in opposition to Church traditions, they dare to perform the Sacraments according to the old *Trebnik*. Such people, if they do not repent before God with all their hearts and do not abstain from these actions, shall be put to shame on the day of God's Terrible Judgment. If the above-mentioned priests are true Christians and have been ordained by an Orthodox bishop, then even if in pandering to human license, they perform a Sacrament according to the old *Trebnik*, the Sacrament remains complete, and there should be no doubts about this. But the priests will come under God's judgment as tempters of many Christian souls. For as the Lord said, 'Whoever causes one of these little ones who believe in me to sin, it would be better for him to have a great millstone fastened round his neck and to be drowned in the depth of the sea' (Mt. 18:6). These priests, who have been placed by the Holy Church as pastors and keepers of Christ's verbal flock, ought to obey the Church in everything, as she is their true mother, and use the revised *Trebnik* when performing the Sacraments, instead of performing them, to the great sorrow and temptation of Christian people, according to the old *Trebnik* which has been abandoned by the Church. They also should flee and remove themselves wholeheartedly from any association with schismatics and should tearfully encourage others to do the same. For such teaching and guidance of Christians they would be made worthy of receiving their reward from Christ God on the day of His righteous reward.

"Here is your next question. 'Certain priests have left the Church and their bishops and are living among the schismatics. Can any Sacraments be performed by such priests, i.e. Baptism, Confession, Marriage, and the other holy acts of the Church, or will grace fail to follow in such a case? Be so kind as to inform us about this, for the sake of the catholic truth itself.'

"My answer is that priests who have left the Church and their bishops and live among the schismatics become one with the schismatics, and together with them they blaspheme the Orthodox faith, the entire Church of God, the Holy Mysteries of Christ, all the Sacraments of the Church, and the whole episcopal and priestly order. For all these blasphemies alone, such priests are unworthy to be called priests, but are pseudo-priests, or, more correctly, non-priests. They have been excommunicated from the Church, are estranged from it, and have been defrocked by their bishops. So how can they perform the Holy Sacraments of the Church; or how can the Sacraments of the Church be performed by such people? This is absolutely impossible, for the Holy Spirit does not perform the Sacraments of the Church through obvious enemies of God, who are bound not only from their bishops, but from the entire Church. The force of the bishop's authority to bind can be seen from the following. The reliquary of a certain martyred saint was inside the altar table, and whenever the deacon would exclaim, 'all who are catechumens, depart,' it would, through God's invisible power, leave the church and remain in the porch to the very dismissal, after which it would return into the church and stand in its usual place. The reason for this was that this holy martyr had been bound by his starets for some sort of disobedience. When the starets came and loosed him, the reliquary immediately stopped leaving the church and stood firmly in its place in the altar table. Oh, how powerful is divine obedience, when the very blood of the martyr, the starets disciple, which was poured out for Christ, could not loose the binding of the starets, until the starets who had bound him did the loosing himself! And so, if the binding of the starets, who was not a bishop but a simple monk, was so powerful, how much more powerful is the bishop's binding! For only to the apostles and their successors the bishops was given and is being given the supernatural grace to bind and loose from Christ the Savior, who said to his disciples, 'Whatever you bind on earth shall be bound in heaven, and whatever you loose shall be loosed in heaven.' And so, being bound from their bishops, the said priests are eternally bound both on earth and in heaven. Having been cast off from their bishops, they became alienated from the grace of the priesthood and all priestly activity and cannot perform a single Sacrament. Orthodox priests who are defrocked justly, by conciliar action, are placed on one level with laymen and together with them participate in the prayers of the Church and partake of Holy Communion. And if they would dare to serve the Divine Liturgy or perform other Sacraments of the Church, they are totally cut off from the Church like rotted members, according to the twenty-eighth Apostolic Canon.

"In a book of canons written in Moldavian I found a question and answer corresponding to my answer to this question you are asking me. The question, asked by St. Methodius, Patriarch of Constantinople, is: 'If a priest is ordained by a deposed bishop, can he serve or not?' The answer, by Theodore the Studite, is: 'A tree of the wilderness cannot bear good fruit.' Likewise, a bishop whose grace has been taken away, cannot ordain priests, for he does not have the episcopacy. Without episcopacy, neither can he convey priesthood. If he does ordain anyone, the person remains unordained and cannot perform the Liturgy or any other priestly acts, as he is a simple layman. If a person has something, he can give it to another, but if he does not have it, how can he give it?

"From the above answer of Theodore the Studite it is clear that priests who are justly deposed according to the Apostolic Canons are totally cut off from the Church should they dare to perform priestly services after this.

"Your next question consists of the following: can a Christian who has suddenly died while drinking wine be buried according to the Christian rite and commemorated by the Church? For many of your priests, as you say, considering these to be suicides, do not give them a Christian burial and do not commemorate them. You ask me this for the sake of love and Christian benefit, and to resolve this puzzle according to the rules. My answer is that I had a great desire to resolve this puzzlement of yours according to the holy rules, but because of my lack of skill, I could not find anything about it in the canons, and so I am puzzled as to how I should answer you. On the two memorial Saturdays, during cheese-fare week and before Pentecost, when all the deceased Orthodox Christians are commemorated, many different forms of sudden death are mentioned, and the Catholic Church commemorates Christians who have died through them and asks God for the salvation of their souls. But this form of death, i.e. sudden death from overindulgence in drink, is not mentioned, and this would lead to the conclusion that the Holy Church does not pray for such people... I would think that it is about them that the Holy Spirit says, through the Apostle Paul: 'Do you not know that the unrighteous will not inherit the kingdom of God?... Neither the immoral, nor idolaters, nor adulterers, nor homosexuals, nor thieves, nor the greedy, nor drunkards... will inherit the kingdom of God' (1 Cor. 6:9). Is not one who dies suddenly while drinking wine and without confessing his sins and partaking of the Holy Mysteries of Christ guilty of causing his own sudden death? Had he been drinking a little wine in moderation, he would not have died such a terrible sudden death. It would seem that such a person can be classed with suicides, and this is why your priests do not dare to bury them according to the Christian rite and commemorate them. Therefore I ask your love not to be upset by this, for this matter lies under great doubt and perplexity. If anyone were able to find in the holy canons a statement on this by the Church, then no one would have any question about it and would confidently follow the Church's statement.

"Your next question is the following. Can a priest absolve a humble penitent for his weakness without assigning a penance and admit him to Holy Communion, or is this impossible?

"It seems to me that your question is not well put. Is the person repenting for great or small sins, and is his weakness spiritual or bodily? Let us suppose that he has a bodily weakness. If his bodily weakness is such that he is approaching death and does not have time to undergo penance for his sins, then, even if his sins were great but he humbly repents of them, the priest should absolve him from his sins and give him Holy Communion without penance. But if he is not so desperately ill and is able to undergo penance, then the priest should not absolve him without penance, since the penitential act is the third step of the Sacrament of Penance, and it should not be done away with except for mortal necessity. It should be explained in greater detail what the penitential act is and how it is assigned for sins. The Apostolic Canons, which John of Damascus places on an equal footing with the books of the Divine Scripture, depose all ordained clergy from their rank for their sins, while the laity are excluded from participation in the prayers of the Church and in Holy Communion. This is how the Holy Catholic and Apostolic Church, on the basis of these apostolic canons and under the Holy Spirit's guidance, treats the transgressions of the whole multitude of ordained and non-ordained Orthodox Christians. Those of the ordained, i.e. bishops, priests, and deacons, who have fallen into lesser or greater sins, it either temporarily suspends from priestly duties for lesser sins, or forbids them from performing these duties for the rest of their lives, but does not prevent them from receiving Holy Communion. Monks and laymen are excluded from Holy Communion for a brief period of time for lesser sins and for a longer period for greater sins. No other rule or penance is applied by the Church to the non-ordained for their sins. The reason for this is that the early Christians partook of Holy Communion very frequently from the apostolic times in the entire Church of Christ out of their inexpressible love for Christ the Savior. Whenever they happened to fall into lesser or greater sins, they would be excluded from Holy Communion and from standing with the faithful for a briefer or longer period of time. They would stand in penitential areas determined by the Church, first in front of the church doors, where they would fall down with tears and entreat everyone coming into the church to pray to God so that He would forgive their transgressions. Eventually, they would be allowed to stand in the atrium near the church doors and they would listen to the singing and reading in the church, but would not enter into the church itself. After this, they would be allowed to stand in the church proper behind the ambo at all services, and only during the Divine Liturgy, when the deacon would proclaim after the Gospel, 'Depart, ye Catechumens,' they would go to the atrium and remain there till the end of the Liturgy. Then they would be permitted to stand with the faithful but not to have Holy Communion. Finally, having been absolved from the penance, they would be allowed again, as before their transgressions, to have Holy Communion with faith and love. Now how did they behave during the penance? They would always sigh from the depth of their hearts, weep and wail, keep away from all evil, and compel themselves to do good deeds and diligently fulfill the Gospel commandments. When the other Christians would receive Holy Communion, their minds would be filled with the realization that they are not worthy of Holy Communion for their sins, and inflamed with the divine fire of unbearable and inexpressible desire for Holy Communion, they would entreat Christ God with many tears to enable them to partake of his holy and pure body and the immortal fountain of his pure blood, once they have spent the period of their penance purely and without defilement. Having foreseen such a sincere repentance on the part of Christians who have been excluded from Communion for their sins, the Holy Spirit did not institute any other penalty or penance for sins.

"One should know that the Church gives bishops the authority, when they observe the worthy fruits of repentance, to shorten penitential periods determined by the holy canons. I also wish to inform you that I made a diligent search of all the holy canons to see if there are any penances in existence without exclusion from Holy Communion, and could not find any. But it is awesome to contemplate how terrible and severe is the punishment allotted to those who dare give Communion to transgressors and who receive Communion without such a penance. The Church likens both to Judas.

"Your next question consists of the following. When the particles for the living and the dead are taken out at the proskomidia, is it equally effective when a separate particle is taken out for each person as when one particle is taken out for many people? We ask you to enlighten us sinners about this also.

"My answer is that the particles which are taken out at the proskomidia for the living and the dead, as soon as they unite with the pure Mysteries of Christ, partake of the holiness and grace of the Holy Spirit and give the same benefit and grace to those for whom they are offered, be it a separate particle taken out separately for each or one general particle taken out for many. And this is clear from the very order of the proskomidia, for when he has taken out the fourth prosphora, the priest takes out of it only one particle for the whole clergy and for all living Orthodox Christians in the entire Church of Christ. Likewise, he takes out one particle of the fifth prosphora for all deceased Orthodox Christians. The Catholic Church believes and confesses that, although only one particle is offered for all living Orthodox Christians, and only one for all the deceased, the same benefit is bestowed to them through the grace and holiness of the Holy Spirit as if a separate particle would be offered on behalf of each Orthodox Christian. For the almighty grace of the Holy Spirit is never spent, as it is the same and equally effective in the bloodless sacrifice both in the form of one particle for each person separately and one particle for many.

"You go on to ask if it is possible for those having particular desire and zeal to ask the priest at the proskomidia to commemorate the names and take out the particles for those saints whom they might wish to commemorate out of their love for them, especially those whose names are not mentioned in the service book. Can their names be submitted for the proskomidia for special commemoration of these saints, so that they would pray for us sinners?

"My answer is that although what you have written in your question does not seem incorrect to you, all of the ranks of the saints are commemorated by the nine particles offered in their honor, even if all of them are not mentioned by name. If a priest, heeding the desire and zeal of certain lovers of Christ, would be prevailed upon to offer particles in addition to these nine in honor of certain saints not mentioned in the service book, he would place the new particles among the rows of the earlier ones and would create a fourth row of particles taken out for saints. If he should wish to take out particles for a greater number of saints, a fifth row of particles taken out for saints would be created. This is because the particles taken out for saints ought to be placed next to the particles for the saints, and not elsewhere, separately from the nine particles. If a priest were to dare to do this, he would destroy the order of the whole Liturgy, which has been maintained steadfastly by the entire Orthodox Church from the time the Christian Church began, and would introduce into the liturgical order a new practice, heretofore unheard of. It is from such innovations that various heresies and schisms usually arise, and may Christ preserve all who correctly believe in him from them. Those who have faith and love for the saints should be content with nine particles and should not seek to take out special particles in honor of certain saints. And let them call upon the prayers of those saints, so that through their prayers, they may obtain mercy and forgiveness of sins from God.

"You ask further if a priest can administer Holy Unction by himself or not, since you have a custom that only a priest with a deacon and a junior deacon can perform this Sacrament.

"And I answer that it says in a book on the profession of
the Orthodox faith that this Sacrament should be performed
by a number of priests, and this is in total agreement with the
Holy Scriptures, which say: 'Is any among you sick? Let him
call for the elders of the church, and let them pray over him,
anointing him with oil in the name of the Lord' (Jas. 5:14-15).
Thus it cannot be done by one priest, which would be in dis-
agreement with the Holy Scriptures and contrary to Church
Tradition. St. Symeon, Bishop of Thessalonica, says in his book:
'Is it possible for one priest to perform Holy Unction? One
priest should not perform this sacrament, for it is said, 'Let
them (sic) call for the elders, and not just one priest, and this
order has to be observed. Just as a bishop is not consecrated
by one bishop, so is Holy Unction not performed by one priest'
(Ch. 283). Why are there seven priests in Holy Unction, and
why even three if there are not enough priests? The brother
of the Lord does not indicate the number of priests, but
custom has established that seven shall be called. I consider
the basis of this to be the seven gifts of the spirit of Isaiah, or
the seven priests of the Old Testament who blew their trum-
pets around Jericho seven times at God's command, thus
causing its walls to collapse, so that these New Testamental
priests might destroy the evil city, and the cruel walls of
sinful offerings. Perhaps, in imitation of the Prophet Elisha,
who prayed seven times over the youth and restored him from
his deathbed, the New Testamental priests should restore the
dead soul by their sevenfold prayer. Or just as the Prophet
Elijah, having prayed seven times, opened up heaven, which
had been concealed by sin, and let the rain fall down, so shall
these, after praying seven times, put an end to the drought
of sin and let the rain of mercy from God and remission of
sins fall down. Such, it seems to me, is the meaning of the
sevenfold number of priests. Sometimes, when there is a
shortage of priests, only three are summoned, and this should
not be condemned, for this points, first of all, to the dogma
of the Holy Trinity, and also to Prophet Elijah's testimony
about the Trinity, when he resurrected the dead son of the
Zarephath widow, after praying over him and prostrating

himself three times. But let us not seek out too much about the number, but instead hold to the ancient tradition. One priest does not perform Holy Unction. We see from these words by St. Symeon that it is not right for one priest to perform the Sacrament of Holy Unction; when necessary, at least three priests should perform it. I found in one Slavonic book that even two priests can perform this Sacrament if necessary, but I did not find this in the Greek books. Enough said on this matter.

"I answer your last question, in which you ask me how you can be saved while living in the world with wives and children, in the following manner. Who can include in a brief word everything relating to the matter of salvation? I can only give you my advice for you to read the Divine Scriptures and our Holy Fathers with the greatest zeal, for to them is given the understanding of the mysteries of the heavenly kingdom, i.e. the true sense of the Holy Scriptures. In their soul-enlightened teachings, we can find in their entirety, all instructions necessary for spiritual salvation, which inspire anyone wishing to be saved to perform various good deeds and flee any deeds contrary to God. Reading their teaching zealously and diligently with faith and love, and with the fear of God and complete attention, you will have constant encouragement for various good deeds necessary for your salvation. And I, with all my unworthiness, recognizing that you are seeking instruction from me, can answer the following. The most merciful God saves the souls of Orthodox Christians through the Orthodox faith, good deeds, and his grace. The Orthodox faith is the one which is contained in the One Holy Catholic and Apostolic Church, and without this faith it is impossible for anyone to be saved. Good deeds are Gospel Commandments without which, as without the Orthodox faith, it is likewise impossible for anyone to be saved. The Orthodox faith without good deeds is a dead faith, and good deeds without the Orthodox faith are dead deeds. Whoever wishes to be saved must unite the two, and in this way, through the grace of Christ God, who said, 'Without me you can do nothing,' he can try to attain salvation. One should know that

Christ the Savior made good deeds equally obligatory for all
Orthodox Christians, be they monks or laymen living in the
world with wives and children, and seeks and demands from
everyone the most zealous performance of his commandments,
so that those who violate them and do not repent will have
no excuse and will not be able to respond at his awesome
Second Coming. All Orthodox Christians, male and female,
of all ages and ranks, the healthy and those lying in their sick
beds with various illnesses, and the weak and aged, can all
fulfill Christ's commandments, with the help of God's grace,
without any difficulty through only their good will and spiritual
humility, and in this way they can be saved. The Gospel
commandments, at least the most important and most general
ones, are so necessary for salvation, that if only one of them
was unfulfilled, there can be no salvation for the soul. These
include love for God and neighbor, meekness and humility,
endurance, wholehearted forgiveness of a neighbor's transgressions, lack of condemnation, lack of hate toward one's
neighbor, love for one's enemies, the bestowal of both spiritual
and bodily kindness toward one's neighbor, and other
commandments of Christ indicated in the holy Gospels. It is
necessary to try to observe them with all zeal, especially
loving God wholeheartedly with the entire soul and reasoning,
as well as one's neighbor as oneself. One should, following
Christ's meekness, resist the passions of anger unto blood and
be in peace with everyone, which is so necessary that Christ
himself said to his disciples many times, 'peace unto you,
peace I leave unto you, I give you my peace.' Where Christ's
peace is present, there Christ dwells. Christ does not dwell
in a soul that does not have the peace of Christ. And endurance
is so necessary for salvation that Christ says, 'By your endurance
you will gain your lives' (Lk. 21:19). Gaining lives is nothing
other than the salvation of souls. And one should have
endurance not only for a particular period of time, but until
death itself, for whoever has endured till the end will be
saved. Whoever wholeheartedly forgives his neighbor, will
himself not be condemned by God. But who can briefly
enumerate all the Gospel commandments which anyone who
wishes to be saved should keep and observe as the apple of

the eye? Meekness, the foundation of all the Gospel commandments, is just as necessary for salvation as is breathing for
human life. All the saints would save themselves in various
ways, but without meekness, no one saved himself and cannot
do so. Therefore anyone wishing to be saved has to consider
himself, wholeheartedly, the least of all before God, and to
regard himself alone as being guilty of each of his transgressions, without blaming anyone else. Fulfilling in this way,
with God's help, all of the Gospel commandments and
submitting before God, he becomes worthy of God's mercy,
forgiveness of his sins, and reception of God's grace. Through
God's mercy, he attains the salvation of his soul with total
certitude. In addition, Orthodox Christians ought to observe
meticulously all the Church commandments as well. The
sacrament of Confession consists of true repentance before
God, departure from one's sins, a firm resolve, with God's
help, no longer to return to them, confession of all sins to
the confessor, as to God himself, absolution of these sins, and
the acceptance of any penance assigned to him for these sins
according to the order of the Church. I will say the following
about preparation for Holy Communion. One should approach
Holy Communion with wholehearted confession, fasting and
tenderness of heart, at total peace with everyone, having heard,
according to Christian custom, all the Church rules, not
undergoing penitential discipline forbidding communion,
having fear and trembling, and with love and prostrations
proper to the One God, so that the Communion would be to
the remission of sins and life eternal. On the subject of how
to conduct one's own life at home and that of wife and
children, you can find most perfect instructions in the writings
of St. John Chrysostom and other saints.

"And so, my answers to your questions which, at your
fervent request or rather at your insistence, I had to write
against my will, have come to an end with God's help. As for
you, lovers of Christ, who have written these questions to me,
forgive me, a sinner, if I was not able, according to your
wishes, to give you the proper responses, because of my lack
of skill, to your questions about the holy canons. I could not
find the appropriate answers to all of the questions. Upon

receiving my answers, read them attentively, and should you find in them anything in agreement with the Holy Scriptures and the true mind of the Church, then follow it. And if in my answers I have erred in anything as a human being, then do not follow my error, but hold to the healthy mind and reasoning of the Catholic Church in everything, and in this way you will never fall into error. Let the God of love and peace be with all of you. Amen."

Concluding with this, the presentation of Starets Paisii's letters which were at our disposal, we shall now go to the description of the last days of his life and of his death.

CHAPTER V

The Last Years of Starets Paisii's Life

We have described Starets Paisii's life and activity during his stays at Dragomirna and Niamets as that of a leader of a monastic community, a toiler over the correction of patristic texts, and as a defender of true monasticism and Orthodoxy in his correspondence with various people. Many years of his life went by unnoticeably in these diverse labors and cares, and finally, he approached the departure from this temporal world to the eternal which none can avoid.

The starets' last years at Niamets were darkened by the terrible ravages of the war which had broken out nearby. According to the starets' biographer, a bitter struggle was again burgeoning between the three empires of Russia, Austria and Turkey. The countryside was filled with troops, the seas were covered with ships, and the towns and settlements of Moldavia were emptied. Local inhabitants disappeared into the mountains and forests, and the Niamets Lavra became filled with refugees who found room both inside and around the monastery. When Austrian troops came near and occupied the Moldavian foothills, the refugees felt safe from the Turks and started returning to their homes. But this security did not last long. The Turks gathered their strength and pressed the Austrians, who retreated to their border. The village of Niamets was taken by the Turks, who entered it without shooting or bloodshed, not counting three people who were killed for the resistance they offered to the Turks. A rumor spread in the monastery that the Turks had occupied a village fifteen miles away and were advancing toward the monastery. An indescribable horror overtook those who were in the monastery and seeking refuge there. The boyars sent soldiers to investigate, but frightened off, they returned without discovering anything certain. Not knowing exactly what the Turks were doing, the inhabitants of the monastery did not know what steps to take. Some urged that the monastery gates not be shut, and that everyone come out and beg the Turks to spare them. Others advocated locking the monastery and giving armed resistance to the Turks. Finally, a monk volunteered to go, with the starets' blessing, to the village and find out what was taking place. He reached Niamets safely, walked freely throughout the entire village, and found our from one of the peasants that the Turks had left Niamets. When the monk brought this news to the monastery, everyone calmed down. But the joy did not last long, for the Turks returned to the village again. Then the boyars and the starets moved to Sekul, while the rest of the monastery's inhabitants ran off into the woods. This was the second week of Great Lent. Finally, the Austrians came again and forced the Turks to retreat. In the meantime, Russian troops also entered Moldavia. Prince Potemkin, commander-in-chief of the Russian army, arrived in Jassy along with Archbishop Amvrosii of Slavensk and Poltava. Archbishop Amvrosii wished to see the famous Starets Paisii and came to the Niamets Monastery, where he was greeted by the starets and the entire monastic community with great honor. This was in 1790. After two days at the monastery, Archbishop Amvrosii served a Sunday Liturgy, at which he elevated the starets to the rank of archimandrite. Thus Paisii Velichkovskii, native of Poltava, received the rank of archimandrite from Archbishop Amvrosii, likewise of Poltava. After staying a few more days at Niamets and blessing everyone, Archbishop Amvrosii left the monastery and was seen off by the whole community with great gratitude and glory. Archbishop Amvrosii is known for his holy life and his uncorrupted relics are in the Monastery of the Exaltation of the Cross in Poltava.

After these events, four years went by in the usual labors and cares for the starets and the brethren. In 1794 the starets, as before, was working tirelessly, writing letters, working on translating the Fathers, and overseeing the community's life, but he was growing noticeably weaker. According to his biographer, Starets Paisii received brethren and visitors only from morning till noon during the last years of his life. He spent the rest of his time working alone in his cell. Only confessors could come to him during this time. Once a year the starets would visit the dwellings of his pupils, whom he would bless, praying that God would preserve them without harm from any evil. Shortly before his final illness, he ceased doing translations personally, but continued examining and correcting them to the last days of his life. After the fifth of November, he felt particularly weak and had to remain in bed, where he spent four days. He felt better on Sunday and wished to attend Liturgy. When he came into church, he sat in his usual place. During the Communion Verse, he went into the sanctuary and received Holy Communion. After the service he felt so weak that he was barely able to return to his cell, supported by some of the brethren. Over the next three days, the starets grew weaker. Onorii and Martirii, the brethren who were serving him, would not allow anyone to see him except for those who were the closest to him, since the starets wished to die in total silence. On the fourth day, sensing the approach of death, the starets received Holy Communion once again. He then called to his side the two senior confessors, Sofronii for the Slavic brethren and Silvestr for the Moldavians, and presented his peace and blessings through them to the whole community. The starets appointed no successor for himself, leaving that to God's will, the choice of the Mother of God, and the wishes of the community itself. Thereupon, he quietly passed away, as if asleep, on the fifteenth of November, 1794, at the age of 72. Immediately after the starets' death, the news was sent to Metropolitan Iakov. The Metropolitan entrusted the burial to Bishop Veniamin of Husi, later Metropolitan of Moldavia. When the news of the starets' death became known, a great numer of people gathered at Niamets, including laity, monks, priests, boyars, and simple folk of both sexes. They waited three days for Bishop Veniamin, and then gave up and the whole assemblage held memorial and burial services for the starets in the great church of the Ascension on the right side to the entrance. Bishop Veniamin arrived on the day after the burial and that morning served a Liturgy and memorial service. And a few days later, after a vote by the whole community and the Metropolitan's blessings, according to the rules of Paisii's brotherhood, he appointed Father Sofronii, the senior confessor of the community, as the starets and head of the monastery. A tombstone was later erected at Starets Paisii's grave, on which the following inscription was written in Rumanian and Slavonic: "Here lies our blessed Father, the Hieroschema-monk and Archimandrite Starets Paisii, a native of the Ukraine, who came to Moldavia from Mount Athos with sixty pupils, and gathering many brethren here, renewed the life of the community. He departed to the Lord in the year of 1794 on the fifteenth day of November, during the time of the righteous Voevode Michael Sudzhu and his beatitude Metropolitan Iakov." One of the starets' pupils wrote a "Funeral Dirge" to the deceased from all his spiritual children (see Appendix 3 at the end of the book).

From the first days following the starets' death, the brethren of the Niamets monastery were completely certain of the power of his prayers for all who faithfully and lovingly asked for his heavenly intercession. This confidence was expressed by the fact that soon after his death a special service was compiled, (verses and canon) "To our Blessed Father, the Starets Hieroschema-monk and Archimandrite Paisii in which the deceased is glorified as a great holy man of God, whose prayers grant spiritual salvation and bodily health to the faithful." In order to obtain an idea of this service, let us cite a few excerpts from it.

From the verses of "Lord I call . . .": Having ascended to the height of virtues, O our Father Paisii, you lived the monastic life, teaching, instructing and convincing us not to neglect the way which is pleasing to God. Through your zeal you have imitated the lives of the saints of old. You have been a good example for everyone, and had to endure many troubles until all became convinced of it by your great patience, monastic feats, and love. You have also written for us testimony from the Holy Scriptures.

You were a skillful physician, for you healed with great

facility those who came to you. You did not reproach them for the attack of illness, but as one skilled in patience, you placed in their hearts the perception to stay away from harm. Since your healing had effect to the very depths of wounds, you would heal completely, dismissing all of them in joy and peace, so they may fearlessly come to your healing, O our Father Paisii.

Constantly sitting in your cell and surpassing all in your mind, you discussed various spiritual and bodily afflictions and applied your healing and pleasing ointment to all, O Father.

From the canon: You were both ill and had many bodily wounds, but by your blessed manner and humble words you healed those who came to you, O Father Paisii.

Sedalen: Once a year you left your cell, O Father Paisii, and surveyed your pupils' dwellings, riding forth, viewing, and blessing the cells of each one of them as the sun was setting; and you sang with tears presenting them to God, saying, "Guard this small flock and protect it from the wolves that destroy it."

Forgive, O gentle Father, in your blessed and humble manner, me for violating your commands, for disregarding your holy will, for being more envious and evil than any man and for fulfilling my own will even more than the devil, and pray that God give me time for repentance.

I alone have walked in your light, and have not felt your light. I alone have eaten your sweet food and do not recognize my nourisher. I alone have drunk your sweet drink, and have not felt the sweet spring flowing out of your lips. I alone am the sheep who has lost its way from your flock, O good shepherd. Be not angry at me and beseech God to give me time for repentance.

When he was still alive, Starets Paisii was known for his unique gift of ardent and tearful prayer, during which his always radiant and magnificent face would become even more radiant and enlivened with the internal ardor of prayerful feeling. Here is what his cell-servant tells us in his biography of the Starets:

One day, still in Dragomirna, I came to him before
Vespers and intended to knock on his door to find out
if I could come in, but since the door was open, I
walked right into the cell after saying a prayer. Seeing
the starets lying down, I said, 'Bless, Father.' The
starets did not respond. I looked at him and saw that
his face looked as if it were flaming, while usually it
was white and pale. I was terrified. After standing for
a while, I repeated myself in a louder voice. The starets
did not respond again. It became clear to me that the
starets was engrossed in prayer, which explained why
his face was aflame. After standing a little while longer,
I went out, not telling anyone about what I had seen.

Much later, the same pupil saw the starets' face become radiant
while conversing with the brethren two more times. Besides
the gift of prayer, the starets, in certain instances, showed the
gift of foreseeing future events. Thus he foretold the terrible
death of the Voevode Gregory Shica. Shortly before the
Voevode's death, the starets saw a dream several times in
which a sword was hanging on a hair over the Voevode's
head. Soon afterward, the Voevode's head was indeed cut
off at the Turkish sultan's order, which caused the starets to
weep a great deal. Another time the starets was very sorrowful
about a certain brother from his community; he often reminded
him about mending his ways, but the brother would not listen.
Three days later, the brother drowned. In another case, the
starets implored a brother not to leave the monastery, and
finally tearfully said to him, "Brother, listen to me, for you
will not see the place to which you wish to go." The brother
did not listen and died along the way after four days, which
likewise caused the starets to weep. There were also instances
of miraculous healing through the starets' prayers, which due
to his profound humility, he totally attributed to the intercession of the Theotokos.

Besides these gifts of grace, the starets had many other
gifts which enabled him to successfully perform the service
which God had appointed to him on earth. These included:
the gift of wisdom and intellect, and together with this the

gift of profound self-knowledge, about which speaks St. Isaac of Syria, the teacher of silence whom the starets loved greatly: "Whoever is able to see himself is more blessed than one who has seen an angel"; the gift of proficiency in Greek and Slavonic; the gift of understanding the great meaning of the ascetical works of the Fathers; the gift of teaching and the building up of a monastic community; the gift of counsel, which he offered to all who required helpful instruction correctly and precisely, in accordance with the Fathers' teachings and instructions, and thanks to which they excelled in patience, humility and love; the gift of spiritual strength, which enabled him to remain, in all sorrows and temptation, calm and steadfastly confident in Divine Providence; the gift of the fear of God, which enabled him to faithfully keep all of God's commandments and be prepared to lay down his life for any of them; the gift of the love for God, which was ignited from his early youth, never leaving him and burning even stronger, so that he also kept others warm with his love and ardor, grieved over everyone and sympathized with all, without turning away anyone who requested help and consolation; the gift of love for peace, which enabled him to preserve peace, not to be offended by anyone, and not to despise anyone; the gift of patience and meekness, thanks to which he never appeared angry or upset, but always remained clear, meek, and patient; the gift of gentleness and childlike simplicity along with a profound intellect; the gift of consolation, by which he could pacify and calm down the saddest and most downcast person with his words; the gift of profound humility and self-criticism, which enabled him to take the blame for all unpleasant incidents which took place in the community; and finally, at the foundation of all these gifts and as a result of his unwavering performance of God's commandments, his constant maintenance of a pure heart, and unceasing internal prayer, there was his acquisition of the grace of the Holy Spirit, which caused a continuous stream of divine teachings to flow from his lips, delighting souls and withering all the evil passions. It was due to all these gifts that Starets Paisii was able to perform his great work, i.e. "to renew the deteriorating monastic order, restore fallen community life, implant in it thrice-holy obedience, enlighten with his teaching those abiding in the darkness of ignorance, and to instill wisdom through the correction and new translations of patristic and theological books from the Greek into his own language."

Part Five

Starets Paisii's Pupils on Mount Athos, in Moldavia and in Russia and the Growth of Orthodox *Starchestvo* in the Eighteenth and Nineteenth Centuries

"The kingdom of heaven is like leaven which a woman took and hid in three measures of meal, till it was all leavened"

(Mt. 13:33).

Starets Paisii's Pupils on Mt. Athos, in Moldavia and in Russia and the Growth of Orthodox Starchestvo in the Eighteenth and Nineteenth Centuries

Even if all the work done by Starets Paisii Velichkovskii would have amounted to his being an example of personal holiness, his organization of a monastic community on the basis of ancient patristic principles, and his corrections of patristic books, this would have been of no little importance to the Orthodox Church and Orthodox monasticism and society. But Starets Paisii has accomplished more—he created a school for spiritual life, reawakened a great spiritual movement in Orthodox monasticism, ignited the hearts of many with love for the spiritual life, and aroused a yearning for the internal monastic feat, for spiritual activity. Many outstanding ascetics were brought up in Orthodox monasticism under Starets Paisii Velichkovskii's influence and they totally mastered his precepts. Through constant prayer, unceasing attention to themselves, self examination, internal struggle with thoughts, obedience and humility, careful study of the Fathers, and the observance of the Gospel commandments, they achieved a high level of spiritual life and exerted great influence not only on their monastic brethren, but also on laymen, some of whom were highly educated not only secularly, but also theologically. Starting from the second half of the eighteenth century, this spiritual movement continued developing during all of the nineteenth century, up to the Revolution. It would be very interesting to follow this

movement in all its details—to study the ways and methods
by which it spread, be introduced to its principal representatives,
and to trace its influence on society and the people.
Unfortunately, the unfavorable circumstances of the present
time do not allow us to fulfill this task properly. Thus we
will have to limit ourselves to just a pale and superficial
account of this extraordinary movement and to reduce this
account practically to a mere list of names.

We will start by indicating Paisii's influence on Mount
Athos. Even when the starets was still living at Mount Athos
he had, besides his community of brethren at the Skete of
St. Elijah, a great deal of spiritual charges, interlocutors, and
friends who sought his spiritual guidance. Among them was
the Greek Patriarch Seraphim who was living in retirement at
the Pantokratoros Monastery. The Patriarch Seraphim loved
Starets Paisii very much, would visit him at his monastery,
would often invite him to his own, would hold lengthy talks
with him about spiritual life, and was very sorry to see him
leave for Moldavia. We also know that many monks would
come to Starets Paisii for confession and conversation from
many of the Athonite monasteries, sketes and cells. Sometimes
there were so many that the starets' own brethren would not
have a chance to speak with him, and they would start
grumbling. The traces of Starets Paisii's influence at Mount
Athos did not disappear with his departure to Moldavia. His
traditions and rules are still being kept at the Skete of
St. Elijah and other monasteries. The tradition of Starets Paisii
arose with particular force at Mount Athos in the nineteenth
century, with the appearance of Starets Arsenii, a pupil of
one of Starets Paisii's Moldavian pupils who had a great
influence on all the Athonite monasteries and died in 1846.
Among Arsenii's allies and successors were the schema-monks
Nikolai, Andrei, and Nikodim, and after them the
Hieroschema-monk Ieronim, the confessor of the Russian
Monastery of St. Panteleimon, who had particularly great
influence at Mount Athos and beyond it, and who died in
1885, and Makarii, the archimandrite of that same monastery,
who died in 1888. Through the work and cares of these
startsy, there arose in Caucasus the New-Athonite Monastery,

which also took on Starets Paisii's traditions and kept them in the person of its superior, Hegumen Ieron, and other startsy-monks, till the most recent time.

Starets Paisii also had a great influence on Moldo-Walachian monasticism. His closest associates both at Mount Athos and in Moldo-Walachia were all Moldavians. Such was, for instance, Father Vissarion, the starets' first pupil, and the first member of his brotherhood and helper in organizing his community. He died around 1776. Fathers Makarii and Ilarion, who helped Starets Paisii in correcting and translating books, were two more of his pupils in Moldavia who we can name. Ilarion was later confessor and superior of the Sekul Monastery, while Hieromonk Makarii, who had lived with the starets at Mount Athos, apparently later went to Russia where he was superior of the Molchansk Hermitage. Of the other of the starets' pupils in Moldavia, we shall first name those who became after his death his successors as confessors and superiors at the Niamets Monastery. The first one, Archmandrite Sofronii, the senior confessor of the Slavs at Niamets, headed the monastery for over ten years immediately following Starets Paisii. It is known that he made a trip to Kiev at the starets' request to obtain religious books for his monastery. He later corresponded with Starets Paisii's pupils in Russia, namely Father Afanasii in Briansk and Mariia Petrovna Protas'eva.

After Father Sofronii, Niamets was headed by Dorofei, whom the starets had sent to study at the theological school in Bucharest, Dosifei, the confessor and head of the infirmary at Sekul during Starets Paisii's time who sat up with the patients entire nights, consoling and comforting them in every way, and Ioann. All three of them were Slavs. After Father Ioann, the first Moldavian superior, Silvestr, was elected. He had been the confessor of the Moldavians during Paisii's time. To the list of Starets Paisii's pupils in Moldavia we may add Onorii, head of the infirmaries at Dragomirna and Niamets, who enjoyed the starets' unlimited trust, took care of him during his final illness, translated the Fathers, and died a year after Paisii; Martirii, who along with Onorii took care of the starets during his final illness; Irinarkh, the confessor whom the starets had sent to Prince Konstantin with the letter in which the starets refused to be moved to Niamets; Iakinf, likewise a confessor at Niamets, who had remonstrated with Feopempt, the blasphemer of mental prayer and who had done other services for the starets; another Ioann, schema-monk of the Transfiguration Skete at the Niamets Monastery, who became the starets of the Vorona Monastery in Moldavia and died at a very old age in 1843; Platon, schema-monk of the same Transfiguration Skete, who left behind the collection of Starets Paisii's works he had copied himself, which are now in the library of the New Niamets Monastery and who wrote the starets' autobiography; Mitrofan, a schema-monk who spent over thirty years as Starets Paisii's cell-servant and compiled his first biography; Archimandrite Feodosii, who headed the Merlo-Polyansk Skete in Walachia and was later summoned along with his pupils to Russia by Prince Potemkin to set up the Sofroniev Hermitage (a letter to him from the starets has been preserved in which he gives a detailed account of his work in translating and correcting patristic books); Gerontii, who studied at the theological school in Bucharest together with Dorofei; Grigorii, later to become a metropolitan, who wrote a biography of the starets; Hierodeacon Stefan, translator of the lives of the saints, schema-monk Isakii, and others. Among the keepers of Paisii's traditions were also Neonil, a disciple of Starets Sofronii, and Feofan, Neonil's disciple, both of whom transmitted Starets Paisii's traditions to the New Niamets Monastery. We must also add German, who was Feofan's successor. Besides these pupils and successors of Starets Paisii, he had many other helpers in Moldavia in copying, correcting, and translating patristic books, whose names have already been mentioned elsewhere. We should also note the bishops who sympathized with the starets and supported him. Such were Metropolitan Gavriil, who had placed Dragomirna at the starets' disposal, Iakov, and Veniamin. We do not have enough information about the further spread of Paisii's influence in Moldavia. We only know that many monasteries in Moldavia

We have much more information about Starets Paisii's and Walachia were headed by his pupils.

pupils in Russia. A particularly large number of his pupils went to Russia, and under their influence a great revival of spiritual life took place in our monasteries, interest and love for the reading and study of books were aroused. There appeared startsy and superiors of monasteries who kept Starets Paisii's precepts and introduced his community rules and the practices of monastery life, as well as bishops who sympathized with his orientation and gave him their protection and support. Many educated lay people were also attracted to this spiritual movement, while some of them left the world, entered monasteries, and became outstanding figures on the lines of Starets Paisii. The general result was a profound and widespread spiritual movement which did not abate within Russian monasticism up to the time of the Revolution. Let us enumerate as many of the participants in this movement as we can. First of all, let us mention those who, when the starets was still alive, turned to him from Russia for spiritual guidance. These included the starets' childhood friend the priest Dimitrii who most probably served in Poltava, the monks of the Monastery of the Exaltation of the Cross in Poltava, a group of devotees of righteousness from northern Russia, and the abbess of the Arzamas community, M. P. Protas'eva. We see from her correspondence with Archimandrite Sofronii, the starets' successor, that the latter sent to her monastery icons, Starets Paisii's portrait, and manuscript copies of the Fathers translated by Starets Paisii, including the *Philokalia,* the book of St. Barsanufrios, the *Twelve Homilies* of Symeon the New Theologian, and others, asking him to obtain from the Metropolitans Platon and Gavriil the permission to print these books. Others who had spiritual contact with the starets by correspondence will be mentioned later.

The spiritual movement in Russia under the influence of Starets Paisii can be divided into three main currents — northern, central and southern. The northern movement had as its main centers the Solovetsk Monastery, Valaam, the St. Aleksandr Nevskii Lavra, and the Monastery of St. Aleksandr of Svir. The central movement was concentrated mainly in Moscow, in the Vladimir Province, in the Optina Hermitage of the Kaluga Province, in the Briansk Monastery of the Orel Province, in the Roslaul forests of the Smolensk Diocese, and in the Monastery of Belyi Bereg. The southern movement was centered around the Ploshchansk Hermitage of the Orel Province, at the Glinskii Hermitage of the Kursk Province, and others. These monasteries should be regarded only as the most notable or originating points of Paisii's movement, which actually encompassed not tens but, as we shall see, hundreds of Russian monasteries.

In the extreme north, at the Solovetsk Monastery, the sower of Paisii's traditions was Hieroschema-mank Feofan, who has been mentioned before. Upon the death of the Kievan starets, the recluse Dosifei, Feofan moved to the Solovetsk Monastery, to where he carried Starets Paisii's precepts. At the Lavra of St. Aleksandr Nevskii, a group of Paisii's admirers and followers was formed even while the starets was alive, headed by Bishop Gavriil of Novgorod and Ladoga. Starets Paisii sent Metropolitan Gavriil a translation of the *Philokalia* from the Greek written in his own hand. The metropolitan had this translation examined by a group of learned instructors from the theological academy, and he recommended that as they correct the translation they should consult certain startsy with experience in the spiritual life saying that although these startsy were unfamiliar with the subtleties of Greek, they have mastered the content of the Fathers by their lifetime experience, and could therefore give them helpful suggestions in correcting the translation. The metropolitan also had the *Philokalia* printed in St. Petersburg. Those who grouped around the metropolitan included his cell-servant Feofan, who later became hegumen of the Novoozersk Monastery, Hegumen Nazarii of the Valaam Monastery, Hierodeacon Filaret of the St. Aleksandr Nevskii Lavra, who later became starets of the Novo-Spasskii Monastery in Moscow, Starets Paisii's pupil Afanasii, who had brought the *Philokalia* to the metropolitan, and others.

The Schema-monk Feodor and the Hieroschema-monk Kleopa were the pupils of Starets Paisii who worked at Valaam and at the Monastery of St. Aleksandr of Svir. They left Moldavia for Russia in 1801. Kleopa was a native of the Ukraine, while Feodor was from Karachev in the Orlov

Province.* They lived many years in Starets Paisii's monastery, received the tonsure from him, and were solidly instructed by him and established in the spiritual life. Upon arriving in Russia they first lived at the Chelna Monastery in the Orel Diocese, and then at the Belyi Bereg Hermitage of the same diocese, located among remote and at the same time almost impassable Briansk forests. There they became close with the monk Leonid who was, like Feodor, a native of Karachev and came from the merchant class. In 1811, Leonid and Kleopa moved to Valaam, where Feodor also joined them. They spent five years at Valaam, learning mental activity according to Starets Paisii's instructions, and had to suffer for this from ignorant adherents of external feats. In 1816 Starets Kleopa died at the Valaam Monastery, while Feodor and Leonid moved to the Monastery of St. Aleksandr of Svir, where they received the attention of Emperor Alexander I. Father Feodor died here in 1822 on the very day of Christ's Resurrection, and a few days later, Father Leonid went with his pupils to the Optina Hermitage, where he remained to his very death on October 11, 1841. While living at Valaam and the Monastery of St. Aleksandr of Svir, the startsy had spiritual contact with the St. Aleksandr Nevskii Lavra and had like-minded brethren and pupils everywhere. At Valaam their pupils were Starets Hegumen Valaam, who later moved to the Optina Hermitage and died there, and Evfrimii, the confessor at the Valaam Monastery. Evfrimii, in turn, had as pupils Hegumen Damaskin of Valaam and

---

* Starets Feodor, born in 1756, left Starets Paisii's monastery for a while to stay with the hermits Onufrii and Nikolai, who lived in silence by the Poliana-Vorona stream, about four miles from the skete of the same name. Onufrii, who was born in Chernigov into a noble family, came to love Christ from his youth, was a fool for Christ six years in his youth, after which he went to the Ukraine with his friend Hieromonk Nikolai, and then to Moldavia, to Starets Paisii, with whose blessings he settled in the desert with Nikolai and lived there with him twenty-five years. Starets Feodor also lived with him five years. After Onufrii's death, Feodor and Nikolai returned to Paisii, and after Paisii and Nikolai died, Feodor returned to Russia. At the Niamets library, there is a manuscript of a patristic book, which Nikolai copied for Onufrii. How little money meant to Feodor can be seen from an incident when he gave five rubles which had been given to him for travel expenses to the first poor peasant woman he met.

Ilarion, who carried Starets Paisii's traditions to the Nikolo-Babaev Monastery of the Kostroma Diocese. Damaskin, the famous hegumen of Valaam, had as pupils Archimandrite Agafangel of the Monastery of St. Aleksandr of Svir, Schema-monk Agapii of the Valaam Monastery and the silent Schema-monk Ioann of the Valaam Monastery. Agafangel had as a pupil Hegumen Navrikii of the Valaam Monastery.

Still another pupil of Starets Paisii did his work in the northern section. This was Arsenii, who left the Briansk forests for the St. Nikandr Monastery in Pskov. His pupil was Gerasim, a monk from the Solovetsk Monastery. In some of the northern monasteries Starets Paisii's traditions were borrowed from the monasteries of the central section and therefore will be mentioned elsewhere.

Let us turn to the central section. Here we should first of all mention Kleopa, a pupil of the starets different from the Kleopa mentioned above. This Kleopa lived with Starets Paisii for a long time, first at Mount Athos, then at the Drago-mirna Monastery and probably at Sekul, and went to Russia before 1778, where he became the superior of the Ostrovsk Hermitage of the Entrance of the Theotokos in the Vladimir Diocese. This was an outstanding ascetic and a keeper of mental activity. He introduced in the Ostrovsk Hermitage the cenobitic rules of Mount Athos, which his pupils later took to other monasteries of central and northern Russia. Starets Kleopa's pupils included Ignatii, who originally was at the Sanaksar Monastery, under the guidance of Starets Feodor Ushakov, and later at the Florishchev Hermitage in the Vladimir Diocese. Starting in 1778 he was the superior of the Ostrovsk Hermitage following Kleopa, and later the Peshnosk Monastery in the Novgorod Diocese, and with Metropolitan Gavriil's blessing introduced the cenobitic rules there. In 1795 he was transferred to the post of archimandrite at the Simonov Monastery in Moscow to establish cenobitic life, and died there in 1796. It is said about him that he was everywhere an example of exalted living, particularly of humility and lack of acquisitiveness. He was generous to beggars, sympathetic to the unfortunate and full of love to his brethren. Another one of Starets Kleopa's pupils, the Schema-archimandrite

Makarii, who followed Ignatii as the superior of the Peshnosk Monastery till his death in 1811, has a special place in the history of Russian monasticism and *starchestvo*, since 24 of his pupils ended up as superiors of monasteries. He was in spiritual contact and in correspondence with Starets Paisii, who presented him with a staff as a gift. He put the Peshnosk Monastery in internal and external order. Untiring and knowledgeable in domestic work, he was even more tireless and experienced in feats of spiritual life. He had a strict appearance, but his soul was full of fatherly love. He had no possessions, sharing everything with his brethren, was affable with everyone, and the simplicity of his heart, together with his spiritual wisdom, attracted general favor and respect. Metropolitan Platon entrusted him with the restoration of declining monasteries and held him up as an example to other superiors.

The Peshnosha Monastery was the source of both the cenobitic rules and monks capable of upholding community life for many monasteries. Thus, the following monasteries received their rules and organizational principles from Starets Makarii: Golutvin, Meeting of the Lord in Moscow, St. Kirill of Novoozersk, and the hermitages of St. David, Optino, Berlinkov, St. Catherine, Medvedev-Krivoozersk, and others. Among Starets Makarii's pupils we will name Avraamii, later superior of the Optina Hermitage, Maksim, superior of the Peshnosha Monastery, Schema-monk Ignatii of the Konev Monastery and the superior of the Zadne-Nikifor Monastery, and others. This Ignatii had as spiritual daughters Mariia, the hermit of Olonets, and Anastasiia, founder of a women's community which later became the Podansk Convent. Starets Kleopa's pupil was the remarkable ascetic Feofan, the hegumen of Novoozersk, whom we have mentioned as the cell-servant of Metropolitan Gavriil. He personally visited Father Makarii at Peshnosha in order to receive from him the cenobitic rules for his monastery and to ask for a few brethren to organize community life. Hegumen Feofan was a starets of the Modensk Monastery, the St. Aleksandr Nevskii Lavra, the Usting and St. Kirill Monasteries, and the St. Filipp Iran Hermitage. His spiritual daughter was Mavrikiia, the abbess of the Gorets

Convent. Feofan's successor at the Novoozersk Monastery was his pupil Arkadii. Paisii's traditions were transmitted from the pupils of the startsy Kleopa, Ignatii, and Makarii to the Golutvin Monastery in Kolomna, which was headed by Samuil, a pupil of Makarii and Ignatii. Samuil's pupil was Nazarii, while his pupils were the Schema-monk Ioannikii and the hermit Makarii, who walked the same path of internal spiritual feats.

The next point from which Paisii's movement spread in central Russia was Moscow. Here there were two focal points of this movement—the Simonov and Novospasskii Monasteries. The monk Pavel, one of Starets Paisii's pupils, went to live at the Simonov Monastery. In 1812, he suffered greatly at the hands of the French, who beat him so much that he remained in a sickly state for the rest of his life. Arsenii, another pupil of Starets Paisii, also lived at the Simonov Monastery. Pavel's pupil was Hieromonk Iosif, locum tenens of the Simonov Monastery. The Simonov Monastery was also, as we mentioned, headed by Archimandrite Ignatii, the pupil of Kleopa of Ostrovsk, who was appointed to this post for the purpose of organizing a community. Two remarkable startsy at the Novospasskii Monastery were the Hieromonk Filaret and Aleksandr, pupils of Paisii's pupil Afanasii, who at one time lived at the Florishchev Hermitage in the Vladimir Diocese. Schema-monk Afanasii (not the same Afanasii who brought the *Philokalia* to Metropolitan Gavriil), a former captain of a hussar regiment with the last name of Zakharov, lived with Starets Paisii for over seven years and accepted the tonsure from him. With the starets' blessing he took many extracts from the Fathers' instructions on prayer, humility, patience, obedience, love and other virtues. By force of necessity, he was allowed to go to Russia with the monks Amvrosii and Feofan in 1777. He underwent much trouble here, and spent time at the Gorokhov Monastery, the Florishchev Hermitage, the Belyi Bereg Hermitage, and the Ploshchansk Hermitage of the Theotokos in the Orel Diocese, where he was of great benefit to many through his life and teachings. It was at the Ploshchansk Hermitage that he died in 1825. Whenever Starets Afanasii would come to Moscow from the Florishchev Hermitage, he would visit the Hieromonks Filaret and Aleksandr of the Novospasskii Monastery, and held religious discussions with them about mental activity according to Starets Paisii's teachings. Both of these startsy knew about Starets Paisii, loved and respected him, and made use of his translations of the Fathers, while Father Aleksandr even corresponded with him. Thus, both of these monks from Novospasski stood very close to Starets Paisii and made plentiful use of his spiritual treasures. It is possible that knowing Afanasii, they also knew Amvrosii, another pupil of Starets Paisii, who lived at the Gorokhov Monastery and was noted for his special gift of prayer.

Hieromonk Filaret was a native of Viazma, a member of the well-to-do Puliashkin family of merchants. Sensing an early repulsion to the secular life, he joined the monastery at the age of thirteen, and from his childhood he delved deeply into the readings of religious literature, which was plentiful in his father's house. Later he spent a few years at the Sarov Hermitage, and then became hierodeacon at the St. Aleksandr Nevskii Lavra under Metropolitan Gavriil. From Petersburg, Filaret moved to Moscow, where he spent some time first at the Simonov Monastery and then at Novospasskii, where he spent over forty years in one cell, rarely venturing outside the monastery gates. Only on quiet summer evenings, when human traffic would cease, would he come out with his friend Aleksandr and another starets named Mikhail, who held to the same teachings, for a private journey around the monastery walls. Having spent many years in feats of monastic silence, Starets Filaret devoted the rest of his life to the active service of other people, offering advice and consolation to all who requested them, disregarding their person and rank. His cell was filled daily with people of diverse callings. Dejected with sorrow, oppressed by life, troubled by doubts, possessed by passion, and overtaken by trouble from all directions, they would come to him to pour out their troubles before him and to receive consolation and instruction from him. His remarkable meekness, extreme humility, ardent love for his neighbors, and the beauty and power of his profound spiritual intellect were expressed with particular clarity in his discussions. It often happened that because of the large number of visitors, he would not have time to eat or rest, in spite of his painful illness. And in spite of all this, he found time to read and copy the Fathers. Only shortly before his death (he died in 1842 at the age of 84) was he not able to provide his counsel to those needing it, for because of a stroke his tongue could pronounce little besides his usual calling upon the names of the Savior and the Mother of God. Starets Filaret was the confessor of Nataliia Petrovna Kireevskaia, the wife of the famous Russian writer and philosopher Ivan Vasilevich. Through her he exerted his influence upon her husband, interested him in the spiritual life which was taking place in Russian monasticism, disposed him toward deeper study of Orthodoxy, and contributed to the development of his spiritual closeness with the startsy of the Optina Hermitage. In addition, Father Filaret was spiritual guide for Dosifeia, a nun of the Ivanov Convent in Moscow whose high quality of spiritual life was exemplary. The fate of this nun is somewhat mysterious, and many have considered her to be the daughter of the Empress Elizaveta Petrovna. Dosifeia, on her part, had a great spiritual influence upon the Putilov brothers, famous ascetics who as monks became Moisei of Optina, Isaiia of Sarov and Antonii of Malo-Iaroslavets.

As for Filaret's friend Hieromonk Aleksandr, later archimandrite of the Arzamas Monastery, it is known that he was born in the same year as Filaret, i.e. 1758, and came from an Orthodox family of Polish nobles. He knew Polish well. Devoted to the Orthodox Church, he especially liked the book *The Rock of Faith* by Metropolitan Stefan Iavorskii and the works of St. Dimitrii of Rostov, whose book *The Spiritual Alphabet* he recommended to all who entered the monastery and urged its lifetime study. He received his training at the Kiev Academy. Then he took a position in the civil service. We do not know how much time he spent there, but he was later to say himself that when he was still young, he began the monastic life at the Moscow Novospasskii Monastery. When he was in Petersburg with the monastery's superior he was tonsured by Metropolitan Gavriil, who also ordained him hierodeacon in 1793 and hieromonk a month later. He always enjoyed the metropolitan's favor and maintained a constant correspondence with him. Also in 1793 he was appointed deputy and treasurer of the Novospasskii Monastery, but four years later, he gave up both positions and remained at the same monastery, spending his time in prayer and in studying the Fathers who underwent the performance of the mental prayer of Jesus, and received the great schema in his cell.

When His Eminence Gavriil was in Moscow for Emperor Paul's coronation, he had many talks with Father Aleksandr and invited him to the Novgorod Diocese, but he refused, not wishing to leave his privacy and his friend, who was pursuing the same goal as he was. Living at the Novospasskii Monastery, he had contact with Moldavian and Athonite startsy, made use of their advice, and whenever they came to Moscow on miscellaneous business, he would receive them and be of great help through devoted Moscow acquaintances. Likewise, with great eagerness, he helped those who sought after the monastic life. Under this guidance many of them carried out a diligent monastic life. Some of his pupils were superiors of monasteries. In 1810 Father Aleksandr was ordained archimandrite of the Arzamas Monastery of the Savior, from which he conducted an extensive correspondence with his spiritual children and admirers in Moscow. Living very modestly, but receiving large amounts of money because of his position, he would give everything away to the brethren, the monastery workers, indigent students of theological academies, and everyone who was in need. Only forty kopecks in change and no clothing remained after his death. Before his death he did not take any food for eighteen days, except for a few drops of water, consuming only the bread of life, the Body and Blood of the Lord. He died on April 29, 1845, having served in the priesthood 52 years.

In order to show what the starets was like, we shall cite a few excerpts from his letters. When the young ascetics Timofei and Iona Putilov, who were under Father Aleksandr's spiritual care, were setting out to live at Sarov, Starets Aleksandr gave them the following exhortation: "This is what I advise my brethren in Christ Timofei and Iona to do upon their arrival at the Sarov Hermitage: 1) While living there, go to the brethren and deal with only those whom the superior and confessor specify. 2) Undergo obedience without complaint, and should you be burdened by anything, humbly request to be transferred to something else, and submit if you are not transferred. 3) Remember and live there, without stepping out anywhere, for even if you do observe any seeming discomforts or temptations there, you will not expel them from within yourselves and will take them along. You will find them tenfold in another place and as you wander about they will start increasing, until they return you to the world completely. But if you start obeying your superiors and will accuse yourselves, and will regard temptations concerning brethren as your own ailment and infirmity, you will remain at peace with everyone in everything. 4) Even if your work of obedience will be burdensome, it only seems that way due to disobedience and stubbornness, for you will see others of obedience peacefully carrying out the same work although they are weaker than you. Incidentally, should you, according to your wishes, be left without a work of obedience, you will be so overcome by thoughts that you will not be able to cope with them. So do not refuse work of obedience, but seek it. 5) For your eternal spiritual benefit always remember that any temptation is defeated by humility, self-reproach, and patience. Let the Most Merciful Lord enlighten and teach you, help and preserve you, and conceal you from the nets of the enemy left and right. 6) While undergoing obedience, beware of sudden bursts of energy and watch your health, for you shall answer to God if, due to mindless fervor, you will somehow harm yourselves and burden your neighbors. If you become incapacitated, you will no longer be serving the brethren, but the brethren will be obligated to serve you, and in such a case you will have a bitter life, from which may God deliver you."

In that same year Starets Aleksandr wrote to Timofei Putilov, "I am rejoicing heartily that the merciful Lord has not allowed you and Iona to wander about the world and to defile your souls with deception. Endure for the sake of God and do not forget that your struggle is not unto flesh and blood, but to the principalities and so on. It is better for us to struggle against thoughts according to John Climacus than against conceit. And it is no good for us to be passionless, for demons generally heave for the sake of our conceit, knowing that we can perish from our own pride and remain unrepented apart from their craftiness. You write that thoughts stand in your way. If you hold back the wind, then you can also hold back thoughts. And the Fathers say that it is possible for a monk to be passionate but not to fulfill his passions. Consequently, we will be condemned for the fulfillment of passions, not simply because we have them and are overcome by thoughts. Even the first Adam realized through his sense of discernment that the apple was good to eat, but was condemned for eating the apple and not for this knowledge. And God has commanded him not that he should not acknowledge the fruit's goodness, but that he should not eat it. Therefore do not put your souls in confusion with any thoughts, since you do not like them and do not derive pleasure from them. If you have a confessor and trust him, reveal to him all your thoughts and struggles. But do not accept your mind at all, as it is damaged and defiled by sins, and do not trust yourselves in anything till your death. Most of all I ask you to be obedient without reasoning and humble yourselves before everyone. According to the teachings of the Fathers, only humility can bring salvation, and without it we shall not avoid eternal condemnation even if all the virtues are present. What concern do we have with the visual aspects of life, if only God would preserve us from active sins? God will give you wisdom, if you only endure for His sake."

Father Aleksandr writes to a certain Andrei Stepanovich that Christ should not be sought outside oneself, but inside: "I cannot give you a decisive response regarding your intention and desire to visit Jerusalem and Mount Athos. My advice is that you find yourself a poor monastery which is isolated from the world somewhere in your own country, and in it try to find Jesus Christ not on Mount Athos, but in your heart. For it is impossible to find Him anywhere except in our hearts. And if the Lord will vouchsafe you to find Him in your Heart, then even the most crowded square will become Jerusalem and Mount Athos for you. One of the saints once said, if there is a buried treasure in your house, and you do not know about it, then for you it is as if this treasure never existed. This is precisely how each one of us searches for Jesus Christ in all kinds of places, not knowing that He always abides within us. May Almighty God illumine your heart and point out to you the place where Jesus Christ dwells."

Another very important place in central Russia where the spiritual developments coming from Starets Paisii were being fostered was the Svensk Monastery in Briansk of the Orel Diocese. This was, in the early nineteenth century, the dwelling place of Monk Serafim and Schema-monk Afanasii, the same one who took the *Philokalia* to Metropolitan Gavriil. Schema-monk Afanasii, who had been a senate secretary, left the world, wandered all over Mount Athos and Moldavia, lived at the monastery of Starets Paisii (who entrusted him to his pupil Sofronii), and did translations and transcriptions of the Fathers. In 1805, when he was already living at the Svensk Monastery, he was instructed by Starets Sofronii to stay out of monastery affairs and to live in silence. He died at the same Svensk Monastery in 1811 in the arms of the Schema-monk Afanasii (Zakharov) to whom he first gave his remarkable anthology from the works of the Fathers. While living at the Svensk Monastery, Starets Afanasii, along with Starets Serafim, exerted spiritual influence upon the future superior of the Optina Hermitage, Timofei Putilov, who had been living there for a while. Another person who was able to discover the activity of the spirit from the startsy was the monastery's superior, the famous Filaret who later became dean of the Moscow Theological Seminary, Bishop of Kaluga, and Metro-politan of Kiev, and who was a supporter of monasticism and *starchestvo*.

All these encounters and instances of living together at the Briansk Monastery merit our special attention. As we shall see later, the connections which would have repercus-sions elsewhere were established. A group of hermits from the Smolensk Diocese who lived at the end of the eighteenth and the beginning of the nineteenth centuries in the sketes of the Roslavl forests was in spiritual contact with the Briansk Monastery. This unique group of Russian hermits had a close relationship with Starets Paisii. It included both immediate pupils of the starets, such as Dosifei, who spent forty years in the Roslavl forests and Arsenii, who later went to the St. Nikandr Monastery, in Pskov, and those who did not know him personally, such as Hierodeacon Anastasii, Afanasii, who was confessor at the Svensk Monastery during his last nineteen years, Arsenii from the Hermitage of Belyi Bereg, and Moisei and Antonii Putilov, who later moved to the Optina Hermitage along with the hermits Ilarii and Dorofei.

We shall now turn to the Optina Hermitage, one of the greatest and most famous monasteries in the history of Russian *starchestvo*. This hermitage was restored out of its state of neglect by the famous Metropolitan Platon of Moscow, who named as its superior Avraamii, a pupil of the Peshnosha archimandrite.* This appointment placed the Optina Hermitage into the sphere of Starets Paisii's spiritual influence, since Avraamii, a pupil of Makarii, a fervent admirer of Starets Paisii and a keeper of his traditions, took these traditions to the Optina Hermitage as well. Here he introduced the cenobitic rules and raised the level of spiritual life. Actually, even before Avraamii the Optina Hermitage was not a stranger to Starets Paisii's influence. As early as 1800 the monk Feofan, Starets Paisii's pupil, settled there. He was a native of the Vladimir Province, had served in the Black Sea Cossack Regiment, left the military due to illness, spent some time at the St. Sofronii Hermitage, with Archimandrite Feodosii, from which he went to Moldavia to Starets Paisii where he lived three years working as a cook. Upon the starets' death, he returned to Russia and joined the Optina Hermitage. He was extremely non-acquisitive, very meek, a strict faster and a great master of prayer. His zeal for the feat of fasting once inspired him to spend all of Great Lent entirely without food. He revealed this to one of his brethren who was close to him

---

* Metropolitan Platon was himself a great admirer of Starets Paisii. In the library of the Niamets Monastery there is a book of homilies by St. Macarius the Great which Metropolitan Platon had sent to Starets Paisii with the following inscription: "To the venerable Father Archimandrite Paisii, the spiritual guide and instructor of the Niamets Monastery, this book, inspired by similar feats of a glorified man, is being sent by the humble Platon, Metropolitan of Moscow, with a request for blessings and for prayers pleasing to God. Moscow, third day of July, 1971."

in spirit: "I believe," he said, "that I will not die from this fast." The brother tried neither to discourage nor encourage him in his undertaking. And Feofan ate nothing during the entire fast, except for drinking warm water once a week. Throughout the forty days he performed the whole service in his cell, made many prostrations, heated the cell himself and appeared alert. One day, noticing that Feofan had lost much weight, a brother said to him, "Father, you have greatly exhausted yourself." "Do not worry," answered Feofan, "Christ the Savior poured out all His blood for me on the cross, and I still have plenty of blood." Having carried out this self-accepted feat with God's help, he partook of Holy Communion at the end of Great Lent. Later, he made another attempt to perform this feat, but caught a cold, developed a violent cough, and gradually growing weak, died in 1819. When a brother asked him if he was afraid of anything in his hour of death, he answered, "I would gladly be delivered from this life," lifted his hand for the sign of the cross, and quietly departed to the Lord.

In 1821 the Kaluga Diocese was headed by His Eminence Filaret (Amfiteatrov). A great lover and admirer of monasticism, and especially of Starets Paisii, he, as did Metropolitan Platon, gave particular attention to the Optina Hermitage, and for the greater progress of monastic life in it decided to establish there a skete named in honor of John the Baptist. For this he invited his acquaintances, the hermits of the Roslavl forests Dosifei, Moisei, Antonii, Ilarii, and others, who became the founders of the famous skete at the Optina Hermitage. A few years later Father Moisei became superior of the Optina Hermitage, and his brother Antonii superior of the skete. In this way the spiritual life of the Optina Hermitage became concentrated in the hands of the experienced keepers of Paisii's traditions. In 1829 they were joined by Hieromonk Leonid (Lev after the schema), a pupil of Starets Feodor who had come from the St. Aleksandr of Svir Monastery, and with his arrival the famous Optina *starchestvo* began at the Optina Hermitage.

In this way, the numerous threads of Starets Paisii's spiritual influence joined together at the Optina Hermitage as in a knot through his various pupils. Thus, the monk Feofan brought the spiritual leaven which he had received at the Niamets Monastery directly from Starets Paisii himself, Avramii brought Starets Paisii's traditions, which he had received from Kleopa of Ostrovsk, Moisei and Antonii brought the traditions of the two Afanasiis, Serafim of Svensk, and the hermits of Roslavl, and Leonid brought the traditions of Feodor and Kleopa of the Ukraine. It was this combination of diverse spiritual influences that resulted in the remarkable growth of the Optina *starchestvo*.

Having settled at the Optina Hermitage, Starets Lev soon acquired great influence and extensive fame not only among the monastery's brethren, but also among the neighboring population and pilgrims to the hermitage. Through his superior way of life, wisdom, insight, gift of healing, mercy for the suffering, directness, and bold reprobation of the depraved, no matter what their position would be, Father Lev drew general admiration and love. All sorts of people began coming to him for helpful advice and consolation in their sorrows from various towns and villages—nobles, merchants, artisans, peasants, and clergy. With each year the crowds grew larger. Each person after being received by the starets with fatherly love, would reveal his spiritual wounds before him and would find comfort in what he said. Many of those who had bodily ailments or were possessed obtained help from his prayers and holy ointment from the vigil light burning in front of the Our Lady of Vladimir icon in his cell. Through his positive influence both on the brethren of the monastery, of which he was the superior and confessor, and on the pilgrims, Starets Lev contributed greatly to both the internal and external improvement and well-being of the Optina Hermitage. Many brethren from various places would gather under the hermitage's roof, seeking wise guidance in spiritual feats. Knowing Starets Lev's spiritual experience and giftedness, Father Moisei, the superior of the Optina Hermitage, would entrust all who came to live there to the starets as their spiritual guide. Gifted with spiritual reasoning and having a sharp memory and the gift of speech, Father Lev would give spiritual instruction to everyone from the Fathers and the Holy Scriptures. When in public, the starets preferred to conceal his high spiritual state through the extreme simplicity of his speech, which was marked by the unique combination of the spiritual force of the Scripture and vivid expressiveness of the popular language. In addition to his daily work at the monastery, the starets would receive numerous letters from various people asking him to answer their puzzling questions, and because of his love for his neighbors, the starets would either write or dictate the necessary responses. Father Lev died at the age of 72. During his final illness he repeatedly called upon the name of the Lord, but finally calmed down, crossed himself, blessed the brethren, and peacefully placed his soul into the hands of God.

In view of the great role played by the Optina Hermitage in the history of Russian *starchestvo*, let us name its more outstanding and famous ascetics and startsy, and also those individuals and monasteries upon which it had particular influence. Having received the basic leaven of Paisii upon its restoration, the Optina Hermitage became intimately linked with Starets Paisii's spirit and precepts. Everything in it, including the monastery's rules, the order of services, the general organization of life, and spiritual condition of each separate brother, are amazingly coordinated with each other and bear the seal of a particular spirituality, enlightenment, and joyful peacefulness. Having barely crossed the threshold of this monastery, a pilgrim immediately senses God's proximity, the particular blessedness of its spiritual atmosphere, and unwittingly grows closer to God, and assumes a radiant and joyous manner. The Optina Hermitage maintained these spiritual features and this prolific influence for over one hundred years, up to the Revolution.

From among the remarkable ascetics and startsy of the Optina Hermitage we should first mention its famous superior Moisei, who headed it for over thirty years and who died in 1862. Son of a Moscow merchant, he, along with his brothers Aleksandr and Iona, was under the spiritual guidance of the Moscow startsy Filaret and Aleksandr and the starets Sonifeia. Later, he lived at the Sarov Hermitage with his brother Iona, from which he moved to the Svensk Monastery in Briansk, where he made use of the guidance of Starets Paisii's pupils Afanasii and Serafim, lived with his brother in the sketes of the Roslavl forests under the guidance of Dosifei, Dorofei, and Arsenii, and, finally, moved to the Optina Hermitage where he remained till his death. He was a strict keeper of Paisii's traditions and his cenobitic rules, initiated the Optina *starchestvo*, brought spiritual and material well-being to the Optina Hermitage, and was himself known for his holy life and spiritual experience. While guiding the life of the Optina community, he did not leave without guiding others who sought counsel from him. Thus his spiritual guidance was extended to Moisei, superior of the St. Tikhon Hermitage in the Kaluga Diocese, and to Hieroschema-monk Aleksandr, a recluse at the Gethsemane Hermitage at the Trinity—St. Sergeis Lavra, whose pupil was Hieromonk German, confessor at the Gethsemane Hermitage, who later became the superior and abbot of the St. Zosima's Hermitage in the Vladimir Diocese.

Father Moisei's brother, Father Antonii, lived with him in the Roslavl forests and took part in the organization of the Optina Skete. He was its first superior, after which he spent fourteen years as the abbot at the Mal-Iaroslavets Monastery in the Kaluga Diocese. After resigning this post he spent twelve years in retirement at the Optina Hermitage, where he died in 1865. Like his brother, he was noted for the high level of his spiritual life and had a special gift of comforting the sorrowful. His letters and notes, which were published by the Optina Hermitage, are remarkable. Hieroschema-monk Iosif of St. Nikolai of Ugreshsk Monastery, in the Moscow Diocese, was under his spiritual guidance.

In addition to the above there were many other remarkable ascetics at the Optina Hermitage. These include the following: Archmandrite Melkhizedek, a pupil of Ignatii of Ostrovsk, whose positions were superior of St. James Monastery in Rostov, the Monastery of the Savior in Arzamas, and the Monastery of the Savior and St. Euthymius in Suzdal, and acting superior of the St. Aleksandr Nevskii Lavra, and who died while in retirement at Optina; Hieroschema-monk Starets Ioann, a former schismatic and pupil of Starets Lev who was tonsured by Father Moisei and left behind several writings against the schism. (While proving the correctness of Orthodoxy, he bore wonderful testimony to it by reaching into a boiling pot of water for a handful of sand at the bottom. He died in 1849); the Monk Ilarion, who joined Optina at the age of eighty and remained there sixteen years; Vassian, a starets, schema-monk, and great faster who in all his 45 years as a monk never drank tea or wine, never ate fish or milk except for Pascha, and twice underwent a total forty-day fast; Hieroschema-monk Iov, Starets Makarii's confessor and a great lover of silence; Hieroschema-monk Pimen, Starets Amvrosii's confessor and a pupil of Lev and Makarii who distinguished himself through his outstanding simplicity and quietness.

We shall now turn to Makarii, the next famous Optina starets. He came from the Ivanov family, members of the landowning gentry in the Orel Province. In his youth he was thinking of marriage, but one time he visited the Ploshchansk Hermitage in the Orel Diocese and was so taken by the beauty of monasticism ("all the monks seemed as earthly angels to him"), that he decided not to return home and remained at the monastery for good. His instructor at the Ploshchansk Hermitage was Starets Paisii's pupil Schema-monk Afanasii (Zakharov), the same one under whose influence were the Startsy Filaret and Aleksandr, and through them Moisei of Optina and Ivan Vasilevich Kireevskii, all of whom later worked with Starets Makarii on the publication of Starets Paisii's translations. What an amazing network resulted from the spiritual threads coming from Father Paisii! Father Makarii lived at the Ploshchansk Hermitage twenty-four years. After Starets Afanasii died, Father Makarii and Father Lev grew closer spiritually and began a correspondence, the result of which was Father Makarii's move to the skete of the Optina Hermitage. For seven years the Startsy Makarii and Lev lived together at the Optina Skete. They were bound together by the closest of friendships and were of the same mind. They would write together to their spiritual children under a common signature. But their personalities were totally different. Father Lev, who was of the merchant class, was direct, somewhat coarse, and full of practical wisdom, although he did have a gentle heart. Father Makarii, who was a noble, was mild, meek, enjoyed working with books, and in his youth, before joining the monastery, he played the violin and liked to sing. But they were both equally great practitioners of true spiritual monasticism. After Father Lev's death, Father Makarii continued as a starets for nineteen more years while serving simultaneously as head of the skete after Father Antonii, and died in 1860. Just as Father Lev, he gathered around himself many pupils who wished to train in monasticism under his guidance. Among them were many educated men with whose help the starets undertook the publication of Starets Paisii's translations of the Fathers. As we said, a particularly close collaborator in this task was Ivan Vasilevich Kireevskii, Father Makarii's spiritual son, who lived at Dolbino, his estate not far from the Optina Hermitage. Ardent cooperation in publishing books was given to the starets by his Moscow friends and admirers, including Metropolitan Filaret of Moscow, Father F. A. Golubinskii, professor at the Moscow Theological Academy, Professor Shevyrev of Moscow University, and others. Thus, Starets Makarii's work and concern gave root at the Optina Hermitage to the publishing activity which continued even after his death.

Two years after his death Father Makarii was followed by Archimandrite Moisei, superior of the Optina Hermitage, and three years later, by his brother Abbot Antonii. In this way death overtook the main personalities who established *starchestvo* and strict monastic community life at the Optina Hermitage. But the work they had started did not dwindle after they died. The work of the first generation of the Optina startsy was kept and continued by the new starets, Hieroschema-monk Amvrosii, and by the new superior of the monastery, Archimandrite Isakii. Starets Amvrosii, whose surname was Grenkov, came from a family of clergy and was born in 1812 in the village of Bolshiia Lipovitsy in the Tambov Province. After completing an ecclesiastical school and a theological seminary, he spent some time as a tutor in a family of landowners, and then as an instructor at an ecclesiastical school in Lipetsk. In 1839, at the advice of Starets Ilarion Troekurovskii, he went to the Optina Hermitage, which he joined under the spiritual guidance, first of Father Lev, and after his death, of Father Makarii. Exhibiting a lively, cheerful and sociable personality, a kind and gentle heart, a penetrating mind, experience in life and wisdom, a lofty spiritual nature, and a profound gift of prayer and knowledge of the human heart, Amvrosii, after Makarii's death, naturally took his place and united in himself the spiritual qualities and gifts of both his predecessors. He had a great spiritual influence not only upon the brethren of the monastery, but also upon outsiders of every rank and calling, financial status, and educational level, starting with the poor and ignorant peasant woman, weeping over her dying turkeys, and ending with metropolitans, grand dukes, senators, writers, and philosophers, who would come to him with difficult and complex problems of inner and outer life, seeking advice and consolation, and no one would leave from him without obtaining the necessary help and moral support. Thus, the following words of the apostle, carved out later on his tombstone, were actually fulfilled in him: "To the weak I became weak, that I might win the weak. I have become all things to all men, that I might by all means save some" (1 Cor. 9:22). In spite of his extreme weakness and the illness which kept him in bed most of the time, he would receive visitors from morning till late at night, with a small break for lunch and a brief rest. This activity continued without interruption for as long as thirty years.

During the last ten years of his life, he added to his cares the upkeep and maintenance of the populous women's community of Shamordino, which he founded eight miles from the Optina Hermitage, and which supported an orphanage, a school, an almshouse for sixty elderly women, and an infirmary, in addition to a thousand nuns, most of whom had no means of their own and were sometimes sick and aged. With the help of devoted spiritual children, among whom we cannot avoid mentioning the Kliucharev, Perlov and Bakhrushin families, the starets not only supported this huge monastery, but also erected there a magnificent church and refectory of rare beauty. In the midst of such a large population and such cares, the starets did not cease his work in book publishing and also carried on an extensive correspondence.

When in 1891 Starets Amvrosii died, everyone felt the collapse of a tremendous moral and material support for a great many unfortunate and miserable people, and there was nothing pretentious in the great general sorrow and loud weeping which accompanied his burial.

While Starets Amvrosii was at the Optina Hermitage, the superior there was Archmandrite Isakii. He came from a wealthy Kursk family of merchants named Antimonov. In his youth he sold livestock and frequented fairs. Having decided to join the monastery, he went to the Optina Hermitage without his father's knowledge and appeared to Starets Lev. As usual, the starets was sitting surrounded by people, weaving sashes, his usual handicraft and conversing. The young Antimonov settled down behind everyone. Suddenly he heard the starets calling out loudly, "Vaniushka!" Since he did not think that this call was addressed to him, a fashionable little dandy from the city, Antimonov remained calmly seated. However, the people grew agitated, started shoving him, and saying, "Go on, the starets means you." Struck by the starets' insight, Antimonov came up to him and after speaking with him stayed at the monastery for good. First he was a pupil of Starets Lev, then Father Makarii, and finally, Starets Amvrosii, upon whose instructions, which were a total surprise to him, he was appointed superior of the monastery after Father Moisei's death. Father Isaakii was profoundly humble and pious and practiced silence. He died at an old age in 1894.

We can name additional Optina dwellers. Hierodeacon Palladii came to Optina from the Ploshchansk Hermitage during Avraamii's time in 1815 and lived there 46 years. Hierodeacon Mefodii was bedridden with paralysis for 22 years. He could say "yes, yes" and "Lord have mercy." Lev Tolstoi knew him and liked to point him out as an example of great suffering and endurance fostered by the Christian faith. There was the blind Schema-monk Karp, about whom Starets Lev said, "Karp is blind, but sees light," and Hieroschema-monk Gavriil, the founder and starets of the Belokopytov women's community. Hieroschema-monk Feodot was the confessor and starets at the Gethsemane Skete and the Paraclete Hermitage of the Trinity—St. Sergei Lavra. Hieroschema-monk Ilarion,

confessor and head of a skete, was Starets Makarii's cell-
servant, and later shared the work of *starchestvo* with Starets
Amvrosii. The novice Elisei was a forest warden who spent
52 years at Optina, refused salary increases, and was Starets
Amvrosii's favorite guest. Hieromonk Kliment (Zedergolm)
was Starets Amvrosii's pupil, clerk, and partner in book publishing, whose story is especially remarkable. He was the son
of Moscow's chief Lutheran pastor, a very learned and serious man who was deeply devoted to Lutheran teachings.
Father Kliment graduated from the philosophy department
of Moscow University, where he did very well, and was preparing to become a professor. Dissatisfied with Lutheranism,
he came to know Starets Makarii through his Orthodox Moscow friends, felt the beauty and truth of Orthodoxy, converted
to the Orthodox faith, became a monk, and settled at the skete
at Optina, where the strictest ascetics lived. There he became
Starets Amvrosii's most devoted pupil and helped with clerical
work and book publishing. His correspondence with his father
about his conversion to Orthodoxy is quite interesting. Also
interesting is his biography by the famous Russian writer and
philosopher K. N. Leont'ev, who was Starets Amvrosii's spiritual son.

Let us continue our list of outstanding Optina dwellers.
Konstantin Nikolaevich Leont'ev was Russian consul in the
Near East, a highly educated man, a creative Russian thinker
who hated and rejected socialism as a tendency toward a general
leveling and depersonalization and who acknowledged that
the world lives and is saved by beauty. He wrote the book
The East, Russia, and Slavicism. When he was at Mount
Athos, he lived through a serious illness (cholera) and was
healed miraculously through prayer before the icon of the
Theotokos. After this he became a deeply believing Orthodox
Christian, having sensed with special power the truth of two
Orthodox principles—about eternal torments and eternal bliss.
After moving to Optina in the seventies of the last century,
he met Father Amvrosii and became his devoted pupil. Before
Father Amvrosii's death he went to the Trinity—St. Sergei
Lavra, became a monk and died in 1892. Another was Elavian,
a pupil of the Startsy Lev, Makarii, and Ilarion, and a strict

ascetic. There was also Anatolii (Zertsalov), a hieroschema-monk and head of the skete following Father Ilarion's death. A pupil of the Startsy Makarii and Amvrosii, he was from an ecclesiastical family and a seminarian. Together with Iosif, he was Father Amvrosii's successor as starets. He was known as a performer of mental prayer and was confessor for the Shamordino sisters, dying in 1894. Hieromonk Daniil Bolotov came from a prominent noble family and was the brother of the Schema-nun Sofiia, the famous first abbess of the Shamordino community. A graduate of the Academy of Arts, he was an outstanding iconographer and portraitist, and a very educated man. This pupil of Starets Amvrosii was unusually kind and pure in heart, and painted Amvrosii's best portrait. He died in 1907. Hieroschema-monk Iosif, Starets Amvrosii's cell-servant and his successor as starets, was a humble and meek starets. Starets Amvrosii would say to his spiritual children about him, "I gave you wine with water to drink, but Iosif gives you pure wine to drink." He died in 1911. Archimandrite Venedikt, who came from the married clergy, was Anatolii Zertsalov's successor as head of the skete and as starets. After being widowed, he turned to Starets Amvrosii for advice and joined Optina upon his instructions. He served as Father Amvrosii's clerk and as confessor for the Shamordino sisters. He died as archimandrite of the Borovsk Monastery. Iuvenalii (Polovtsev) helped the Startsy Makarii and Amvrosii in their book publishing and later became superior of the Glinskaia Hermitage, acting superior of the Kievan-Pechersk and St. Aleksandr Nevskii Lavras, Bishop of Kursk, and Archbishop of Lithuania. Leonid Kavelin, likewise a partner of Makarii and Amvrosii in book publishing, was later acting superior of Trinity-St. Sergei Lavra. Ksenofont, archimandrite and superior of Optina, was a humble, strict, silent, and pious keeper of Optina traditions and came from a peasant background. The last startsy at Optina were Hieromonk Nektarii, a performer of mental prayer and pupil of the head of the skete and Hieromonk Anatolii, who was Starets Amvrosii's cell-servant and later became his generally recognized successor.

With these final names we conclude our far from complete

list of the outstanding deceased Optina ascetics who have
kept Starets Paisii's precepts. Through its continuous spiritual
growth, the Optina Hermitage became a powerful spiritual
center, out of which the spirit of true Orthodox monasticism
developed extensively throughout all of Russia. Lev Tolstoi,
who observed the Optina startsy closely and acknowledged
that Christian feelings were deeply rooted in the Russian
people, says in one of his letters that these feelings have been
cultivated among them by the Russian monasteries and their
startsy.

Now let us name those monasteries and people to whom
was extended the spiritual influence of the Optina Hermitage
and its startsy. Starets Antonii of Optina, upon being appointed
superior of the Malyi Iaroslavets Monastery, brought along
Starets Paisii's traditions. His work was continued by Archi-
mandrite Pafnutii, who had previously been the head of the
skete at Optina. Starets Lev planted *starchestvo* at St. Tikhon's
Hermitage of the Kaluga Diocese through his pupil Gerontii.
Besides Gerontii, we also know of other ascetics at St. Tikhon's
Hermitage. Its confessor was Efrem and its superior was
Moisei, a pupil of the Startsy Lev, Makarii, and Moisei of
Optina. At the St. Nikolai of Ugreshsk Monastery of the
Moscow Diocese there were Starets Lev's pupil Ilarii, the
monastery's superior, and Abbot Antonii's pupil, Hieroschema-monk Iosif. *Starchestvo* was planted at the Belev Convent by Father Lev through his spiritual daughter Anfiia, who
endured much grief for her devotion to Father Lev, and also
through Abbess Pavlina, mother superior of the Belev Monastery, under whom this monastery especially flourished. Likewise, the St. Boris-Our Lady of Tikhvin Women's Hermitage
of the Kursk Diocese was under Starets Lev's spiritual guidance. Other pupils of the Optina startsy included Makarii,
superior of the Mozhaisk-Luzhitskii Monastery of the Moscow
Diocese; Nikodim, abbot of the Meshehev and Malo-Iaroslavets Monasteries; Ilarii, starets of the Meshehev Monastery; Makariia and Abbess Tikhona, mothers superior of the
Kashira Convent; Aleksandra, founder of the Belokopytov
Convent of Our Lady of Kazan and Archpriest Andrei, priest
at the convent; Archimandrite Agapit, superior of the Likhvin

Monastery, who wrote the best biography of Starets Amvrosii;
Abbot Serapion, superior of the Odrino Monastery; Hieroschema-monk Antonii, confessor at the Kievo-Pechersk Lavra;
Archpriest Father Georgii Kossov of the village Spas Chekriak
in the Orel Province, who was famous for his praying abilities
and gifts of insight and healing, and who built a magnificent
stone church, a school, an orphanage, and an almshouse in
his poor and remote village; the Schema-nun Sofiia (Bolo-
tova), who was Starets Amvrosii's spiritual daughter and
pupil, and the first mother superior of the Shamordino Monastery of Our Lady of Kazan, and upon whose death Starets
Amvrosii said, "O Mother, you obtained grace from God!";
Abbess Efrosiniia, the blind second mother superior at Shamordino; and the Abbesses Ekaterina and Valentina, the latter
being the last mother superior at Shamordino.

Starets Makarii exerted his spiritual influence upon convents
in Velikie Luki, Viazma, Kursk, Serpukhov, Sevsk, Kaluga,
Elets, Briansk, Kazan', Ostashkov, Smolensk and others. Likewise, many convents are connected with Starets Amvrosii's
name, and certain of them owe their creation to him. Those
under his guidance included St. Boris' Hermitage, the Kashir,
Belev, and Bolkhova Monasteries. He gave his blessings to
the creation and organization of the Gusev Monastery of Our
Lady of Abhtyrba in the Saratov Diocese, the Kozelshehina
Monastery in the Poltava Diocese, the Piatnitakaia convent,
the St. John the Baptist Hermitage in the Orel Diocese, the
St. Nicholas-Our Lady of Tikhvin community in the Voronezh
Diocese, and, finally, the Shamordino Hermitage of Our Lady
of Kazan.

In speaking about the spiritual influence of the Optina
Hermitage. We cannot remain silent about its influence upon
the Russian intelligentsia as well. We have already mentioned
I. V. Kireevskii, Father Kliment Zedergolm, and K. N. Le-
ont'ev. Let us also mention N. V. Gogol', who corresponded
with Starets Makarii and Archimandrite Moisei, Professors
Shevyrev and Iurkevich of Moscow University, and those who
paid visits to Starets Amvrosii, including F. M. Dostoevskii,
V. S. Solov'ev, Count A. K. Tolstoi, Grand Duke Konstantin
Konstantinovich, and Count Lev Tolstoi, who, even in the final

fatal days of his life was first of all drawn to Optina, to its startsy. There lived at Shamordino Lev Tolstoi's sister Mariia, about whom Starets Lev said when she was yet a child, "This Masha will be ours." It must be said about Shamordino in general that hundreds of educated women whose names are impossible to list found refuge there under Starets Amvrosii's wing.

It still remains for us to examine the southern branch of the Russian *starchestvo* which originated from Starets Paisii. We know the following immediate pupils of Starets Paisii who were in the southern part of Russia. The monk Gerasim was tonsured by Starets Paisii and upon leaving for Russia, dwelt at St. Sofronii's Hermitage in the Kursk province. Hieroschema-monk Liverii lived in the Ekaterinoslav Diocese and died at a very advanced age in 1824. One of his pupils was the learned monk Makarii, Dean of Students at the Ekaterinoslav Theological Seminary, who later became the famous leader of the Altai mission. A most extensive influence in the south was undoubtedly exerted by the famous Hieroschema-monk Vasilii (Kishkin). He came from a noble family of the Kursk Province, travelled a great deal and stayed a long time at Mount Athos and with Starets Paisii in Moldavia. Upon returning to Russia he became head of the Belyi Bereg Hermitage, and afterwards lived at the Kremenets Monastery, Savior Hermitage, Korennaia, Glinsk, St. Sofronii and St. Boris Hermitages of the Kursk Diocese, Pukhov Monastery of the Chernigov Diocese, Ust-Modveditsa Monastery of the Don Diocese, and Sevsk Monastery and Ploshchansk Hermitage of the Orel Diocese. He left numerous pupils at all these places and died in 1831. He had the good fortune to hear Tikhon of Zadonsk speak, and was a friend of Bishop Antonii of Voronezh. He was an outstanding ascetic who from his youth showed chastity, humility, patience, and love for those abusing him. Among his pupils we know Starets Lev of Optina, who was under his guidance at Belyi Bereg; Serafim, the former superior at Belyi Bereg; Arsenii, who lived in the Roslavl forests; Schema-Hierodeacon Melkhizedek, Schema-monk Makarii of Belye Berega, and other ascetics of this hermitage, which, it should be said, was likewise a prominent center of the movement which Paisii inspired. Other pupils of Starets Vasilii included Schema-monk Afanasii of Mount Athos, Hierodeacon Anastasii, who lived at the Svensk Monastery and the Roslavl forests, Archimandrite Melkhizedek of St. Simeon's Monastery in Moscow, Archimandrite Moisei of Optina, and Abbess Avgusta of the Ust-Medveditsa Convent.

The famous ascetic of Glinskaia Hermitage, Filaret, with whom the Glinskaia branch of Russian asceticism began, was also Vasilii's pupil, as well as being a pupil of Starets Archimandrite Feodosii from Moldavia. We can name the more famous ascetics of this branch: the Monk-starets Feodot, who had the gift of insight; Hieroschema-monk Makarii, also an insightful starets who attained a high level of spiritual perfection; Martirii, a great faster who would not eat for whole weeks and who enjoyed solitude and silence; Schema-monk Evfimii, who was Father Filaret's cell-servant; the hermit Hieroschema-monk Panteleimon, who is buried in the skete which he established at the spot of the appearance of the miraculous icon of the Nativity of the Theotokos; Hieromonk Antonii, who was assistant to the community's confessor and a practitioner of silence; Hierodeacon Serapion, who saw his guardian angel and fingered his rosary beads for three hours after his death; the monk Dosifei who had the gifts of insight and healing, and who was allowed the honor of hearing angelic singing at Starets Feodot's deathbed; Schema-archimandrite Iliodor, who for eight years was abbot of Rykhlov Monastery and superior of Sts. Peter and Paul Monastery of the Chernigov Diocese; Schema-monk Lavrentii, who was Archimandrite Iliodor's pupil and his successor as starets; Archimandrite Innokentii, who was a pupil of many startsy, mostly Starets Makarii, and who possessed a heart filled with love and the gift of healing; Hieroschema-monk Iliodor, a master of prayer who foretold his own death a year in advance; Schema-monk Arkhipp, who possessed the gifts of insight and prayer and guided the spiritual life of the schema bearers; the insightful ascetic Luka, and many others.

Among the individuals who did not belong to the community at Glinskaia Hermitage, but who utilized its spiritual guidance, we know the following: Abbess Filareta of the Annunciation Convent in Ufa, who was a pupil of Filaret of Glinskaia; Archimandrite Makarii of the Altai Mission, who was later superior of the Trinity Monastery in Bolkhova and was known for his biblical translations and gift of insight; Feodosii, who was confessor at the Hermitage of the Holy Mount in the Kharkov Diocese and a pupil of Filaret; Hiero-schema-monk Ioann, who was a recluse at the Hermitage of the Holy Mount and a pupil of Father Filaret; Ioannikii, also a confessor at the Hermitage of the Holy Mount and a healer of the possessed; Archimandrite Paisii, superior of the Vysoko-gorskaia Hermitage of St. Nicholas and a pupil of Father Filaret, whose supervision of monks was foretold by St. Sera-fim of Sarov 24 years in advance; Makariia, the insightful schema-nun of St. Gamaliel's Convent of the Chernigov Diocese who was the spiritual daughter of Starets Anatolii of the Glinskaia Hermitage; and Abbess Kleopatra of the Sevsk Convent, to whom Starets Anatolii gave the blessing to join the convent while predicting that she would become an abbess.

To this brief list (which is far from complete) of Starets Paisii's pupils, we consider it necessary to add a list of lavras, monasteries, convents, hermitages, sketes, and communities which received from him or his pupils their statutes, startsy, or superior, or which had his pupils and followers among their brethren. Again, we caution that this list is far from complete.

1) The Skete of St. Elijah on Mount Athos and other Athonite monasteries and sketes which have been under the influence of Starets Paisii and his pupils.

2) The Dragomirna Monastery of the Holy Spirit in Moldavia.

3) The Sekul Monastery of St. John the Baptist in Moldavia.

4) The Niamets Monastery of the Ascension in Moldavia.

5) The New Niamets Monastery in Bessarabia.

6) The Tisman Monastery in Moldavia and other Moldavian monasteries which were under Starets Paisii's influence.

7) St. Aleksandr Nevskii Lavra in Petersburg.

8) St. Aleksandr of Svir Monastery of the Olonets Diocese.

9) The Arzamas Monastery of the Savior of the Nizhni-Novgorod Diocese.

10) The Susev Women's Community of Our Lady of Akhtyrka in the Saratov Province.

11) St. Amvrosii Our Lady of Kazan' Women's Hermitage in the Kaluga Province.

12) The Altai Mission.

13) The Borovsk Monastery of St. Pafnutii of the Kaluga Diocese.

14) Berlukov Hermitage of the Vladimir Diocese.

15) Sts. Boris and Gleb Monastery of the Moscow Diocese.

16) The Svensk Monastery in Briansk of the Orel Diocese.

17) The Hermitage of Belye Berega of the Orel Diocese.

18) The Kashira Monastery of Belye Peski of the Tula Diocese.

19) St. Boris' Convent of the Kursk Diocese.

20) The Belev Convent of the Exaltation of the Cross.

21) The Bolkhova Convent of the Orel Diocese.

22) The Bolkhova Monastery of the Trinity.

23) The Buzuluk Women's Community of Our Lady of Tikhvin, of the Samara Diocese.

24) The Babaev Monastery of St. Nicholas, of the Kostroma Diocese.

25) The Belokopytov Convent of Our Lady of Kazan of the Kaluga Diocese.

26) The Briansk Convent of the Orel Diocese.

27) The Valaamo Monastery.

28) The Velikie Luki Convent.

29) The Viaz'ma Convent of St. Areadius.

30) The Vysokogorskaia Hermitage of St. Nicholas on the Churka.

31) The Vil'no Monastery of the Holy Spirit.

32) The Goretsk Convent of the Novgorod Diocese.

33) The Gorokhov Monastery of the Vladimir Diocese.

34) The Gethsemane Skete at the Trinity — St. Sergei Lavra.

35) The Glinskaia Hermitage of the Kursk Diocese.

36) St. Catherine's Hermitage of the Moscow Diocese.

37) The Elets Convent.

38) The Zadne-Nikiforskaia Hermitage of the Olonets Diocese.

39) St. John's Convent in Moscow.

40) The Krivoozersk Hermitage of the Kostroma Diocese.

41) The Golutvin Monastery in Kolomna.

42) St. Cyril's Monastery of the Novgorod Diocese.

43) The Konevts Monastery on Lake Ladoga.

44) The Kursk Convent.

45) The Kozel'shchina Convent of the Poltava Diocese.

46) The Kremenets Monastery of the Voronezh Diocese.

47) The Convent of Our Lady of Kazan in Troitsk.

48) St. Elias Monastery in Menzelinsk, of the Ufa Diocese.

49) The Kashira Convent.

50) The Kievo-Pecherskaia Lavra.

51) The Kaluga Convent.

52) The Kirensk Monastery of the Irkutsk Diocese.

53) The Likhvin Monastery of the Protection of the Kaluga Diocese.

54) The Leslevsk Hermitage of the Smolensk Diocese.

55) The Medvedev Hermitage of the Vladimir Diocese.

56) The Modensk Monastery of the Novgorod Diocese.

57) The Malyi Iaroslavets Monastery.

58) The Meshehev Monastery of the Kaluga Diocese.

59) The Mozhaisk Luzhitskii Monastery of the Moscow Diocese.

60) The Molchansk Hermitage of the Kursk Diocese.

61) The Novoozersk Hermitage of the Novgorod Diocese.

62) The Novospasskii Monastery in Moscow.

63) St. Nicholas of Ugreshk Monastery of the Moscow Diocese.

64) New Athos in Caucasus.

65) St. Nicholas-Our Lady of Tikhvin Women's Community of the Voronezh Diocese.

66) The Ostrovsk Hermitage of the Entrance of the Theotokos of the Vladimir Diocese.

67) The Optina Hermitage of the Entrance of the Theotokos of the Kaluga Diocese.

68) The Odigitriia Convent in Cheliabinsk.

69) The Odrino—St. Nicholas Monastery of the Orel Diocese.

70) The Ostashkov Convent of the Tver Diocese.

71) The Peshnosha Monastery of the Moscow Diocese.

72) The Palei Ostrov Hermitage of the Olonets Diocese.

73) The Padansk Convent of the Olonets Diocese.

74) The Paraclete Hermitage of the Trinity—St. Sergei Lavra.

75) The Ploshchansk Hermitage of the Orel Diocese.

76) The Pskov Monastery of St. Nikandr.

77) Sts. Peter and Paul Monastery of the Chernigov Diocese.

78) The Piatnitskaia Women's Community of the Voronezh Diocese.

79) St. John the Baptist Hermitage in Kromy.

80) The Pochaev Lavra of the Dormition.

81) St. James Monastery in Rostov.

82) The Ryklov Monastery of the Chernigov Diocese.

83) The Roslavl Sketes of the Smolensk Diocese.

84) The Monastery of the Meeting of the Lord in Moscow.

85) St. Simeon's Monastery in Moscow.

86) The Solovetsk Monastery.

87) The Sarov Monastery of the Sarov Diocese.

88) The Suzdal' Monastery of the Savior—St. Evtimii.

89) The Serpukhov Convent.

90) The Sevsk Convent.

91) St. Sofronii Hermitage of the Kursk Diocese.

92) The Hermitage of the Holy Mount, of the Kharkov Diocese.

93) The Smolensk Convent.

94) The Spas-Cherkriak Monastery in the Bolkhova District of the Orel Diocese.

95) The Tikhvin Monastery of the Novgorod Diocese.

96) Trinity Monastery in Kiev.

97) St. Tikhon's Monastery of the Kaluga Diocese.

98) Trinity Monastery in Birsk, of the Ufa Diocese.

99) Trinity—St. Sergei Lavra.

100) The Usting Monastery of the Novgorod Diocese.

101) The Ust-Medveditsa Convent of the Don Diocese.

102) The Monastery of the Dormition in Orenburg.

103) The Ufa Monastery of the Annunciation.

104) The Florishchev Hermitage of the Vladimir Diocese.

105) St. Filipp's Hermitage on the Irapa, of the Novgorod Diocese.

106) The Chelnshaia Hermitage on the Irapa, of the Novgorod Diocese.

107) The Iakutsk Monastery.

We see from the above, how extensive was the scope of Starets Paisii's influence. In Russia it affected the monasteries of 35 dioceses, and the greatest number of monasteries with Starets Paisii's pupils can be found in the Moscow Diocese (14). The other dioceses are Orel (12), Kaluga (9), Novgorod (7), Vladimir (6), Kursk and Smolensk (5), Olonets (4), Petersburg, Tula, Voronezh, Orenburg, and Ufa (3), Kostroma, Pskov, Kiev, and Chernigov (2), and the rest with one each.

The present book was written at a unique moment in time, when not only in Russia, but everywhere a bitter struggle is being fought against the very foundations of Christianity. A drive is evolving to construct human life upon entirely new principles, known as socialistic and communistic, but which would be more correctly called atheistic and materialistic. For two thousand years Christianity has been pointing out to humanity that neither in humanity nor in man who is estranged from the eternal source of life, from God, can the true meaning and justification of life be found. They can be found only in the knowledge of God, in unity with Him, in love for Him, and in conforming one's life with God's will. Outside of this submission to God's will, human life turns into a complete chaos of bitter struggle and mutual destruction.

Christianity has revealed to humanity the most profound mystery of the salvation of the world and man through the Son of God, the God and Man Jesus Christ, who became incarnate and was crucified on the cross, through His Holy Church and His Holy Sacraments, especially the Sacrament of Holy Communion, and through His teachings. In the name of this saving faith he calls men to brotherly unity and peaceful upbuilding of the common life—to the continuous development of all the aspects of human life, including the mental, moral, aesthetical, and material. Christianity does not disparage earthly life, although it regards it as only a preparatory stage for eternal life. It promises immortality to men. Through its view of the world and its practical application of religion to life, Christianity has been training mankind for two millenia, producing a tremendous upsurge in its spiritual capacities and creating great treasures in the works of art, music, architecture, literature, and science, which have ennobled human mores and relationships. It revealed to men a boundless world of a new boundless life.

It is this Christian worldview and the spiritual image of the soul which it creates that are so repugnant to the new man. Their idol is man, whom they regard as the supreme being of nature, while at the same time they do not believe in his immortality. For them man is merely the highest of the animals and his existence is limited to earth. Contradicting themselves, they do not notice the insignificance of human existence, building on a foundation of sand. And while Christianity calls men to universal brotherly unity, they deepen strife, sow enmity, and call for mutual destruction in the name of class interests. And so a great struggle is taking place in the arena of the world — atheism is struggling with Christianity. The Book of Revelation tells us whose side will be victorious. But how many souls are cut off from God in this struggle, from the fullness of a meaningful and happy life! Through his whole life and his whole spiritual image, Starets Paisii Velichkovskii serves as a radiant and attractive expression of the Christian spirit, which is repugnant to the atheistic spirit. From his early youth his soul was already inextricably bound with God through faith and love. He was very far from the proud exaltation of the human personality. He had no other desire besides being a performer of God's will. In this yearning to conform his will to God's, and in his continual spiritual growth in the image and likeness of God, was contained the meaning and joy of his life. But it was not only in himself that he created and bore this meaning and this joy. He spread it all over, and first of all within that large Christian community which was gathered beside him. One can say that this was a commune, but one created not in violence and blood, but by a free will, self-denial, and brotherly love in the name of Christ.

In publishing our book we wish that not only monastics, but all Christians might find in the living example of Starets Paisii Velichkovskii confirmation of the wisdom and correctness of the Christian way and the possibility of its practical realization, on the condition, of course, of total and self-denying obedience to God, of the acceptance of the easy and light yoke of Christ (Mt. 11:30).

Bibliography on Starets
Paisii Velichkovskii

A. Manuscript Sources

1) Manuscript No. 58 of the Imperial Academy of Sciences, Section on Russian Language and Literature, A. I. Iatsimirskii, Collections: "The Account of the assembly of the Fathers, Brethren, and my spiritual charges, all Beloved in the Lord, who gathered in Christ's name around me, who am unworthy; for the sake of the spiritual salvation; this assembly having taken place at the following holy and honorable monasteries: the holy and great Monastery of the Ascension of our Lord, God, and Savior Jesus Christ, known as Niamets, and the holy Monastery of the honorable and glorious prophet, forerunner and baptist of the Lord John, known as Sekul; for which cause this holy assembly has gathered around me, sinful and unworthy as I am." This manuscript contains Starets Paisii's autobiographical notes which he wrote while at Niamets and which break off with his first stay in Moldo-Walachia.

2) Manuscript no. 65 of the same collection: Starets Paisii's letter to monks on the precepts of monastic life and on his own life.

3) Manuscript no. 66 of the same collection: Starets Paisii's letter on silent prayer and other ascetical issues.

4) Manuscript no. 29 of the Petrograd Imperial Theological Academy containing: a) The Life and Feats of our Blessed Father, Starets Paisii: "Escape from the World, His Wanderings, the Gathering of His Brethren, and Living Together with Him" (the biography was written by Schema-monk Mitrofan, a pupil of the starets who was with him nearly thirty years); b) Instructions on the tonsure of a monk; c) A letter to a certain priest Dimitrii; d) A letter to the bishops of the Orthodox Moldo-Walachian land, containing the starets' statutes and order of monastic community life; e) A funeral dirge to the starets; f) A service to the starets.

5) The manuscript collection of Starets Paisii's works from the library of New Niamets Monastery in Bessarabia, containing: a) *Introduction on the Order and Statutes of the Cenobitic Assembly by our Father, Starets Paisii of Blessed Memory*; b) Starets Paisii's letter to the most honorable Feodosii, abbott of the Tsibukan Skete; c) Letter to the same Feodosii, Archimandrite of St. Sofronii Hermitage in Russia (more detailed than the one in print); d) The

accusation against Hieromonk Feopempt, who blashphemed against mental prayer; e) Starets Paisii's responses which he wrote to certain devotees in Russia on certain questions; f) Paisii's short essay on the sign of the Holy and Life-bearing Cross, which ought to be made by all Orthodox Christians; g) Letter to the venerable teacher Kir Nikifor (later bishop of Astrakhan); h) Letter to the desert fathers Onufrii and Nikolai, who lived in silence 25 years by the Vorona stream; i) A brief letter from Paisii to the most honorable Priest Ioann and others. This collection was handwritten by the Schema-monk Platon, a pupil of Starets Paisii, in the eighteenth century.

6) Anthology no. 56 of the Simonov collection of manuscripts in the Moscow Synodal (Patriarchal) Library. This includes *The Life of Our Blessed Father Starets Paisii*, gathered from many writers and compiled by Father Platon in the days of the Voivode Mikhail Grigorevich Strudtsa, with the blessing of His Eminence Metropolitan Kiriu Kir Veniamin, when Makarii was archimandrite of the holy monasteries at Niamets and Sekul in the summer of 1830, at the Niamets Monastery of the Ascension. In addition to the biography, this anthology contains certain of the above-named articles and translations by Starets Paisii.

7) Manuscript no. 47 from the same collection, containing the story by the Solovetsk Starets Hieroschema-monk Feofan of his visit to the Niamets Monastery in the time of Starets Paisii.

8) Sekul Monastery Collection (unnumbered), containing: a) Introduction on the Order and Statutes of the Cenobitic Assembly by Our Father, Starets Paisii of Blessed Memory, along with the Order and Statutes in Eighteen Points; b) The Life and Feats of our Blessed Father and Starets Paisii (by the monk Mitrofan); c) a *Funeral Dirge* to Starets Paisii from his spiritual children; d) a service to the Venerable Starets Paisii; e) The following letters: to Abbot Feodosii of the Tsibukan Skete; a scroll with Starets Paisii's works on mental prayer, divided into chapters; the complaint of the monks of the Poliana-Vorona Monastery to their abbot against Hieromonk Feopempt, who blasphemed against mental prayer, and their general complaint against the same Feopempt to Starets Paisii on June 19, 1793; Starets Paisii's letter to them; letter to the teacher Hieromonk Nikifor (Feotoki) in response to his request to send monks who could teach children in city schools; Starets Paisii's letter dated June 7, 1776 to the desert Fathers Onufrii and Nikolai, on the subject of the latter's illness.

9) Collection no. 354/111 of the Orel Diocesan Archives, containing excerpts from the Fathers on prayer, humility, patience, purity of heart, and so forth. This was compiled by Schema-monk Afanasii of the Svensk Monastery in Briansk, a pupil of Starets Paisii, who in 1810 gave it to another of Paisii's pupils, Schema-monk Afanasii Zakharov, who was the teacher of Hieroschema-monk Makarii, the Optina starets.

10) The collection *On Monastic Feats*, containing excerpts from the Fathers about spiritual life. It was written by Archimandrite Moisei, superior of the Optina Hermitage, while he dwelt in the Roslavl forests as a youth in the years 1812-21. This is interesting for studying the nature of the activities performed in their cells by Starets Paisii's followers in Russia.

11) Manuscript no. 143 of the Niamets monastery. Words on Fasting By Our Father Abba Isaac of Syria From Among the Saints, the Faster and Hermit, who was Bishop of the Christ-Loving Town of Nineveh, Written in His Own Language, as Told by Our Venerable Fathers Abba Patrick and Abba Abraham, who Were Wise and Silent, and Who Kept Silence at the Lavra of Our Father Sabbas From Among the Saints. Translated by the Blessed Starets Paisii. This was transcribed by Durii in 1798. It is a remarkable example of the aesthetic quality of the work of Starets Paisii's pupils.

12) Manuscript no. 150 of the Niamets Monastery. The Life and Feats of Our Blessed Father Starets Paisii, his escape from the world, his wanderings, the gathering of brethren around him, and their life together with him.

13) Manuscript no. 155 of the same monastery. Chapters by Our Blessed Father Starets Paisii against slander about Him from a certain Starets Afanasii, Written on Holy Mount Athos. (They were copied into a special book by Hieromonk Nafanail of Niamets in 1837.)

14) Manuscript no. 398 of the Rumanian Academy in Bucharest (Akademia Romana). This contains excerpts from Paisii's answers to questions.

15) Manuscript no. 485 of the same Academy—*Instructions for the Tonsure.*

16) V. Kazanakli, *Paisii Velichkovskii and His Significance in the History of Orthodox Monasticism.* St. Petersburg, 1888-1889. A thesis manuscript recommended by Professor I. S. Palmin of the St. Petersburg Theological Academy as a valuable aid.

17) Manuscript no. 20 of the Orel Diocesan Archives: the manuscript of the Ploshchansk Monastery and a 1758 anthology on spiritual activity.

18) Manuscript no. 54 of the Orel Diocesan Archives: *Inner Treasures* (eighteenth-nineteenth centuries).

19) Manuscript no. 58 of the Orel Diocesan Archives: *An Ascetical Anthology on Mental Prayer.*

20) Manuscript no. 59 of the same collection: *A Collection of Ascetical Articles on Mental Prayer.*

21) Manuscript no. 37 of the New Niamets Monastery: *The History of the Beginning and Construction of the Holy Monastery Named in Honor of the Ascension to Heaven of Our Lord and Savior Jesus Christ.*

22) Manuscript no. 38 of the same monastery: *Introduction to Community and Gospel-based Life.*

23) Manuscript no. 96 of the same monastery. A collection of essays and letters of Starets Paisii, written by Archimandrite Andronik.

24) A. P. Orlovskii, *A Table of Russian Starchestvo, Starting From the Starets Archimandrite Paisii Velichkovskii.*

B. Printed Material

1) *The Life and Writings of the Moldavian Starets Paisii Velichkovskii With the addition of Prefaces to the Books of Sts. Gregory of Sinai, Philotheus of Sinai, Hesychius the Presbyter, and Nil Sorskii, Written By His Friend and Co-Faster Starets Vasilii of Poliano-Merulsk, On Mental Sobriety and Prayer.* Published by the Kozelsk Optina Hermitage of the Entrance of the Theotokos, Moscow, 1892.

2) *The Life and Writings of the Moldavian Starets Paisii Velichkovskii.* Publishing for the New Niamets Monastery of the Ascension in Bessarabia, Odessa, 1887.

3) *The Moldavian Starets Paisii Velichkovskii, 1722-1794.* A brief biographical account with an appendix containing Starets Paisii's teachings on mental prayer. Written by Archimandrite Amvrosii, Dean of the Volynia Theological Seminary, Pochaev, 1902.

4) "Paisii Velichkovskii, a Laborer of Righteousness in the second Half of the Last Century," *Poltavskiia Eparkhialniia Vedomosti,* 1897, nos. 22-23.

5) "Paisii Velichkovskii and His Significance in the History of Orthodox Monasticism," *Kishinevskiia Eparkhialniia Vedomosti,* 1897, nos. 18-24.

6) *The Life Histories of the Native Laborers of Righteousness of the Eighteenth and Nineteenth Centuries in Twelve Books.* Published by St. Panteleimon's Monastery on Mount Athos. These books contain information both about Starets Paisii and his pupils in Russia.

7) Professor A. I. Iatsimirskii, *The Renaissance of Byzantine-Bulgarian Mysticism and Slavonic Ascetical Literature in the Eighteenth Century,* Kharkov, 1905.

8) Iatsimirskii, *Research in the Collection of Russian Language and Literature Section of the Imperial Academy of Sciences.* Vol. LXXIX, 1905. This contains a description of Slavonic manuscripts from the Niamets Monastery which were written by Starets Paisii and his pupils.

9) Our Father St. Isaac of Syria, Bishop of Nineveh, *Spiritual-Ascetic Homilies,* translated from the Greek by Starets Paisii Velichkovskii. Published by the Kozelsk Optina Hermitage of the Entrance of the Theotokos under the supervision of the starets and Hiero-schema-monk Makarii. The preface contains Starets Paisii's account of his translation work.

10) *On Mental or Inner Prayer.* Written by the blessed starets, Schema-monk and Archimandrite Paisii Velichkovskii. Translated from the Slavonic. 1902.

11) N. Popov. Manuscripts of the Moscow Synodal (Patriarchal) Library. No. 11 (2), Simonov Collection. (On Starets Paisii's manuscripts).

12) V. E. Buchnevich, *Notes on Poltava and Its Monuments.* Poltava, 1882.

13) I. F. Pavlovskii, *Poltava.*

14) G. Levitskii, *Sketches of Folk Life in the Ukraine in the Second Half of the Seventeenth Century.* Kiev, 1902.

15) Askochenskii, *Kiev With the Academy, Its Oldest School.* 2 vols.

16) D. Vishnevskii, *The Kiev Academy in the First Half of the Eighteenth Century,* Kiev, 1903.

17) Antonovich, *Research on Gaidamachestvo According to the Acts of 1700-68.* Kiev, 1876.

18) Archbishop Filaret, *History of the Russian Church,* Period 5.

19) Professor Golubinskii, *A Brief Sketch of the History of the Orthodox Churches in Bulgaria, Serbia, and Rumania.*

20) Bishop Arsenii of Pskov, *Research and Monographs on the History of the Moldavian Church,* St. Petersburg, 1904.

21) *An Athonite's Letters About Holy Mount Athos,* eighth edition, Moscow, 1895.

22) *The Russian Cenobitic Skete of St. Elias the Prophet at Mount Athos, Kievskaia Starina,* January 1893.

23) Prince A. Dabizha, "The Ukrainian Monastery at Mount Athos," *Kievskaia Starina,* January 1893.

24) *The New Niamets Monastery,* Kishinev, 1881.

25) *Solovetskii Paterik,* Moscow, 1895. This book contains the account by the Starets Hieroschema-monk Feofan about his stay at Niamets with Starets Paisii.

26) K. N. Leont'ev, "On Starchestvo," *Russkoe Obozrenie,* 1891. "Starets Amvrosii of Optina," *Grazhdanin,* 1891. "Reminiscences About Archimandrite Makarii" (Afonskii), *Grazhdanin,* 1889.

In 1938 Father Sergii Chetverikov's book, *The Moldavian Starets Schema-Archimandrite Paisii Velichkovskii* was published in Estonia in two parts. In comparison with Father Sergii's manuscript, this edition was significantly abridged. The present edition of Father S. Chetverikov's work is based on his manuscript. "An Outline of the Growth of Orthodox *Starchestvo* in the Eighteenth and Nineteenth Centuries," compiled under Father S. Chetverikov's supervision, could not be reproduced for technical reasons.

The Instructions of Archbishop Rafail Zaborovskii of Kiev to the Professors and Students of the Kiev Academy

The Instructions of Archbishop Rafail Zaborovskii of Kiev to the Professors and Students of the Kiev Academy.

1) In accordance with imperial order, the Academy will admit for the acquisition of knowledge any free individual of any station or calling, as long as he practices the Eastern Christian faith and has scholastic aptitude.

2) Faculty members should always serve as lofty examples to students of faith in God and of love in particular. They should also be examples of humility, politeness, good upbringing, education, and both of inner purity of the soul and of the outer neatness of body and clothing.

3) On feasts and days when classes are not being held both instructors and students, especially resident students, are always, except for a valid cause, required to attend all church prayer sessions, services, and especially the Divine Liturgy, in the company of the overseer.

4) All the students of our Academy, both residents and non-residents must undergo confession and approach the Mystical Supper of our Lord and Savior once during each fast and twice during Great Lent, according to ancient custom, with the appropriate preparation and repentance.

5) All students must without fail arrive at the Academy for the very beginning of studies in early September, and await the final school recess in mid-July. If any student should leave the Academy before vacation, especially without the knowledge and blessing of the prefect and professor, he will undoubtedly be punished. Likewise, none of the students should wander about the city asking for handouts without the Academy's permission. Care should also be taken that

the undeserving not be accepted as candidates for the highest academic degrees, and also that the students would not occupy the most deserving places without their own merits, according only to the instructors' indulgence and partiality. Otherwise, the undeserving will be placed on one level with the deserving, and the negligent with the exemplary, which will cause some to lose their inclination to study, and others to become increasingly mired in indolence.

6) At the first Academy bell the students are to go immediately to their classroom. At the second bell the analogists, infirmists, grammatists, and syntacticians should sit at their benches. The instructors enter in the following order: those of the first two schools before the third bell, teachers of grammar and syntax immediately after the third bell, teachers of poetry and rhetoric after the fourth bell, disregarding any personal needs. They should faithfully execute their direct responsibilities toward their classes with fiery zeal and in as simple a manner as possible, thinking of their students' benefit rather than boasting of their minds. They should remain till the end of the lesson, before which none of the instructors or students can leave their school, except for extreme necessity. At the conclusion of each lesson there should be no delay in the classrooms, but upon the final signal all the schools, led by their teachers, should enter the church in an orderly manner to offer to God at least brief prayers and to give Him thanks.

7) All members of the community are strictly accountable, and instructors and teachers in particular, to make it a rule that both in the collegial schools and the seminaries, and both among themselves and the students, to speak only in Latin, and the students should have the *calculum* with them for daily use. Also, in the lesser schools, from analogy to philosophy, students should expound and present exercises alternately in three languages—Slavonic, Polish, and Latin. In philosophy and theology constant discussion (without which knowledge cannot be perfectly assimilated) and frequent disputations should take place as a matter of course. And Latin should be spoken always and everywhere by the examiners of cell schools, expecially by teachers, except for analogists and infirmists who study mostly in Polish and speak in it.

8) Each lower school should everywhere yield its place to the higher school and should render honor to it even through external signs of respect. In case of any insult from a student, especially one who is not a member of the community, no one should take it upon himself to avenge the insult, but should await satisfaction on the part of the authorities.

9) All members of the community should always be present at all academic ceremonies regardless of the day, including Sundays. In the case of a greater directive, all the members of the senior brotherhood are expected, and those not belonging to it are expected in the case of a lesser directive.

10) Students who are the most successful in their studies and who are known for their good character ought to be preferred to the others, and the most deserving should be distinguished by the Academy from the undeserving. And students who hold little promise and are indolent and intractable must be admonished frequently, while those who do not hold any good promise at all, such as drunkards, brawlers, rabble-rousers, telltalers, and cheats are to be expelled from the Academy as being incorrigible, so that the good would not be spoiled in bad company. Nonetheless, even if some possess impeccable morals, but turn out to be so dull-witted, that neither the Church nor the country can expect to derive any benefit from them, they should be dismissed from the Academy so that they would not waste their time and would choose the manner of life which would enable them to be more of use to themselves and others. In this way the Academy will have a reputation not so much for the quantity as for the quality of its students. This is intended particularly for the teachers' consideration.

11) Students of any school should in no case behave violently against anyone, especially against teachers. Such brawlers should be severely punished or preferably expelled.

12) Teachers and especially proctors should not treat those over whom they are in charge too strictly or too leniently. They must hold to the middle in this matter, as commanded by their duty of enlightenment and politeness, and should also beware of scolding students in abusive language, both in public and at home.

13) No student, without the permission of his instructor, and especially of his proctor, should dare to be away from school or to go anywhere from his dormitory. If he does so, he is subject to punishment.

14) No member of the community should wander about at night, but instead everyone is obliged to be in the dormitories going about his own business. Any idle or drunk student who is caught by his senior must invariably be subject to a fine or punishment.

15) Each proctor, as part of his duty, should watch over the students entrusted to him, no matter where he happens to be with them, so that they would conduct themselves with humility, intelligence, and politeness. Should any proctor start ignoring his duty or himself spend the night at home because of some dissipation, or conduct parties, or proceed to use food, drink, and other community property for his own benefit, wasting it dishonestly, or if he should exceed his authority, he will be immediately dismissed from his position.

16) Students should not bring with them to the Academy any firearms, nor can they fire a gun or a pistol. They should dress modestly and appropriately. Even if anyone should be dressed fashionably, this does not give him the right to change accepted Academy customs and ridicule the dress of others.

17) Each subordinate member of the community must in any

case display every possible obedience and respect to his senior, as long as this is not in opposition to divine and human laws. One should not obey nor cooperate with his seniors in a dishonorable matter.

18) Individuals of suspicious behavior shall not be tolerated in the student dormitories. Likewise, it is not permitted to rent apartments and to live in houses which either suspect or defame by something of a criminal nature. This is done to avoid encounters with bad company.

19) Students can in no case attend spectacles at which gladiatorial or boxing contests take place, even to watch them. But so that they would not remain in a constant state of tension, they are allowed on certain days to play on musical instruments appropriate to a student. Likewise, other dignified games are not forbidden for a brief period of time to restore morale.

20) No student, without the permission of the prefect and his professor, should disturb persons in high places with requests, or address panegyrics to them, draw pictures, or generally do anything special of this sort. It is likewise wrong both for students to select their proctors and for proctors to select their pupils at will without the prefect's permission.

21) It is essential that each student, whether he completes his course of study or leaves the Academy before completion for a valid reason, receive from the prefect upon graduation an open record of his scholastic progress as a general confirmation of his education. For this the school prefect is obliged to enter annually into the Academy Library, for future reference and any occasion, both private annual listings compiled correctly by the instructor of each school and containing the name and evaluation of each student, and to provide a general listing of all students, compiled with every care according to the order and worth of each school and containing the name, nickname, religion, birthplace, parents' occupation and financial status, and each student's age and amount of knowledge.

22) The prefect of the Kiev Academy, whose good direction must be obeyed by all students of all the schools and even their teachers, is obliged without question both to diligently observe and carry out these directives himself, as well as to compel all members of the community to observe them. Violators of these rules are to be reprimanded and appropriately corrected.

APPENDIX II

A Sermon on the Monastic Tonsure[*]

A monk is a spiritual warrior, who, like the warriors of the world, must equip himself with arms for successful victory over his enemies. The strife of Christ's warriors is directed against the flesh, the world, and the devil. The Savior commands us to take up the cross against the devil. He commands the flesh to resist by rejecting father, mother, son and daughter.

He says about the world, "If we gain the whole world, what does it profit us?" The witnesses of our strife are God and the angels, the devil and his angels. The battlefield is the space between the righteous and the sinners. His home is his body, his rider is his soul. His chieftain is his mind and his weapons include faith as his shield, patience as his helmet, diligent prayer as his spear, and unhypocritical humility as his bow and arrows. The leaders of the satanic host include pride, gluttony, uncleanliness, murder, vanity, rage and anger. These are commanded by the devil, who strikes the soul like an arrow. The second army of satanic might is the malice of this world. Our very bodies rise up against our souls, through overeating, drunkenness, the lust of fornication, indolence, and other passions. This difficult struggle of the visible nature with the invisible man is helpless without God's help.

The first step in the struggle against this world is to abandon it, reject its voluptuousness, the deceptive contemplation of its beauties, perishable wealth, and its temporary gladness, and to accept Christ's voluntary poverty. It is to hasten from out of the darkness of sin to the promised land, to the purity and sinlessness of a God-pleasing life. Remove yourselves from the world through the irreversible journey. And in this way you will defeat the enemy, and with this triumph you will gladden heaven and cause sorrow for the demons. And should the enemy overcome you and capture your soul, then, even if you acquire the wealth and beauty of all the world, there will be

---

[*] Taken (with slight abridgement) from manuscript no. 279 of the St. Petersburg Theological Academy and no. 485 of the Akademia Romana in Bucharest.

333

no profit to you. Do not be disturbed by the thought of forsaking your dear ones—father and mother, wife and children, sister and brother. They remain in their worldly cares, like the dead burying their dead. As for you, hasten to do God's work and withdraw from worldly wisdom to the heavenly, where Christ dwells forever. Actually, you should only stay away from those relatives who hinder your salvation and think of the worldly, saying "Gather, O son, the wealth of the world, acquire land, plant grapevines, gather many servants, and be glad in all the days of your life." You should flee from such parents, for instead of light they point to darkness, and to death instead of life. But parents who give good advice and lead us to God and to His service should be loved, honored as saints, and their will and advice should be followed.

Prevent excessive eating and drinking and fornication through fasting. Defeat indolence through vigilance. The body is not only our enemy, but also is our friend. We can use our body for fasting, shedding tears, bending our knees, and offering alms. Without our bodies, relying only on our soul, we cannot do these things. The body preserves the soul from pride, for the soul, being of a higher order as the image of God, may be carried away by conceit. But when it remembers its body it stills its conceit. Therefore St. Gregory says about the body that it is the "merciful enemy" and an "insiduous enemy." So do not be captives of the nether world of the body and death but turn toward the lofty world and to the boundary of immortality and you shall become the inheritors of its light. And if you defeat the first armies of your enemies you will be able to take up arms against the devil himself and vanquish his host. Just receive all of God's weaponry, which is threefold, consisting of faith, patience, and prayer, by which all of the enemy's forces are destroyed and driven away. Pride is driven away by humility, vanity by self-denial, and fornication by chastity. You will defeat your enemies by the cross even more. Through patience you should crucify yourselves on the cross and die to the world and sinful living. And then God's angels will come out to meet you, rejoicing, and Christ the King of Glory will receive His victory-bearer and will glorify him before the assembly of His radiant angels, before the patriarchs, prophets, and apostles, will number him among the host of the righteous, and will give him a place in His heavenly kingdom.

What is a monk? A monk is a performer of all of Christ's commandments, an abyss of humility, a pillar of endurance, an unforgettable memory of death, an unceasing source of a tearful torrent, a treasury of purity, a castigator of the perishable, a defier of all that is beautiful and delusive in this world, voluntary mortification, an everyday martyr and worker, a God-pleasing sacrifice, an ever-bearing lamp of spiritual wisdom, an enlightened mind, a secret observer of everything visible and invisible, a fast-paced prayer, contemplation of God, a pure heart, a mouth unceasingly praising God, the abode of the Holy Trinity, a spectacle for the angels, and a horror to the demons.

A monk is called *inok* because he has a different life, not bodily but spiritual, a different activity, a different period, different food, different clothing, and different work. He is called black-robed, for he has sorrowful black robes. He is called a monk (*monachos*), meaning solitary, untroubled, and obliged to abide alone with the One God. The first lawgiver for monasticism was Melchizedek, the priest of God on High, who lived without a wife or progeny in the desert. The second was Elias in the Horeb Desert. And the third was John the Baptist in the Jordan Desert, who had no possessions, did not know meat or wine, and wore a hair-shirt. The monastic order was established by the Lord Jesus Christ Himself and by His Apostles. The Lord lived in chastity, poverty, and non-acquisitiveness. Likewise, the apostles, having forsaken everything, followed after Christ. Monks follow Christ's teachings and counsel, and show zeal for the apostolic life. They forsake all of the world's joys, reject marriage, merriment, bodily comfort, and impermanent wealth, and walk after Christ, taking up their cross and wandering in deserts and mountains. Instead of radiant homes they live in dark caves. Instead of wives and children they live with the beasts of the world and birds of the air. Their bed is the earth and their cover is the sky. Monks have accepted the cross of daily patience, in order to serve the Lord completely. The apostle says, "If anyone fasts and offers prayer, let him be separated from his wife for a while." Monks are continually fasting and praying even until death. And the Old Testament commands, "Those drawing near to the Lord should leave their wives." Monks are always working, always serving the Lord—therefore they leave their wives even until death, working for God in purity. Although heretics disparage monks for disdaining marriage and meat, this is not so. A monk rejects marriage and meat not because he disdains them, but out of abstention. From the creation of the world to the Flood people did not eat meat or drink wine. And according to the Law of Moses, the Nazarites neither drank wine nor ate meat. And Daniel with the three youths shunned the meat of Nebuchadnezzar. And Moses and Elias, and the Lord Himself did not eat meat or drink wine forty days. John the Baptist did not eat meat or drink wine all his life. The same is told about St. Matthew the Evangelist and the Apostle James of Alphaeus. Monasticism brings out all of the Christian virtues. Christ was an example of purity, poverty and obedience even unto death, a death on the cross. In following the Lord the monks likewise commit themselves before God and are obliged by oath to maintain true purity and chastity, voluntary poverty, and unhypocritical obedience.

Monastic life is divided into three categories: a) cenobitic community, b) skete dwelling, and c) eremitic. There is also a fourth category consisting of willful monks living like brigands, each with his own purpose, his own will. They act as hypocrites, not as monks. As for monks in one of the three categories, they should adorn themselves with great virtues, humility, love, fasting, and prayer.

So therefore, monks, do not be slaves of indolence and infamy, but work for the Lord, bring about your salvation in fear and trembling, adorn your minds with thoughts about God, for this is the true monastic activity, and perform diligent prayer with your mouths rather than enjoying sleep and dreams. Do not seek the perishable goods of this temporal age but the everlasting goods of the future. If you do this, you will be God's true servants. And your Lord says, "Where I shall be, there my servant shall also rule with me, in the glory of my kingdom." Amen.

A Funeral Dirge

To Starets Paisii From His Spiritual Children.*

A

1) The image of your face, o wondrous Paisii,
   Could be sketched by an artist without any great skill.
   But the fine quality of your mind was so amazing
   That none could describe it in words,
   Only the light of the sun can describe your mind.
   You alone were like the one sun.

B

7) Your spirit burned like a flame with piety,
   And illumined the whole Church through dogmatic teachings.
   You introduced the correct monastic rules,
   Wholesome discussions and morals grew from this.
   You revealed the teachings, dividing them among nations.
   So that they may glorify the creator in various tongues.
   They followed the new splendor of the Church,
   And learned how best to serve Him.
   Reading and singing became so beautiful,
   That the whole world was amazed as if awakened.

---

* Written by Hieroschema-monk Ioann Diakovskii, a native of the town of Luboch. Diakovskii was of "great learning," a preacher in Kiev's St. Sophia, who died four months after Paisii.

Note: The author's unique numeration of the verses apparently denotes the more significant years in the starets' life—his birth, entry into school, departure from the world, tonsure into the mantiia, acceptance into the priesthood, etc. The total amount of verses corresponds to the length of the starets' life in the world.

C

17) You who thoroughly adorned the Church,
Were also a wise housebuilder.
Not having done the least thing without counsel,
Not having left any needed word unanswered,
And knowing how to hold the true measure in your hands,
You vividly described God's treasured providence.
You did not neglect your own when you had authority,
Nor did you reject the stranger in the least.
You closely watched those who worked well,
And to each a good reward was written in your heart.
You were long-suffering and of good judgment in all things,

D

29) Only your shoulders could bear such labor,
As many wise men were not able to do.
With a radiant face, you had a noble appearance.
It would not be shameful for rulers to labor under you.
Your speech is meek, it is humble in its counsels.
It has been dissolved by the salt of grace.
Your words have been faithful and true,
Your tears have shed authentic testimony.

E

37) You were generous in need and without pride in honor,
You could also bless the Most High without flattery.
You could wisely repel disgraceful blandishment,
And truly escape from worldly vanity.
While you admonished your opponent with incomparable skill,
Not a single vile word fell from your lips.

F

43) You were a comfort to sojourners and a respite
                                                   to the overburdened,
A physician to the sick and a healer to those of unsound mind.
Alms flowed from you like a river,
God satisfied the poor through your hand.

G

47) All the virtues dwelt manifestly in you,
    As well as unquenchable love for the Fathers.
    You spent days and nights without sleep for their sake,
    And led them into the light out of the darkness of indifference.
    For you enjoyed translating them into many tongues,
    So that the last ages may know the feats of the ancients.

H

53) The soujourners were amazed by your most wondrous word,
    They came together, ready to obtain benefit for their souls.
    Coming to you with perservering hope,
    And returning to their homes with complete joy.

I

57) Our hearts wished to be illumined by you forever,
    But alas, the dark year came to put out your light.
    Your light did not go out, no, it only hid itself,
    It only moved from the worldly sphere to the sphere of lights.

J

61) Therefore, shine on earth and pour out your comforting rays,
    The Most-High has made his dwelling in you.
    Your memory, O blessed one, shall remain in glory,
    And will shine as long as the world lasts.

K

65) We, your spiritual children, were born of you,
    Led from out of the darkness of ignorance into the light.
    We give thanks to the Eternal God on high,
    Who gave us you as a pastor to lead us all above.
    We put our trust in all your prayers, O father,
    And we bow our heads to you, be you dead or alive.
    Do not forget your flock while praying.

L

72) Be our intercessor, so that we may enter into eternal joy.
                                                    Amen.